SPYGIRL

SPYGIRL

True Adventures from My Life as a Private Eye

AMY GRAY

Villard New York

Library of Congress Cataloging-in-Publication Data

Gray, Amy.
    Spygirl: true adventures from my life as a private eye / Amy Gray.
       p.   cm.
    ISBN: 0-8129-7152-3
    1. Gray, Amy.   2. Private investigators—New York (State)—New
York—Biography.   I. Title: Spygirl.   II. Title.

HV8083.G73A3 2003
363.28'9'092—dc21   2003047982
[B]

Villard Books website address: www.villard.com

Book design by Meryl Sussman Levavi/Digitext
Printed in the United States of America on acid-free paper

9 8 7 6 5 4 3 2

First Edition

For P.B.S.

✪ AUTHOR'S NOTE

All of the characters and the events in this book are real, although some names and situations have been changed, and some individuals and incidents have been conflated to protect the innocent, the guilty, and to cover my ass. Where the narrative strays from rigorous nonfiction, my intention has been to remain faithful to the essence of characters and events I've written about. To my parents: The drugs and rock 'n' roll are made up. And I've never had sex.

SPYGIRL

⟳ ONE

Everyday life is the greatest detective story ever written. Every second, without noticing, we pass by thousands of corpses and crimes.

—FRANZ KAFKA

Money Over Broke-Ass Bitches

This is written on the wall in the stairwell of my new office building. It's my first day at work, but instead of thinking about that I'm thinking about this comment. "Who *are* these broke-ass bitches?" I'm thinking about those broke-ass bitches, and wondering who's spending money on them and pissed off about it when I see a two-hundred-or-so-pound guy storming down the stairwell at me. Close up, his face is red and scarred-looking. Rivulets of busted blood vessels spread all around his nose and chin, even in his eyes, which look like they're crying red, and tributaries seem to be spreading down the creases in his face to his gullet. I duck down into the corner of the winding stairs below more graffiti written in blood-colored ink that says STRANGER THINGS HAVE HAPPENED.

"Unlikely," I say out loud.

I had arrived on the first morning of my first day in a close-fitting Italian gray flannel suit that hadn't fit well since I'd bought it on sale at Daffy's two years earlier. Being nervous is an excellent diet. In the last several weeks I'd lost the five or six pounds that I'd accumulated since the last time I was this nervous.

I'd spent fifteen minutes in the lobby of my new building, pushing the up arrow on the elevator until Tommy the Building Super and All-Around Troubleshooter came and got me. It was 8:50 A.M. No one else was at work yet.

"It ain't working. Follow me, sweetheart." Tommy winked and led me outside, across an icy sidewalk, where we reentered on the other side of the building. He pulled on a huge steel arm to open the service elevator. Nothing happened. A few more tugs on the cargo winch yielded nothing, so he took me back past the elevator and unlocked the stairwell. "Go on up, honey." The office was on the fifth floor. As far as stairwells go, this one was particularly rank-smelling and sketchy. Years of people taking pisses and treacherous flights down these stairs had left a sticky patina on the wood floors. After the red-faced bull of a guy blazes past, I sit down on the stairs to catch my breath.

I realize my Starbucks latte is sideways across my Italian wool–wrapped lap. From a few floors above me, I hear what sounds like the approach of another desperate character. The sound grows louder. *Boom. Thud. Crack.* "Mutherfucker" muttered. *Boom, boom, boom. BOOM!*

Bounding past me, red-faced, is my new boss, George, holding a baseball bat, wearing no shirt, and Tevas. He jumps over the five steps I'm sitting on and keeps on going. "Hey, Gray," he mutters on his way down. Following him down minutes later are Evan,

Gus, and Wendy. They are investigators in my new office. They're all out of breath and grayish-looking. Everyone else is late for work; as I later learn, they always are. "You picked a great first day," Evan says, smiling.

"What's going on?" I demand, standing up as my empty latte cup primly rolls off my lap and down the stairs. Was this the disgruntled subject of an investigation come to exact revenge? What had I done with myself?

A Short Runway to a Sure Death

At the same time I was preparing with half an eye to start my new job as a private investigator, with the rest of my attention I was planning for the end of the world.

On New Year's Eve, 1999, two days after I'd accepted my new gumshoe assignment, I roamed New York City's icy streets with an exhilaration that can only come from the knowledge of—and acceptance of—impending doom. A layer of ice enveloped the city in what seemed like the perfect embodiment of our inexorable destiny: clear, unmoving, and deadened. I got up at ten-thirty and jumped out of bed—absolutely out of character—and walked over the Brooklyn Bridge, and then along Centre Street, up through Chinatown, then over to Mulberry Street through NoLita, and then over to the Lower East Side by way of Rivington.

It was a tour of mourning for the New York that I was just starting to fall in love with. A New York that, with its inimitable defiance, appeared perfect and vivid in a way that seemed to taunt its unalterable fate. I was leaving the second job I'd ever had in my short working life, as the assistant (read: slave) to two top New York book editors (read: frustrated writers who have watched their friends get rich on the NASDAQ while they struggle to maintain summer shares in Southampton) and my new enterprise seemed to present only more doubts—a blank, vast expanse of the unknown. I hated that feeling of Not Knowing. In comparison, total chaos seemed more manageable and more plausible.

I was on Broome Street just off Mulberry when it started to snow, at first cautiously, and then, like a gift, the sky cast millions of tiny grayish particles down, each one a miniscule and vast testament to the unknowable. The air hung with the honeyed smell of bread from the nearby Angel's bakery, and with the smoky perfume of an incoming storm. Surveying the city, I breathed in the rush from passersby, recording the contours of an archway of crumbling cement in a public garden on the Bowery, the pink shock of a child's earmuffs against the flecking of snow.

"Jesus Christ mudafucka!"

I felt a moment of lightness, and then in a clumsy ballet of sinking limbs I slid into an icy puddle, my foot wincing below me and my left knee giving out with a pop. I was kneeling in the middle of Clinton Street, right off Delancey, and a pock-faced taxi driver with a white turban and a bushy unibrow was slamming the door of his taxi, saying, "Miss, what da hell are you doing, Jesus! Miss, Goddamn muda . . ." A skinny Puerto Rican woman with a tiny white chihuahua in a stroller was staring at me, and a crowd of busty girls on the other corner, scratching their butts and chewing gum. "She *crazy*," I heard a Puerto Rican grandma saying to nobody in particular, as I limped around the block into a McDonald's.

The bathroom key, which was tied to a toilet plunger, was given to me reluctantly by a girl at the counter who had nails with little palm trees painted on them. She kept asking, "Kin I help da *next* person?" I locked the door, washed my face, and realized with horror and some perverse satisfaction that the arm of my white parka was steeped with blood. The quiet spell of my witness-bearing was broken, transformed by my blood, the apotheosis of my suffering. I took off my coat and tried to wash it a little, and steeled myself to at least walk by my new office in the Flatiron District.

From Avenue A I hobbled along up to Stuyvesant Town and caught the M1 bus over to Sixth Ave. Out the window of my bus, separated by a wall of condensation and fingerprints, I willed everything outside to be reduced to its most elemental essence, and tried to savor the New York to come that would be a mass of small clues, a snarl of exquisite singularity with no grand theme. When I walked by a Bed, Bath & Beyond, a block from my new office, I gave up strolling and hailed a cab to my friend Andrew Levy's apartment in Chinatown. Andrew was a publishing friend who was working as a business-book editor, even though he really wanted to launch his own nail spa just for men.

"Hi, pumpkin pie! To what do I owe this pleasure?" he chirped as I brushed past him, grabbed a can of frozen juice concentrate out of his freezer, and collapsed on the floor, clutching it to my knee.

"I'm fine. I just got hit by a fucking cab." I started to get up and planned to throw myself onto his bed and summon a much-deserved shower of pity.

I didn't realize he had company. Standing above me was a blond, curly-haired pre-Raphaelite work of art who was naked but for Andy's ancient pee-stained GI Joe sheets wrapped around him like a toga.

"Andrew . . ." I paused, looking around for him. "I didn't mean to interrupt your . . . fun?"

"Um, darling, I tried to tell you when you buzzed up." His face was beety. "We met last night at Colin's art opening . . . remember I invited you to that . . . didn't I? Amy, meet Cristoff, Cristoff, Amy . . ." He trailed off. I normally would have been pleased to see Andrew getting some action. But this windfall was ill-timed. He put me in a cab whispering the send-off, "Angel pie, he's *titanic*." Now I would have the image of his German hunk's extraordinary member in my fertile unconscious for the near and distant future. Not to mention my jealousy that my gay friend's boyfriend was much cuter than any of my boyfriends, current and former. The End of the World couldn't come soon enough.

Apocalypse Averted

On what was supposed to be the Night to End All Nights, I sat in my boyfriend Elliott's parents' Upper West Side apartment with our friends Patrick and Lily, and at eleven fifty-nine and thirty-six seconds we were all holding hands in a candlelit Ouija-style circle over Elliott's camp trunk-cum-living-room-table, waiting breathlessly as Dick Clark called out the seconds to oblivion, 8 . . . 7 . . . 6 . . . 5 . . .

We were enthusiastically preparing for the greatest man-made disaster since Hiroshima. Y2K, I had surmised, would be my generation's assassination of JFK, blackout of 1965, and Challenger disaster all rolled into one. In my fantasy, in a moment of Luddite poetry, the whole of New York's infrastructure would collapse because our ATMs and elevators, electricity, Motorolas, and Lotus Notes would simply halt. The result would be an enormous, open, undetermined time-space where now there was none. The excruciating void of my future would then have a structure and modality. It would be a tangible entity to be shared and not to bear alone. An offering for my generation.

But it was not to be.

At least eight seconds after the Big Ball hit the ground, I remember pushing my hand to Elliott's mouth, struggling to eke out a First Kiss, and shouting, "Oh My God, it's happening!" A shudder shook the room and a chorus of collisions and explosions and screams and bursts of light followed. I squeezed his hand and then everyone ran to the window to watch and wait for the last blow. I hobbled over, wincing as I felt a swelling pain in my left knee from my earlier fall. This was it. The city was erupting in a final dazzling burst.

The groans of a great city in the throes of its final moments thundered around us. When we realized—about fifteen minutes later—we probably didn't have a cataclysm on our hands, but a fuckload of fireworks and screaming drunk people, Elliott deflatedly opened four bottles of Korbel—one for each of us. We were, after all, on Eighty-second Street, and a straight shot up Broadway, transformed into a huge sound tunnel from the Times Square Millennium 2000 debacle. We scanned the television for some signs of crisis.

"How can this be happening? What about the electricity grid? What about that guy in Vancouver with the underground bunker made out of old soup cans I saw on *Nightline* last week!" I was yelling.

"Maybe we should have something harder to drink," Lily said, giving Patrick an Amy's-Losing-Her-Fucking-Mind look.

Barring a stuck elevator in Japan and some AM radio transmission problems in Australia, we had escaped annihilation. Elliott squeezed in next to me on the couch, making a kissy face. Through puckered lips he taunted, "So it looks like it's straight to the bowels of New York for you, Spygirl."

✎ TWO

If you love everything, you will perceive the divine mystery in things.

—FYODOR DOSTOYEVSKY,
THE BROTHERS KARAMAZOV

How to Look Like You Know What You're Doing

Think what you want, but my job as a private investigator is not as glamorous as it seems. Arriving at the Agency for my first interview, I was struck by the aptness of the space. The office was housed in a cavernous loft, but the kind that missed the eighties renovation boom of glass-brick half-walls and the nineties look of iMac-inspired Lucite and brushed metal. There was nothing chic about it. Its six thousand square feet were a vast sea of buckled, bruised, and burned wood-slatted floors and enormous windows in different stages of disrepair, most of which required a claw hammer to open. It once housed a printing factory, so there were deep black burnished grooves in the floor at regular intervals from the scorching machinery settling for thirty years into the hard oak. Some of the windowpanes in the back of the office were punched out or broken. Two, I later discovered, were fatalities of a game of office Wiffle ball, another a casualty of an angry (ex-)investigator who pitched a stapler out the window. The fractures were perfunctorily stuffed with cardboard wedges, seventies-era maxipads, and tube socks.

The Agency represented a prepubescent boy's fantasy of an office. It was dirty. Nothing was breakable that wasn't already broken. There were rat traps and sticky insect tape skirting the perimeters, some soiled with recent (or otherwise) catch. The walls had been painted white maybe four or five years prior, but even with a recent touch-up there was a funny-smelling brown, milky goo that seeped from the upper reaches of the back-left wall. The ceiling was bifurcated by a snaking metal air vent that looked like a massive tapeworm.

Evan Pringlemather was the office manager and highest-ranking investigator. He greeted me at the office door, and took me into a makeshift conference room, created by two cheap plywood walls that sectioned off a narrow corner of the loft. The conference-room wall was dotted with the oily impact of years of office jai alai. ("Yep, that's my ball grease," Nestor, another of my coworkers, once proudly announced.)

First I was interviewed by Evan. Sporting the indie-boy uniform of a too-tight Superchunk T-shirt over a long-sleeve thermal, he was solicitous yet informal. "Wassup?" he inquired, leading me through two French doors with waxpaper windowpanes into the conference room. He wiped some errant orange peels and half a snowball off the table onto the floor and waved for me to sit down.

His hair was bedraggled. Short spikes were molded in two

plains around his face into a craggy faultline at the crest of his head. It was either an au courant half-mohawk, or bedhead.

It turned out he'd gone to Boston University (we both saw the Pixies at the Orpheum in Boston in '89) and he had worked at Calvin Klein as a sort of callboy in the copywriting department for three years before starting here. "This is the only job I've ever liked," Evan told me. Although, he admitted, he did miss working with all those hot CK girls.

Evan said he still did cases occasionally when they interested him, and he was also responsible for deciding which investigators got which cases, so "I'm the guy whose ass you want to kiss."

Then Evan asked me for three words I would use to describe myself. I suppressed my gag reflex. "Okay . . . diligent, articulate, and smart-as-hell." He appeared reflective and took more notes. "A negative quality?" This was the stumper.

I hesitated. "Overly attentive to detail?"

"Nice one!" he responded, impressed. He said he usually answered that question by saying he liked to work too much and sometimes didn't take advantage of vacation time. "Listen," he continued, "since these interviews are bullshit anyway, we can just talk about whatever till Sol comes in here to get you." He winked. We compared notes about what bars we liked, he told me about his girlfriend, who worked in the fashion industry but who he was thinking of breaking up with (long story, he said), and about growing up in New Hampshire, where his mom ran a bed and breakfast and dated a Hell's Angel.

George, one of my would-be bosses, came in. He and Evan looked more like brothers than the manager and his minion. But then George opened his mouth. "That's enough of you, Ding-Dong. I'll take it from here."

What Do You Do to Get Him to Spill It?

George led me to his desk. He had a large shaved head, an upper body like Marky Mark circa the Funky Bunch, and short, sinewy legs. He looked like a He-Man action figure. He was about the same size, too. Even though he was the "brainy behind-the-scenes guy," his stocky five-foot-one frame endowed him with brute force enough for him and Sol, my other boss.

George was expert in the art in not looking at you when he was talking to you. "How-ya-doing-why-doncha-hava-seat," George said, his eyes fastened to an imaginary coordinate thirty degrees below my left shoulder. His chin still tucked in, he thrust his hand out to squeeze mine while walking backward to his desk. He cut to the chase.

"I know you can do this work, you're obviously smart with a fancy education," my soon-to-be-boss told me, motioning air quotes over the word "fancy." He pursed his mouth and seemed to be chewing something before pausing and asking, "Why do you *want* to?"

Why *did* I want to do this? I was caught short. I wanted out of corporate hell. I wanted adventure. I still wanted to be able to go where the boys go and not be begrudged for doing it. I sat there silently.

"This was the job I wanted to have more than anything at age eight." He looked bored and wiped his nose with one big, over-developed forearm.

"That doesn't impress me." My face was hot. "We're not the police. We can't arrest people. We're not lawyers, so can't sub-poena them, and we're not Gambinos, so we can't threaten to break their legs. Being good at this business means making people talk. So say you're calling someone, an acquaintance of a guy you're investigating, and he's hesitant to talk. What do you do to make him spill it?"

"Let them be the heroes."

"That's all they teach you at Brown University?" He laughed nervously and I followed suit, feeling like I'd just walked out of a test and only answered a quarter of the questions.

~~❦~~

Sol was the "people" guy. Since he and George had started the Agency with the seed money from Sol's bar mitzvah savings, he had been the only salesman hocking cases to clients and cold-calling venture capital companies. ("Okay," I heard him say while I was waiting for our meeting, "I'll give ya two cases for 5G. You'll neva do betta.") He spoke like a native Long Islander, which he was. Tall and slouchy, he wore a blazer, khakis, and a tie with Energizer bunnies marching across it.

Sol put me through the interview wringer, too. "I'm choosing between you and two other people," he professed, unapologetically. "Why should I choose you instead of them?"

I thought about it. "I don't know. Maybe you shouldn't."

He laughed and invited me out with the people who would become my new colleagues for beers at the dingy Blue and Gold Bar. I wasn't sure what the invitation meant until, on our fifth beer he told me, "Well, Gray, you sold us," and bought a celebratory round.

That night I took the subway home from the Second Avenue stop on the F train to the Bergen Street stop in Cobble Hill, Brooklyn, and I felt vigorous and brisk with the anticipation of my new job and five Hoegardens. This was going to be as far away as I could possibly hope to be from the belly of the big German corporate publishing beast in which I'd been toiling for so long. Sitting across from a couple of teenagers keenly involved in face-sucking, I joined with the winos and psychotic delinquents bantering to imaginary oppressors, proudly braving the New York City subway system, muttering under my breath, I want to know everything. Everything. Everything. . . .

⊘ THREE

I want to know everything, everything. Everything in the world, everything. I will be a spy and know everything.

—*Harriet the Spy*

Piss and Vinegar

After my stairwell encounter with the scarlet-faced bandit, Sol and George debriefed us. They explained that they tended to be rigid about only taking cases that were "corporate" in nature, meaning that they involved the executives of one company investigating another company and its executives to protect their assets, sometimes an investment, an initial public offering, a merger, or something like that. Or, sometimes, they simply wanted to know if, for example, Mr. A was keeping company with Mr. C, and if so, how much, or whether Mr. B had offshore accounts or shell companies that weren't reported on his books. But not all the cases were strictly corporate. George would make exceptions when he thought he could be effective and enjoy some ball-busting, and he often agreed to take cases for friends of his and any of the investigators that came to him. Bill Mossvelt was one of those exceptions. Gone very, very wrong.

Sol had actually been handling the investigation into the 900-number empire that had earned Mossvelt a gleaming Tudor-style mansion in New Jersey and a garage full of Aston Martins. Our client wasn't the typical stuffy venture capital paper-pusher but a neighbor of George's. He was considering putting a chunk of his savings into the CALL-900-HOT-CHICKS and other classy, upmarket operations Mossvelt was running. George advised against it.

The paint hadn't even dried on the newly touched-up 1980 Corvette Mossvelt had bought when George found dozens of liens on the cars and his newly marble-tiled McManor. The client freaked out. He called a meeting with Mossvelt and told him he had George on his side. He was on to him. He knew what was going on.

Mossvelt was angry. He threatened legal action. He showed up at the office and hung out outside, smoking, leering at the investigators. An anonymous letter sent to George at the office telling him to "rot in hell, asshole" was traced back to Mossvelt (he used his own return address). George was prepared to "cut off [Mossy's] hand and shove it down his blowhole" when he received a menacing talisman from Mossvelt, a platter of rotting hot wings on the front steps. While Evan insisted that the fried chicken still looked okay, Wendy dissuaded him from eating the evidence while George finally called the police. "I *usually* like to take care of these things myself, if I can," he said, visibly irked.

On the morning that was supposed to be my first, Mossvelt walked into our office, offered to blow George's fucking brains out, and squirted him with a fluorescent-green water gun. George felt the wetness trickle down his face and had no idea if it was spit or anthrax spores, and it didn't matter. Either way it was chemical warfare as far as George was concerned. He grabbed his Wiffle bat and swung, hitting all the pictures of his wife and kids off the desk and giving Mossvelt a chance to head out the door. He broke Mossvelt's nose on a second swing near the doorway and eventually tackled him a few storefronts down the block, in front of Justin's, Puff Daddy's southern-style eatery. The next morning there was a small piece in the "Weird but True" section of the *Post* titled, MAN ATTACKS PI WITH WATER GUN.

You Think You're Special? I'll Show You from Special!

My first day on the job after the assault, Evan did not greet me with the same energy I'd noticed in the interview. I returned to a scene that looked more like a combat zone than a workplace. In this case, it was both.

Evan looked bloodshot and hungover. He had a John Player Special gummed to the side of his mouth. I didn't realize we could smoke in the office. Score. "You look tired," I said.

"I think I'm gonna boot," he allowed. "Hey, Gray, let me show you your desk," he said. He led me to a slab of wood across a cheap metal frame and dropped a big orange file with KEENEY on it in black capitals. I could feel fifteen sets of eyes peering sideways from grimy laptops.

My desk had little brown dots all over it. They looked a little like spilled jimmies. I examined this bequest and gave Evan a *look*.

"Rat turds." He said this more declaratively than by way of explanation. Taking aim with one arm, Evan swiped the surface, pushing the nuggets clean off, save for a few stragglers stuck to his sweater. "We're working on that," he said, with air quotes over "working," as if to say, "Don't bet your precious little publishing ass it's gonna get better."

My new desk in the front of the office faced George and Sol. I had inherited the most conspicuous spot in the whole place, and evidently the shittiest piece of real estate. "I don't have anything for you right now, so just keep busy." An hour of solitaire on my new computer later, Evan brought me into the conference room, where two ill-at-ease boys were reposing awkwardly in their seats.

"Gray, this is Noah. Noah, this is Gray. Morgan, this is Gray. Blah. Blah. Blah." Evan sighed and did a half-swivel. "You know the routine." As he lorded over us that day and for a long time to come, Noah, Morgan, and I were the new recruits and were Evan's to abuse "until the next bunch of girls gets here." Morgan blanched. Noah seemed either immune or oblivious to the insult.

Noah was a scrawny, pale-faced kid who had a master's degree in British Renaissance politics. He was also a former child actor on the Nickelodeon classic, *Hey Dude!* (You might remember him as the landlord's son, the one who got his ass kicked in every episode; I didn't.) Later Evan sent around an e-mail with a picture of Noah on the set in britches and another photo of him hobnobbing with the stars of *You Can't Do That on Television.*

Morgan, the other new guy, had taken this job because the online biotech trade magazine he had worked for had filed for chapter eleven, and he needed money fast. He also let drop within three minutes of talking to him that he was a Republican, could trace his family to the *Mayflower,* and that he was "perpetually appalled" by New York, the other investigators, Democrats, and modern culture in general. I felt dirty just talking to him. "We're going to love each other, Morgan," I purred. He shuddered.

My first two days were spent in training. Sol spoke completely in negatives, vigorously displaying his fatalism, saying things like "If you don't want to get fired, don't neglect *anything* in your cases" or "This is how *not* to interview a subject" or "If you can't get the interviews, for *whatever* reason, because the guy's in

Hawaii on vacation or dead—I don't care—it's not gonna make us want to keep you on here." When he left the room for a minute to take a leak, I asked Noah and Morgan, "What's up with this guy?" They shrugged and looked panicky.

On the second day, Sol departed and Evan started to teach us how to search for liens, court cases, and real estate records. The job, he explained, was a combination of sophisticated computer research techniques and skillful interviewing. He used phrases like "second-level search retrieval" and "transunions." Information in some states, we learned, was streamlined and computerized. In other places, it required hiring a research team to dig through dusty files in the basements of court buildings and libraries. New York State seals divorce filings. Alabama has no database for marriage licenses. In Florida, the sale price of homes reported in the public record is rounded up to the nearest hundred thousand. We learned how and where to look, and how to save money doing it. Evan went over office rules with us. We signed dozens of confidentiality agreements, and Evan told us the office policies.

"So the rules are, you have to call me 'Mr. Pringlemather.' No, just kidding. Just don't use *any* of the databases or other resources here for personal stuff. Or if you do, don't get caught." He laughed a little at himself. So did we.

I was swiftly schooled in the seedy mythology of my new workplace, including the story of the legendary investigator Berskow (or Berks, as they called him). He was an investigative phenom and golden boy who, Evan noted for anyone who cared, should be played by Adam Goldberg in the TV movie. Holding court with the recruits, Evan told us that Berks was the best investigator they'd ever had. "He could get anybody to say *anything*," he said, looking rueful.

"Pray tell," Morgan broke in, "why don't we have the pleasure of working with this extraordinary individual?"

"Actually, he had a misunderstanding with management." Evan glanced out the French doors leading to the rest of the office, where the wax paper had been ripped by ornery feet and fists. The coast was clear. "Okay, he got shitcanned," he admitted.

Berks had been moonlighting for another investigative agency, something Evan warned us never to get caught doing. It not only violated his noncompete clause and his confidentiality agreement, but it was an irreparable betrayal. He got paid independently for a case the firm should have handled, even though, at the time, George and Sol had no policy for rewarding investigators who'd brought in business. They'd since instituted a loose practice of giving between 5 and 15 percent of the total billing on the case to whoever recruited a new client, but management had fired Berks for going behind their backs.

Nevertheless, Berskow was still the standard-bearer as far as investigating went. Office policy, I learned, was an ad hoc game, based in part on politics and in part on the hangovers the powers that be had at any one time.

On the day he sacked Berks, Sol had opened a major can of whoopass on the other investigators telling them, among other things, that they were "examples of how to *not* be effective workers," and, "None of you guys are even one tenth of the investigator Berskow was." "That was a shitty day," Evan observed, looking pained. After the evisceration was over, though, Evan said, George handed everyone copies of The Art of War and took them drinking.

━◈━

"Okay, asswipes, time to get fingerprinted." Evan took us a couple blocks over to the Fourteenth Precinct, where we got inked. "Hope none of you guys are felons, 'cause we cross-reference this stuff," Evan warned.

Noah looked visibly agitated. "I was arrested for public

drunkenness and lewd behavior in high school," he whispered to me, almost as a question.

"That's the kind of stuff we *hire* you for," Evan said, over-hearing him.

You Know Where to Stick It

A week into the job, I was sitting at my desk and finally ready to start a case. And my phone was ringing. It was hard to tell, actually. One of the lights on the elaborate matrix was flashing, but the ringers on the phones sounded like they were all coming from the same source. I envisioned George and Sol devising a money-saving scheme that included having only one operable phone ringer.

"Boo?"

"Mu?" It was my ex-boyfriend Ben. We had been broken up for a year at the time, but carried on a vestigial friendship.

While we were dating we spoke in a secret language, a patois of baby talk, infantile gibberish, and a variation of pig Latin words spoken with a lisp and a "b" added to the front. As in "Bamy, bhere bar boo?" He always seemed to trick me back into our old ways, his voice triggering my trancelike response.

"I'm at work," I responded in a barely audible whisper.

"Oh, *okay, then*," he said, annoyed. I was certain that we would never date again, but when I saw him sometimes we hugged for tens of minutes, and I didn't want to let him go. Even at an imposing six foot four, he seemed fragile. He was a magnet for muggers and bullies. Several times during our first year in the city, I came home from writing rejection letters and fetching lattes at my publishing job to find Ben holding an ice pack to a bloodied black eye and a split lip, in a tight, crimson-streaked T-shirt. His wallet had been stolen at knifepoint. He got into an argument with some Jets fans at a sports bar. (He was wearing a Patriots jersey.) He was pistol-whipped trying to cross Washington Square Park at night. We said if we never fell in love with anyone else, we could always just marry each other someday. Even though I didn't mean it, it gave me comfort.

At the time I started at the Agency, Ben wasn't dating anybody and I didn't want to tell him about Elliott because he knew him from college, and that would have made him jealous and pissed-off. But obviously, among our discreet group of friends, word travels fast.

"Sooooo," he whistled, "how's your booyfrieeeend?"

"Ben, I don't want to talk about this."

"Is he giving you the hot beef?" Yes, this was copped from *The Breakfast Club*.

"Fuck off. How's your girlfriieeend?" I teased back.

"She's goood," he said.

"What do you mean? You don't have a girlfriend." He didn't have a fucking girlfriend.

"Yes, I do. I have a new girlfriend. And she's pretty and she's rich and you know her." I felt sick. Why was I jealous of my ex-boyfriend who I broke up with's new girlfriend?

"It's Lisa Saaaks." He said the "a" in "Saks" with the same provocative sing-song he used to talk about Elliott, and for good reason. I did know her. She went to college with us, and her father, Jeffrey Saks, was the owner of the department-store chain. This was a girl who came back from spring break freshman year with a new $20,000 nose and $30,000 breast implants, the teardrop ones before they were all the rage. She had tried to remake herself as a trendy rock 'n' roll chick by not dry-cleaning her sweater sets as often and wearing her hair in ridiculous faux dreadlocks she got at Frédéric Fekkai. She used $100,000 of her daddy's money to do her first ten-minute short film at USC, something everyone else managed with $50 and a Super Eight from the Salvation Army.

"You must be kidding. I hope she gives great head, because that's all she'll do for you."

"Somebody's jealooousss," Ben hissed.

"I am *not* jealous, you're jealous, and I am not continuing this conversation anymore. Good-bye." I hung up. It was 4:55. I *was* jealous, which was exactly his intent, and that made it all the more annoying. I couldn't wait to get the hell out of work and see Elliott, and make myself feel better.

At lunch that day I had munched on Cheetos and a salami sandwich and watched the other investigators shout over their lunches. One of the favorite office parlor games was figuring out who would play who in the TV movie of us. Vinny Gamba, the litigation retrieval manager, was always played by "that short Italian actor with the lisp"—by which everyone always meant Joe Pesci. I didn't ask who would play me, and no one made any suggestions. Then Sol slammed into the room and told us to stop stuffing our faces and get back to work.

The office had the entrepreneurial enthusiasm of a dot-com mixed with the dinginess usually associated with sweatshops and boiler rooms. Sol and George had both grown up in New York working-class families, Sol of Russian and Polish Jews, his father a door-to-door insurance broker, and George the son of an Irish-Catholic cop. They met at a now-defunct New York investigative firm, and, as George delicately put it, they figured, "We can do this crap better than they're doing it, *and* make more money!"

❦

On the train home, I made the face I always make on the subway. It says, "Don't look at me, don't talk to me, don't even think about me." Everybody who rides the subway has this defensive camouflage. It's not that we're mean or cold or indifferent. It's just that if you stop to look at everything, you'll miss your stop. Or worse.

Occasionally this shield is penetrated, usually by cute babies, superior panhandlers, or, when I'm premenstrual, pretty much anything. On the way home, on the illuminated overhead across from me was an advertisement for a dermatologist named Dr. Zizmor. It looked like a fifth-generation copy of an ad from the early seventies, a jumble of weird quotes from patients and lists of procedures and really bad clip art. "Dr. Z," it told me, does "laser, varicose veins, spot removal, acne . . ." It also had a before-and-after picture of a zitty girl and a reproduction of a letter from her in pink bubbly print that said, "Dr. Z, you totally changed my life, Luv, Liza." A rainbow stretched from the end of his name to the beginning of the "Z" in Zizmor. I imagined myself at the end of Dr. Zizmor's rainbow. Not that there was anything wrong with my skin, but I liked the idea that Liza's transformation could be so absolute. Here's before. Here's after.

✍ FOUR

I'm a spy in the house of love . . . I know the word that you long to
hear. I know your deepest secret fear.

—The Doors, "The Spy"

We All Have Our Dirty Little Secrets

Elliott and I were the kind of friends who had spent dozens
of nights together in college, smoking pot and otherwise misbe-
having. Still, we didn't have much to say to each other. We shared
friends and rolling papers, but I didn't *know* him. Junior year in
college I got an indication that there was more to him. My boyfriend then was Ben, and he was away from school, hiking in Arizona with some of our friends. The problem was, I lost my only
copy of the already-pirated key to the dorm where I was living with
him illegally. Student security could send me for disciplinary action if they knew, and adding to the insult, would charge me $75 to
let me into a room I wasn't living in. I, in turn, was renting out the

dorm room where I was *supposed* to be living on a weekly basis to other people. Like freshman boys who wanted some privacy with their girlfriends. Wandering around campus that day, I was hoping to entertain myself until I found someone I knew and found a place to sleep or a key. When I saw Elliott, I was overjoyed. "Elliott!" I exclaimed, as I locked my arm in his. "Thank God I found you." I squeezed my temples and moaned with the force of six hours of futile aggravation. "Arrrrgggh!".

He smiled. "Hey Amy." I didn't think I'd ever seen him smiling like *that* before.

"I'm freaking out."

He took my hand. "You're cold. Relax. What's going on?" He gave me his sweatshirt. A fine mist of rain was falling. Even so, we walked around for hours, from Pembroke to the library and then down around RISD. I felt like I was meeting him for the first time. My stomach was tight from laughing. He told me about his family. Never had I even considered that he had a family before. He suddenly became three-dimensional. His parents, he told me, had divorced and remarried—twice.

"Wow. You're like the perfect Jungian case study," I said.

"Thanks. That was impolitic."

"Sorry. I'm too tired to exercise self-control."

"Hmm. Maybe I should take advantage of that."

We both smiled. "Umm. Maybe."

I seized on this tenderness and guarded it like a state secret. His sweetness was so exclusive, only I knew about it. I could do this: I could mistake a glance, a tiny upturn in a usually scowling mouth, and dream of decades of connubial bliss. Find me your freaks, your disgruntled misfits, your monosyllabic malcontents, your reclusive antiestablishment oddballs. I craved the exclusivity.

That night I slept on Elliott's very hard linoleum floor in his

lilliputian-sized single in a dormitory that could have easily doubled as a prison. At four in the morning I climbed into his bed,
nuzzled my head into his neck. "I've been waiting for you to do
that all night," he whispered. His T-shirt smelled like detergent and
sweat. His lips were preternaturally soft. When Ben came back the
next day, I put it behind me.

Two years almost to the day after Ben and I broke up, Elliott
called me out of nowhere and asked me to meet him for a drink at
the Marriott Spinnaker. This bar-slash-restaurant, which has been
replicated all over the country, is situated on top of a giant rotating
disk overlooking Times Square, perhaps the ugliest view in all of
New York, and it turns 360 degrees every half hour. I marveled
how Elliott was so unafraid to be uncool that he *was* cool. At
twenty-five, I was a publishing lackey; he was a year out of law
school working for a New Jersey–based nonprofit that defended in-
digent clients.

"Amy Gray," he'd said when I met him at a table. He had that
same amused curl in his lips.

"Elliott Reuther," I returned. It reminded me what made me
like Elliott so much—the electric-charged banter, the tit-for-tat
tête-à-tête. Our rapid-fire wordplay made me feel brilliant and in
on the joke that everyone else was outside of. It was heady. I felt my
stomach flutter and my toes curl.

"It's great to see you. You look great—as always."

The strange thing about the Spinnaker, the brainchild of a demented Marriott executive, is that, as you sit sipping your raspberry champagne fizz or whatever, you forget the motion, except
for the slow, almost imperceptible ripples across the champagne
flute. All of a sudden I was facing the flashing pearly whites of a
smiling Gap model; just before I had been at crotch level of a four-
story Al Roker beckoning me to "Watch *Today*." It was unnerving.

"I think this bar is making me sick."

"Don't think about it."

Elliott asked me about my job. I hated it. I asked him about his. "You, unlike me, are doing noble work in the world," I flattered him, "instead of kissing ass and dropping names, which is all I really do."

"Don't give me any credit for being principled," Elliott returned. "I'm doing this work out of pure sloth and selfishness."

"Really?" I had spent the days leading up to our date feeling guilty that my social conscience was grossly inadequate. "So, what are your clients like?"

"They're all toothless whores with seventeen children and crack habits. Seriously. It's hard to defend people that you know are guilty. It's always, 'Listen Judge, Shattiqua has a family to feed, she's not a flight risk, and she can't make bail over $100'—because we bonded her out last week on a child-endangerment charge—'so why don't we let her take care of her children in the nine weeks between now and the hearing?' And then we settle." My illusions of moral inferiority were melting rapidly.

"Sounds depressing."

"It is. That's why I've cultivated total emotional detachment." He swilled his dirty martini with greedy abandon. I was perversely fascinated. "I like winning," he pronounced, "and I like working the courtroom and impressing the judge. But I actually took this job because I thought it would be easy. I didn't want to work eighty-hour weeks at a big firm. Plus, they probably wouldn't have hired me." His law-school grades weren't very good. He told me a story about defending a client who was accused of stalking a former girlfriend.

"So the judge says to me, 'Mr. Reuther, you claim no inappropriate or suggestive contact was initiated by your client.' And I said,

'Judge, that's correct. I don't see any harassment in the content of those messages.' And she says, 'You don't?' And I say, 'No, your honor.' "

His smooth olive skin glistened with a thin layer of oil, and his black, back-swept hair formed a clean arrow at the center of his forehead. He had very Sephardic looks, like Corey Feldman with an extra thirty pounds. Or a dark Bill Maher. I wasn't sure why I was attracted to him, but I was.

"So the judge said, 'Mr. Reuther, I understand in the complaint that Mr. Hernandez said in his messages, 'I put a spell on you because you're mine,' as well as 'I stand at my window, wring my hands and moan.' " Elliott repeated all this with his best uptight-white-guy impression.

"So the judge said, 'Counselor, how do you explain your client's incendiary language?' And I said, 'Your honor, I'll concede to my client having bad musical taste, but not to his being a stalker. These are song lyrics. My client may be a Creedence Clearwater Revivalist, but he's not a criminal.' "

In addition to making the judge laugh, he told me proudly, he got the guy off.

There was something about Elliott's intrepid wickedness that made me laugh and feel nervous. He'd call me up and say he was thinking about me, and it was disarming. I would imagine his indifferent façade retreating, too. Then he'd talk about all the people he couldn't care less about and the social problems that bored him and the clients he'd warned, "Well, if you don't mind getting ass-raped, then go ahead and go to trial," and I wondered if or when I might become the object of his hostility.

When we left the Spinnaker, I was staring in a vortex of flashing light that urged me to "enter my fantasy." Even after excusing myself to the marbleized ladies' room to throw up striking-pink Spinnaker vomit, I knew it wasn't our last date.

❧

New Year's came, with Lily and Patrick. Elliott and Patrick were roommates, and Lily and Patrick were engaged. We held hands, we kissed, and spent the next two days together. I celebrated having "broken the boy seal," having peeled away the layers of resistance like a sour onion.

The Assman Cometh

Although I was dating Elliott at the time, in a purely anthropological sense I was excited about the prospect of working with two dozen boys. I fantasized that being an investigator was to be a fruitful period of fact-gathering for me, amassing a database about people to whom I would never otherwise have access. My peers would also be my subjects, and I would toil alongside them, blending into studied anonymity. I also anticipated a certain base pheromonal attraction one feels to a crowd of guys who have been penned up in a room together for too long.

That is, of course, until I got to know them.

Evan first talked about the Assman in my interview, actually, but at the time I misunderstood and thought he was talking about "X-Men." The Assman was an investigator whose real name was Matt. He was a long-limbed, burly guy who looked a little like he'd stopped working out after high school football and started smoking too much pot. Finally, I fettered my pride and appealed to Assman.

"So, what's the deal, Matt? Inquiring minds want to know. Why does everybody here call you Assman?" Sol was relentlessly soliciting/berating Assman, as in, "Where's Assman's case?" or "Assman, haul it up here!" or "Finish that case or your ass is outta here!"

Matt didn't seem to mind my asking. "Yeah, it's kinda gross, I guess." The previous fall, he told me, his posterior had been hurting for almost a month, just above the tailbone. He complained about it, but Sol told him, "Don't be such a pussy, Assman." And so his name was born. In late November, he was sitting at his desk when he felt a pricking pressure at the point that had been hurting him, and then a wet, viscous relief. "I actually thought Sol was playing soccer with a ball-bearing and was using my seat as the target." It turned out he'd had a pretty deep abscess that had just erupted. Nestor, another investigator who was Assman's best friend and mutual tormentor, called an ambulance, and the whole Agency saw Matt and his leaky butt off to St. Vincent's.

The doctors removed an apple-core-shaped slice from Assman's derriere about three inches deep and a half-inch in diameter. He spent the next three weeks at home, soaking his wound three times a day. "It's pretty nasty," he concluded, "but not a lot of guys have a built-in butt-pouch." He leaned in to me and said, "I keep keys in there when I'm in the field, working a case."

"Stop," I interjected. "I have a sensitive stomach."

Assman and Nestor were the proletariat of the Agency, and I was immediately attracted to their outsider status and subversive bent. Nestor had a lot of things sustaining his victim status. At four feet nine, he was towered over by the freshman college girls we hired out of NYU to do part-time work for us. He had moved to the Lower East Side from Venezuela at the age of eight, and he was an art-school dropout and freelance undercover investigator who'd retired from a highly profitable business selling reconstituted lowrider bikes before he started working at the Agency. We knew he'd been living in New York for at least the past fifteen years, but beyond that his history was murky. Nestor was reticent. Except when it came to busting on Assman.

Although his methods remained fuzzy to the rest of us, Nestor had the most investigative experience of anyone at the Agency, and he was grudgingly regarded as the ballsiest investigator we had. In the early nineties he had worked undercover for another firm started by a former top-ranking CIA operative. For six months, his beat was working The Tunnel and The Vault when Peter Gatien's clubs reigned supreme in a pre-Giuliani Gotham, an investigation that led to Gatien's indictment. He said he had a lot of girls then, because he could get them into the clubs free and had total VIP access. He rubbed elbows with celebrities and hitmen. He hung out with models. When the clubs were shut down, his social life went with them.

I was happy to be accepted by some of the investigators at the Agency. Since my first interview, Evan's chummy banter had devolved into grunts and a vocabulary of crude sign language. He pointed, he shooed, he shushed. Wendy, the only other girl, didn't talk to me. Gus seemed preoccupied and sat on the opposite side of the office. Linus had his head in the clouds. He did manage to talk to some people though, so I supposed his haze just didn't include me. The same story held true for everyone else there, it seemed. I consoled myself by visiting Assman's and Nestor's desks often, to talk shit, smoke cigarettes, and laugh. It was the end of my second week at the Agency, and I left Assman's desk, where he had lured me with bubble rope and Slim Jims. There was a message from Elliott. We had dinner plans.

To Ill a Mockingbird

After work, I met him at his apartment and we went out for a drink. Living as he did on Eighty-second and Second, there were no cool bars within forty blocks. The neighborhood was all leathery-skinned old ladies, dogs, and, seemingly unparented toddlers. We walked past a bar called Quench, which had sleek white leather-upholstered couches and hot-pink bulbs in all the fixtures.

"It's like a modernist bordello," I said.

"Okay, if anybody asks, I'm your pimp." He winked. "And your name is Candy."

"No, I want to be Bambi."

The bar was only about half full. The house special was their chocolate martini, which I ordered, and Elliott got a Manhattan.

"Hey, what's this?" Elliott pulled an oversized binder from the next table. He opened it to a laminated page in the middle with a picture of a brunette smiling too widely in a huddle of other girl-friends whose faces were smudged out.

"She's all gums. Maybe she forgot to put her falsies in."

"Nope, she's wearing them." He pointed to her ample décol-letage as she leaned into the camera. "Listen to this," Elliott started reading, " 'Name: MinervaMilk. Book last read: *To Ill a Mocking-bird*.' It says 'Ill.' That's funny. She must be rereading her sixth-grade reading list."

"Very badly," I added.

" 'Favorite Movie: *Nine and a Half Weeks*.' I think I'm liking what I'm seeing now." When we looked up from the book, we real-ized *all* the people at the other tables were reading these books. Quench was a dating bar. ("Find a friend, a fling, or a forever ro-mance. Quench is the antidote to your romantic thirst.") Just reg-istering cost $250, and each "setup" cost $40 for an e-mail, and $80 for a special phone number and "introduction."

We played around for a while, reading the ads and trying to find people for each other. "Okay, here's the woman you need." I pointed faux-seductively at Elliott, reading, " 'Name: SweetJordana; Most Ideal Date: Tarring and Feathering; Last Book Read: *2001 Contact-Free Ways to Drive a Man Wild*.' "

"Number one: read these ads to them," Elliott winced.

"Seriously." I continued, " 'Favorite Food: whipped cream, Favorite Body Part: neck.' " I noticed Elliott wasn't paying attention to my reading, but kept glancing over his shoulder where a woman was doing an impromptu lap dance for her boyfriend/date/client/whatever.

"Hold on," he said, "I need to get a better view of this." He picked up his Barcelona chair and turned his back toward me. The girl squeezed her boobs together in her hands and shoved them in her companion's face, shimmying to the music. Watching Elliott watching her, I wondered what the fuck *I* was doing there, when SweetJordana or someone like her would be much better.

◑ FIVE

Don't be a spy.

—GARRISON KEILLOR, IN HIS ONLINE ADVICE COLUMN TO A WOMAN
CONCERNED ABOUT HER FATHER'S EXCESSIVE USE OF INTERNET PORN

Perfecting the Art of Mediocrity

In high school, I didn't have a clue what I wanted to do with my life, beyond getting into college. The guidance counselor maintained a closely guarded book of spectrographs organized by college. The graphs were plotted by combined SAT score, on the x-axis, and then GPA on the y, with admittance represented by red dots, wait lists indicated by black doughnut holes, and rejections by black dots. I couldn't stop thinking about the black dots, and how each one of them was a person, with a disappointed family behind them, and a disappointed world to face after their rejection. To me the black dots' despair practically dripped off the pages, representing thousands of dollars misspent on SSAT tutoring, flash cards, math camp, private school, karate lessons, and art therapy, all adding up to nothing. I'd sneak into our advisor's office and smuggle the tome back to my desk. I poured over this book, willing myself into a red dot, resolving through pure single-mindedness and daily prayer to the gods of college admission the oneness of myself and that dot.

When we finally achieved unity, I was at a loss. After the dust had settled, my years in high school seemed like nothing more than the sum of some smudgy purple-inked exegesis in my yearbook. Graduation left a smoky impression of white linen and country club luncheons. I was caught by dread. I had given so little thought to what I actually wanted to do in college that when I received my catalog three weeks after my letter of admission to Brown, I cried. That summer I smoked my first joint, had my first boyfriend, and waited for inspiration to hit me.

In college, my friends and I practiced insulting each other, making bad art, becoming semioticians, and then, having achieved that to varying degrees, rejecting the whole enterprise to embrace a new kind of studied anti-intellectualism. White boys called each other nigga. My girlfriends and I took pride in looking trashy. We also built bongs, and I picked up dirty colloquialisms like "poontang" and "felching."

My college boyfriend, Ben, was a tall, brooding boy I met the first week of school after my roommate, Sarah, took him home with her. It took us two years to fall in love, and then we were inseparable, united by our mutual dependence and our desire to at once eschew the world because "everybody else sucks" and yet still not be disliked by anybody.

I created and discarded many selves. By senior year I applied my skills of clue-gathering to becoming a tamer of unwieldy texts. I wrote a pretentious thesis that strongly favored style over substance, fancying myself the intellectual equivalent of a streetwise

Scotland Yarder—fearlessly willing to bring together elements other people saw as impossible, repulsive, and absurd. One of my advisors wrote in my evaluation that she was "suspicious" of a paper that I wrote so well about "terrible literature." By the time I was done I agreed with her, and I suspected my paper was terrible too.

After graduation, Ben and I moved to a Brooklyn neighborhood called Cobble Hill, which was ungentrified enough that we could afford it, and for Ben to get mugged three times (twice with a gun) on our block. Our windows faced brick walls. I went from studying the panopticon and pornography to desk jobs at one and then another major publishing house, miserably ensconced in the ornery minutiae of forms, typing, and routine. I became sullen, and barely noticed my small reserve of hope fading away from my consciousness. I gritted and bore it for several years, perfecting the art of mediocre typing and barely passable message taking.

It was Eleanor, another editorial drudge and my "pod-mate" (as we called the other overeducated postideologues who populated the plasterboard cubicles in my office), who first inspired my return to the clandestine province of investigation. She and I distracted ourselves from work with rituals like reading our horoscopes every morning off the Yahoo! website. She was a Virgo. One day hers read, "Your fixed star, Mizar, is at its highest point of illumination in the Ursa Major constellation, starting a period of astrological circumstances which foster deep emotional connection and perhaps true love. When he asks, give him your number."

That night she met a guy at a bar who talked to her all night about Charles Bukowski and Tom Waits and his work for the Anti-Defamation League, and at work the next day she thought she must be in love. When she met him for coffee the next weekend she found out he had a girlfriend, a hair weave, and acute male pattern balding. Luckily, a week later at an unbearable Upper East Side mixer for single Jewish cat lovers (she was Irish Catholic and a dog person), she met Bill. He was a nice Jewish boy, and they talked all night about how much they hated anything above Twentieth Street and how much they loved latkes, of which there were a lot at the party. Eleanor adjusted to Bill having a cat *and* a dog. Three weeks later, they were in love.

After they professed their devotion, Bill had to go to Utah, where he was tracking the former cellmate of a guy his firm was investigating. He was a corporate investigator, Eleanor told me, and he was trying to find the prison mate of someone he was investigating for embezzlement and drug-running under the RICO statute. I got daily updates on Bill's progress. Eleanor stopped wanting to read her horoscope, although she let me continue. On his fourth day away, mine read, "Romantic and professional prospects stall, so tread water now. Treat yourself to a great new outfit." That night I dreamt of sleeping in the back of a van parked outside in the hot Utah summer, and waking in the dead of night to scan the vast, black sky and stars for signs. In the day I would watch and draw clues from unlikely places. Subject wears Adidas sneakers. Subject has a nervous tick in his left upper eyelid. Subject eats four bowls of bran flakes. Subject makes numerous trips to the bathroom, etc. In the pantheon of my publishing experience, it seemed that I was always reading about and talking to people who were doing remarkable things with their lives, and yet I was so far from being one of them.

The Odd Days Club and Other Rituals of the Young PI

Now I was supposedly living the life I had dreamt about. Bill and Eleanor had moved to London together, and I had his job.

My second week on the job, I followed everyone onto the fire escape for a smoke. Gus was talking about the Irish tradition of oral history. Gus was short for Gunther. At six feet six, with his head wrapped in a red bandana and a homemade sleeveless Slayer T-shirt stretched across his gut, he was the highest-ranking investigator under Sol and George. He was an expert at database research. I blurted out in my best pseudo-pimp voice, "Yeah, well I can tell you a little about oral history." It was a joke, but they were all aghast for a moment until I broke up laughing and they all followed suit, patting me on the back as we filed back into the office, saying, "Nice one, A. Gray."

That droll display represented a shift from my isolation in the Nestor/Assman camp. Since the two of them baited the other investigators, I had started to feel isolated from the rest of the office. Or maybe I was just being paranoid. I wasn't sure. Until that moment, the three of us had been on different smoking shifts from the other investigators, and we ate lunch at the opposite end of the conference-room table.

After my performance on the fire escape, Nestor and Assman didn't talk to me for the rest of the day, but I took my chances. That night, all the other investigators went out drinking. I had noticed they all left together a few times the week before, but this was the first time I'd been invited along. Assman and Nestor aside, I knew that I was viewed with suspicion by the other investigators in the office. I was only the third woman they'd ever hired, thrown into a sea of guys mourning the loss of a girl-free, belching-friendly office environment. And I was hanging out with the two office outcasts.

"Yo, Gray, wanna go get shitfaced?" This came from Evan, who'd already gotten a head start on the rest us. He led the way, cradling his laptop in one hand and a Papst Blue Ribbon in the other.

"More than you know." I packed up and followed everyone to the 119 Bar, which was a five-minute walk from the office. It was part of an exclusive circuit of dive bars frequented by young PIs, including the greasy spoon Corner Bistro, the grim Siberia Bar, as well as the rank-smelling Alphabet City dive standard, Blue and Gold. My coworkers had a tradition, called the Odd Days Club, which consisted of drinking well into the night at the office on odd-numbered days. But lately they had grown tired of working and drinking and then inevitably (or inadvertently) sleeping in the same place, and had focused their efforts on going out to get drunk. "You don't wanna shit where you sleep, ya know," Gus editorialized.

I devoted time at the bar to chatting with my other colleagues. There was Ronny Finkelman, who grew up in what used to be the largest trash-dumping ground in the United States; that would be the island known as Staten. But he wanted to be an honorary native of Asbury Park, New Jersey. He'd seen Springsteen more times than he could count. Also, admitting he came from S.I. embarrassed him somehow. Ronny had crossed over from being an investigator to being a "marketing guy." I wasn't sure what that meant then, and I'm still not, but I can say that he's the only marketing guy that's come and not gone since I've been at the Agency, and he somehow seems to bring in new clients.

Otis was a former editor at *Guns & Ammo,* who told me he was wrapping up eight years of work on a biography of Ted Nugent. "Yeah," he said, "I'd put him up there with Dylan, and Springsteen for sure." He was shortish and square-jawed, and he was wearing Tevas with socks. It was snowing out. "So, when does it get cold enough for, ya know, shoes?" I asked him. He laughed. "When hell freezes over, man." He turned around and faced the rest the group, crowded in front of the bar. "Hey, can somebody get this girl another drink—she needs to *relax*!"

I finally got to spend awhile talking to Wendy. "Just don't date any of the guys in the office," she advised.

"Nothing to worry about there," I said.

She was a smart and hip (DJ boyfriend, loft in Williamsburg) Californian, so she played up the Valley girl thing too. I told her I liked her leg warmers. She gave me the address for her website, where she sells them along with ponchos and metallic appliquéd drawstring purses. We did shots together.

I don't remember much after that but the taste of the Wild Turkey, Jack Daniel's, and Coke coming up and swishing around my toilet bowl in Brooklyn with the most amazing force.

The First One to Nail This Guy Gets a Free Lunch

The next morning, hopped up on Advil and two Starbucks lattes, I was working glumly at my desk when Sol offered a bottle of Jack Daniel's to the investigator who could better his thus-far-ineffective efforts to dig up dirt on this one guy, a young dot-com entrepreneur. Challenges in the office, I learned, were frequent and cutthroat. This would be my first interview case. Sol assured us our subject was a deserving scumbag—he just didn't have the *proof* yet. He needed one crucial interview to break this case wide open. Galvanized by the provocation, my competitive spirit took hold. I wanted that JD, and I didn't even like whiskey.

I found out where the subject lived and started looking for former girlfriends, lovers, or business partners who may have had a reason to hate the guy. For me, it was easy to begrudge him. At seventeen, when I was studying for the SATs, my subject was a ski bum in Aspen. At twenty-one, when I was working for five dollars an hour in publishing, he was collecting money from his father's rich friends to buy real estate in condominiums in New Hampshire and resell them at obscene markups. At twenty-five, when I finally joined the Agency to make a little more money and investigate him, he was heading an independent wireless ISP and planning an IPO that would net him a million dollars. Our client, a midsized venture capital company, was considering investing in this very offering. Sol told them to hold off.

Unlike private eyes on TV and film, I learned, the Agency staff spent most of its time running Internet searches. My first searches were not fruitful. I plugged Mr. Dot-Com into one search engine and found more than fifteen thousand documents. Adding his middle name, I found one four-year-old picture of him and an "unidentified friend" in a *New York Times* society piece at a benefit for the arts sponsored by some barely nonprofit pro-bono PR group. Not helpful.

I visited Gus in the back of the room.

"Gus, I need your help, and I don't mean kisses," I joked, blowing him one.

"Anything for you, darlin'."

He helped me find a website Dot-Commie had posted for a band he was playing in, replete with pictures of Mr. Dot-Com and his Pearl Jam–loving bandmates posing with a dozen Coronas, and a quote from Kid Rock: "Givin' all my ducats to Uncle Sam. F**k it!" The quote seemed meaningful, but didn't lead anywhere. I considered writing, "Subject has crappy taste in friends and music" on my status report, but I resisted.

Rounding out my more significant findings was a divorce filing from a woman to whom he'd been married for eleven months. I tried to call her, and I got numbers in Arizona and New Mexico, but her family told me she was in Burkina Faso now, with the Peace Corps. They seemed unaware that she had ever been married to Dot-Com Guy at all, saying they knew that she and my subject had dated briefly, but not that they had been married. The folks gave me an address for a post office station forty miles from her camp and assured me she would get any correspondence in "no longer than six weeks."

Unfortunately, the company Dot-Com Guy was running was the only real job he'd had (tenure at his father's investment company aside), so there was no promise in calling there. None of his companies were registered. There were no incorporation records for them and no reported business partners or investors. I spoke to a few former college friends. One told me he was a whippit freak. I thanked him, and we chatted briefly about how he (the friend) was almost prosecuted for selling nitrous-oxide tanks to teens for inhalation. I got off the line quickly. When leaving the office that day, Sol offered a piqued, "You're losing your edge, A. Gray." This was plainly sarcastic, since in my one week of work I had no edge to speak of. From that day on, "A. Gray" was my call sign around the office.

"Kiss this JD good-bye." Sol held the amber bottle in the air and took a pretend swipe from it, wiping his lips.

Insert Foot in Mouth

A month and one day into our affair, Elliott and I saw the movie *Boiler Room*. We were reviewing it for a his-and-her dating site, a job I had gotten through another publishing refugee friend of mine. The site later went bankrupt, though at the time my friend was blessing her stock options and the site was pumping out a torrent of forward-looking press releases and paying $1.50 a word, not to mention the price of our movie tickets.

I was struck by how much our office resembled the grim basement office Giovanni Ribisi sets up in the film—a careless assembly of cheap accommodations, built for quick dismemberment, and a grab-your-employees'-401(k)-plans-and-head-for-the-Caymans kind of ethics. At the Agency, we could pack the place up and jettison the furniture in a few hours, leaving nothing behind but some graffiti on the ceiling above my desk, PUT DICK HERE, an arrow pointing at a dangling metal gasket; skidmarks from Evan riding his mountain bike around the office; and a bad smell around where the refrigerator had been.

After the movie and some dirty martinis, we went back to his house. We were falling asleep and Pink Floyd's song "Fearless" was bleating in the background.

> *Fearlessly the idiot faced the crowd, smiiiiiiling . . .*
> *Merciless the magistrate turns round, frooooowning . . .*

It surged into the kickout, breakout jam part, and I started playing air guitar. Later I hummed along and soon was hovering around sleep. The phone rang at about two-thirty in the morning.

Elliott answered. "Yes, sort of. Well, Amy's here, so I'll call you later," I heard him saying. He fell back down on the bed, sighing in annoyance.

"Who was that?" I asked. His face was framed with the bluish light from the streetlamp outside, but I was clear about the withering look he imparted me.

"It's really none of your fucking business."

I was shot through with an emboldening indignation. I couldn't believe he was treating me like a *chick*, like *some girl, like all the other fucking girls he'd dated.* I had flashbacks to being in college and hearing him with 10 percent of my attention speaking to other people with total detachment about his ex-girlfriends. "She says she wants to stay in touch with me, but I'm like why, I just don't give a shit about you anymore." I remembered him saying the week before, when I asked him to hang out on consecutive nights, "Don't try to take this from A to Z all at once."

I had thought that our history together would give me some

kind of emotional immunity. I realized that sitting around smoking pot *near* somebody for four years does not a friend make. I barely knew him.

"I'm sorry. I didn't mean that." He was reaching for me, shaking his head, but his tone belied his annoyance, like he had to clean up red wine on a white couch and he was pissed off about it.

"I don't give a shit if you meant it or not." Suddenly I was seized with the same hardened indifference that had always fascinated me in him. He begged me not to leave, and I did anyway, in a mechanistic daze that enveloped me like a cloak. He was crying when I left.

When I got home, after running out into the wet, snowy night with hard clarity, my anger melted on my bed, into two little saltwater pools on my pillow, not for the things I was losing with him but for the things I hadn't had.

✺ SIX

The world is full of obvious things which no one, by chance, ever observes.

—SHERLOCK HOLMES

If You Can't Say Something Nice . . .

Elliott left me a plaintive message the following Monday. When he called I was napping in the same position I'd flopped myself down in after work, so I actually just caught the tone of it, which *seemed* to be plaintive. When I went to hit PLAY, the tiny cassette made a screeching sound and ejected itself, also defecating lots of brown silky tape containing the last probable communiqué I might ever get from Elliott.

I turned off the ringer on my phone and balanced cucumber slices on my distended eyes. They started to hurt from the cold, which gave me goosebumps, so I ate them instead. I felt restless. I didn't know what to do with myself. It was a feeling I remembered having had before, and it always hit me as a sort of shock. I had a superstitious ritual that, when I felt it, I would have to say to myself, "I'm lonely." The last time I did this was in the pink downstairs bathroom of my parents' house, where I locked myself during one Thanksgiving dinner in high school. How can I feel lonely when I'm surrounded by so many other people? I wondered. This time, I wrote it down, in big black bubble graffiti on the back of my Con Edison bill, which I then stuffed in my "Pay it fast" file: "I'm lonely."

I went to the liquor store across the street, which was a narrow shopping isle enclosed by bulletproof glass where you would point to the liquor you wanted and they would push it to you in one of those sliding plastic drawer slots like they have at gas stations. I bought a bottle of Lillet. I went home and turned up the volume on PJ Harvey's "Rid of Me."

I wasn't even attached to Elliott. His mind was his big appeal. Plus he was surly. And narcissistic. I was thinking of all the bad things about him I could to convince myself I was happy about being alone. As I was drifting into sleep, I thought to myself, Can't I just be happy about ditching Elliott instead of being *lonely*? I braced myself and fell asleep on my couch at 9:45.

The Hide-a-Jew

The next morning I patted on some concealer and steeled myself. Having a boyfriend had been a nice cover at work, too, while it lasted. It made it easier to blend in and make friends with the guys. I didn't want to tell anybody about the breakup.

"Jesus, did your boyfriend hit you?" Sol was two inches away from the large gray saucers on my face that doubled as my under-eyes.

"Jesus? I thought you were Jewish." I glared at him. "You really know how to make a girl feel like she's the only freak in the room. If you must know, we broke up." Nothing like personal discretion. *I* wanted to hit me. So much for playing my cards close to the chest, for keeping up my game face.

Big Gus walked by us. His nose was red, and he was hacking his way to his desk in the back of the office, practically coughing up a lung. He looked worse than I did, but that didn't keep him from saying, "Late night, Gray?" as he walked by. Do I have a KICK ME WHILE I'M DOWN sign on my forehead? I wondered. "What's wrong with Gus?" I said aloud.

"He's got strep throat." This came from Linus. "Strep, huh?" Sol cleared his throat before commanding to the back of the office, "Gus, uh, when you get a chance, can you make out with Amy?" I started laughing. Linus chuckled with his hand over his mouth, pointing to me and Gus and saying, "Oh shit, he got you guys! Oh shit!" Linus had a Ph.D. in philosophy and a copy of Immanuel Kant's *Critique of Pure Reason* on his desk, along with an Elvis Costello boxed set and a small heart-framed photo of Wynona Judd, "The *queen* of country." He was a recovering Ritalin kid and wore horn-rimmed glasses with the corners duct-taped, because, he told anyone who would listen, he didn't make the ducats at the Agency to get those special screws to fix them.

I had brought in some candy canes that morning I had left over from Christmas. They were a pacifier, an oral fix, a substitute for cigarettes (which cause cancer), pens (which I usually chew till my mouth is blue), or my fingernails (which I bite). Sol noticed me putting them in the middle of the conference table.

"That's funny, I didn't know you were a goy, A. Gray," he remarked. I explained that I'm not, I'm actually 100 percent Jewish, but for like the last six generations, my all Jewish relatives have celebrated Christmas. "My parents are from California," I said to Sol's dubious stare. "Jews on the West Coast are different," I told him.

"So you're not Jewish. You're not Jewish. I mean your name is Gray—what, was it Amy Graystein?" George started laughing from his desk. "Okay, here's a Jewish trivia question. What's the most solemn day of the year?"

I looked at him gravely. "Your mom's birthday." George started clapping, and Evan and Wendy and Linus giggled in the background.

"Nice one, Graystein." He was smiling and his face reddened. "You know what you are? You're a Hide-a-Jew—one of those Jews who tries to 'pass.' " He picked up a candy cane and bit off the tip of the hook. "But you gotta decide: You can't take off Christmas and Rosh Hashanah. Company policy. Take your time—you've got a whole year to decide."

Requiem for a Smoker

I was holding my breath until I thought it was safe to sneak out for a cigarette break. It turned out we could only smoke in the office when our accountant, Adrienne, wasn't there. The smoke irritated her alveoli. We investigators hated her damn alveoli. When I saw Evan and Linus sneak out at twenty-three past ten, I figured they knew what flew and quietly walked out to the fire escape.

"Amus Graymus," Evan said, when I stepped out onto the frigid platform. "Hi, guys," I said. I suddenly felt like crying. I shifted around and sucked down three ciggies while they carried on a debate about why Superman was vulnerable to Kryptonite.

When they left, I sat on the ascending stairs and tears welled up. I took a deeper breath and they came out harder. Now I looked like shit, and I'd have to stay out in the cold until my face wasn't red and patchy. Just then the fire door creaked open and Big Gus stepped out onto the platform.

"A. Gray, how ya doin'," he said with his subtle New York twang. He'd grown up in Texas, actually, but liked sounding like he was from Brooklyn, since now he was. He also was a former dog-catcher and zookeeper who proudly wore a four-inch scar on his right shin, an homage to his favorite client, a mountain lion named Betty. Gus was a hoarder of pop-culture factoids, a repository for every line in every movie or TV show ever made by Dennis Leary, Burt Reynolds, and the entire cast of *M*A*S*H*. I found him a little intimidating, a cross between a hulking biker and a savant, sandy-haired farmboy. He was also one of the many of my new colleagues who seemed suspicious of me hitching my wagon with Nestor and Assman, although he was superficially friendly. I wasn't sure what he thought of me. Maybe he didn't.

"Okay," I squeaked. I was staring at the wrought-iron bars underneath me, giving way to tiers of smaller and smaller plat-forms below. My cigarette fell out of my hand as I went to wipe my lashes clean, and fluttered through the metal to the ground be-neath. It was dizzying.

"Hey, are you cryin'?" He looked closer at me now, and I turned away.

"Nope," I lied, not able to open my mouth, with my hands over my eyes.

"Is it that guy you broke up with?" I wasn't looking at him, but there was a tenderness in his voice that was soothing.

"Uh-huh." If I opened my mouth I'd start bawling.

"Ya know, if that guys treats you bad, then fuck him. I think you're really cool. You don't need that jerk—fuck him!"

"Thanks."

He patted me on the back. "Do you want me to beat the shit out of him?"

"Ha!" I laughed, with visions of Elliott encircled by a gang of Big Gus and Big Gus lookalikes, frail and shaking, all the masculinity in him drained out. I imagined him being tossed like a discarded penny, bouncing through the cracks of the fire escape grates like my cigarette. "That's okay," I said. "Thanks, though."

"No problem. Anytime you need me to—" He took his right fist and slammed into his left hand, indicating a considerable asswhupping. "You just let me know."

I looked up gratefully, for the first time. Big Gus nodded with his bandanaed head and patted me on mine.

"Thanks, Gus."

Before I went back into the office I lit another cigarette and rearranged my face. I surveyed the jigsaw of open sky cut by the backsides and alleyways of the buildings around ours. Concentrating on the white firmament above, I tried carefully not to look down to the graveyard of abandoned butts and injured dreams below.

✌ SEVEN

He examined the sky like a stupid detective who is searching for a clue to his own exhaustion. When he found nothing, he turned his trained eye on the skyscrapers that menaced the little park from all sides. In their tons of forced rock and tortured steel, he discovered what he thought was a clue.

—NATHANAEL WEST, *MISS LONELYHEARTS*

Just Call Me Madam Magnum

When I got back to my desk after a round of high-fives, my voicemail light was flashing, and I felt an unexpected surge of satisfaction. My heart fluttered and I was dizzy. If it's Elliott, that little bastard, I'm not even gonna call him back, I said to myself. I'll be my own valentine. I'll buy myself that Rebecca Taylor peasant blouse from Intermix, the store around the block from my office that had singularly caused my financial ruin. There was the devil inside that store that hid in my gorged credit cards and compelled me to rack up finance charges and late fees. For someone in the business of checking other people's credit, I was uniquely sympathetic to my subjects. Or maybe I'd just have a new Valentine. February 14 was only two weeks away.

Imagine my chagrin when I realized the message was not my newly jettisoned ex-boyfriend, Elliott, but Luke, a wiry neighborhood guy I had met at a Cobble Hill street fair months before. He had a job with the city, and we had talked about zoning laws and Pavement a lot—the band and the hard stuff. He also called everybody "jokers," such as, "That joker's really got to get his act together," or, "What, you mean that joker?" He had the sluggish inflection of a skate bum, the kind of guy who said "stoked," and he wasn't even from Seattle. He grew up in Brooklyn.

He invited me to see a band that night, and, owing to a combination of flattery, and vindictiveness toward Elliott for not having called in the last three days, I agreed to meet him for dinner and to see his friend's band, the Whiskey Whores. After sushi, we headed to Brownie's in the East Village and I slumped into a banquette near the stage, sipping my traditional G&T and sucking down Tareytons. Luke was making the rounds, high-fiving his friends, and I wasn't in the mood for schmoozing.

The first set was a trio jug band, Poncho's Luck, which performed a fifty-minute instrumental homage to Willie Nelson. They were actually good. The second consisted of four fairly straightlaced frat-boy washouts doing an agonizing Hootie-style jam, but with a mildly cute bassist. I kept my eye on him. In the middle of one song, "You're Killing Me," there was a long falsetto part, and I could have sworn the cute bassist was looking at me as he sang, *You slip into my life, and then slip out, No more road to travel, I kick your memory into gravel, and wash it away.* Pretty romantic.

Later, in between their set and the Whiskey Whores, I am in line for the bathroom when Cute Bassist walks by. "Hey," he says, putting his cigarette in his mouth to offer a handshake, "I'm Ethan."

Ethan and I talk for a while, but Luke's not far away and I'm feeling uncomfortable neglecting him, so I'm about to graciously extricate myself from the conversation—while still getting his number—when another guy walks up behind him, puts his arm around Ethan, and introduces himself as Markus, the drummer in the band. But the thing is, it's not just that he's not just a guy in a band, he's Dot-Com Guy, the grand prize in Sol's Jack Daniel's challenge.

Adrenaline pumping, I see my chance for glory and I seize it. These are the moments investigators must live for. Copping a swig from Ethan's Miller Lite (one must make do in dire circumstances), my morph into hyper-PI-mode is complete. I chat him up, and he gives me his number. The amazing thing is this: I stay cool, and say something to Ethan about how I have a friend in town that night and can't chat for long and he seems to buy it. "What's Markus's deal, anyway?" I ask him, holding my breath. "He's a friend of mine from the University of Tennessee," he says (Markus had claimed he went to Yale). I ask him what Markus does; Ethan says Markus made a lot of money from some "online outfit" he set up with his father's money, but that the two of them are planning to open a bar in the Caymans—"With a bowling theme—you know, bowling shirts, roller-girl waitresses." I'm horrified, but outwardly rapt. Such are the perils of the investigator's work today where kids are playing with grownup sums of money and the PR machine keeps financing in the fold long enough for fly-by-night investors to make a nice return, take the money and run. Just call me Madam Magnum, baby.

The next day and four phone calls later, I was on the line with the first of several financiers Markus and company had pursued for investments in their Bowlarama Bar. I was told on condition of anonymity that Dot-Com Guy, who one source referred to as "That little rat bastard," has $250,000 of his investors' money that was supposed to have been funneled into a Skee Ball manufacturing company in East Asia. I got the whole thing on tape, thankfully, and handed it over to Sol, demanding my prize. "What's this?" he demanded. I told him the story, which he got a kick out of, even calling George over to take it all in. Only next time, he promised me, he wouldn't let me off so easy. An anonymous source was okay, but it wouldn't break the case. Keep looking.

The Oenophile's Love Affair

At my desk later that day I got a phone call from my best friend, Cassie, inviting me to an Alphabet City bar called Niagara, where we're semiregulars of the largely nonalcoholic but shamelessly freeloading type. I took her up on it.

Cassie, like so many of my friends, worked for a website as a "content producer." She wrote columns like "Ten Ways to Make a Good Marriage Great," even though she was single, and she had somehow recently started doing a home advice column, counseling people how to remove vomit stains from sisal rugs and how to keep deer out of their garages, even though her apartment was smaller than most garages. Still, Cassie remained an optimist, as demonstrated by her belief that every new night spent at Niagara was full of possibility, despite hundreds of nights that indicated otherwise.

Making plans to go to Niagara was always a ritual of practiced futility, because we inevitably ended up there, although we always went through the motions of exploring other options. Cassie would ask me if I wanted to do something. I'd say, "Sure." Cassie would ask what I want to do. I'd say "How about . . . this place or how about . . . that place," and she'd respond, "No, it's too—" (fill in one of the following) "far away," "crowded," "rank-smelling," "lame," "full of ugly boys," and so on. Then, after a moment of ex-asperated silence, I—or she—would say, "Well, how about Nia-gara?"

On this night, however, she just said, "So you wanna go to Niagara?" upfront and I said, "Sure," and that was that. I told her about breaking up with Elliott. She'd been in L.A. visiting a sort-of-ex-boyfriend, so she wasn't up to speed yet.

"I'm sorry, but I always thought that guy was dis-*gust*-ing." I knew Cassie didn't think much of him, but I was a little offended by her candor. I could have used a little sympathy.

"Listen," Cassie said, "You are so out of his league it's ridicu-lous. He should be begging you to come back, and you shouldn't even be acknowledging his existence."

"I shouldn't?"

"No." She was resolute. "Now let's go flirt with some bar-tenders."

I felt buoyed by her conviction. Cassie was the only friend from high school that I was still close to. Our nights out in New York together so often felt like replays of so many replays of high school: the two of us cutting class (or work), passing notes, and committing other acts of rebellion both small and big, even if there weren't parents or other adults around to affront. Cassie taught me to smoke my first cigarette in the parking lot behind a Friendly's ice cream store. First she had me practice inhaling with a piece of strawberry licorice. "Just fill your mouth with the smoke. Nope, don't breathe it in directly, just like you're filling your mouth with air, not breathing it. Right. And then remove the licorice and now inhale. Good. Now try it again." She was a learned and precise ed-ucator. Later, behind the steamy overlit Friendly's Dumpster, I lit the real thing and I didn't cough or choke once, which was my greatest fear.

⊷

I took the F train to the Second Avenue subway station and walked over to Avenue A and then up to Seventh Street. When I got to Sixth Street, Cassie was waiting on a corner a block away from the bar.

"What are you doing?" I asked her. We were supposed to meet *at* the bar.

"I didn't want to go in alone!" Cassie snapped. She had a thing about that. She refused to go to any social event—even drink at a bar—and arrive alone. She could be alone there, and usually did stay longer than me wherever we went, but arriving alone was out of the question.

Our love affair with Niagara started as an attachment of convenience. In college, when we used to descend on New York on the weekends, the bar was at the center of a downtown drag of dives we frequented. Then, when Cass first moved to the city after school, she lived a block away. Now, six years later, we still make the pilgrimage to our favorite watering hole at least once a week—she from her new fifth-floor tenement walk-up on Avenue B and me from Brooklyn. In addition to the appeal of reliable free drinks (she has vodka cranberry with a splash of seltzer and I have G&T), there is the pull of endless romantic potential: Cass has had crushes on, made out with, and/or dated all of the bartenders there. They are all members of a rockabilly-dressing, punk-rock-sounding band called Hogweed.

For me, the romantic tension at Niagara is negligible, but I go in my capacity as best friend and coconspirator in Cassie's romantic travails. We get waves when we arrive (no ID-checking for us!) and kisses when we leave, although Cass's sometimes involve deep-throat action. I'm the dutiful sidekick, the Watson to her

Sherlock. The Horatio to her Hamlet. The black, joke-cracking supporting actor to her dashing white male lead.

In the glow of the bar's greenly illuminated rows of liquor, we took our usual seats at the end of the bar—the best place for chatting up the bartenders and for spotting hotties' comings and goings. Cass refuses to sit anywhere else, in fact, than at the bar itself, and there aren't always seats available. So sometimes we'll elect some poor innocuous male sitting alone and we'll descend on him with the social equivalent of double-teaming. We squeeze up against the bar on either side of him, and, leaning in seductively in all our water-bra-enhanced glory, we converse with as much ear-splitting vulgarity as we can muster. Efforts are made to talk about "female problems," like urinary-tract infections and menstruation, whenever possible. Like a lamb to slaughter, he invariably offers us his seat and tears off to the remote depths of the bar.

When we got there, the seats were almost all taken, so we staked out a single guy sitting next to an empty bar stool and moved in on him. All we could see was the back of his bald head, since he kept it turned 180 degrees away from us, presumably because he didn't want to give up his seat. "What do you want?" Cassie asked me. She was leaning in over to Stuart, one of our bartender friends and, for Cassie, an occasional suitor. "Whatever you're having," I said. Even though Cassie was making major dough, she never picked up the tab. She passed me a dirty vodka martini and whispered, "You owe me nine please, with tip."

"Right." Cass was as cheap as she was single. We continued talking about Elliott, and Cassie resumed railing about how awful he was. I was just soaking it in, enjoying the armor of righteousness that one gets from laying waste to an ex-boyfriend. Iggy Pop's "Search and Destroy" was thumping out of the jukebox.

I was singing along. "*Somebody will save my soul . . .* Yeah, that's totally true. He's a fucker," I allowed.

And with that the bald guy turned around and flashed us a gorgeous smile and two sweet puppylike big azure eyes and said, "He's stupid." "*Love in the middle of the firefight . . .*"

Cassie rolled her eyes, "What?"

"He's stupid. For blowing it with you. Big mistake." *He was talking to me.* His sweetness was so unexpected that I couldn't help laughing, which I was doing when I finally looked at him dead-on, and I almost departed this life. He was tan, tall, and he was close enough that I could smell him, like Tide and honeysuckle and wheat. I was laughing, and even though he wasn't smiling, he looked amused, his blue eyes revealing an intensity and innocence that was mesmerizing. He had an immaculately chiseled jaw, enticing lips, and a subtle tug in his shirt that hinted at the muscles beneath—an immaculate specimen of masculine form. This was no regular Niagara man, boy, guy, or bartender—he was an angel.

He must be dumb, I figured. Plus, I was only seeing him sitting from the waist up. Maybe he was short, which was a deal-breaker for me. Maybe he had skinny legs. Even worse, maybe he had no legs. There was, I tried to remind myself, no end to how bad this could get. Cass excused herself to the bathroom, and I introduced myself. Gorgeous Boy said his name was Edward, and he was in town from Boston, where he was a third-year resident in cardiology at Amherst. I mentally bracketed "dumb" for further research. I told him I grew up outside of Boston and I used to see bands at the Paradise all the time. He had been to the Paradise. He saw Dave Matthews there. I reinstated "dumb" in full force and added "jock" after it. He also saw Fu Man Chu. I set aside drawing any conclusions for now. By the time my cell phone rang an hour and a half later, I was so engrossed that I didn't recognize the voice on the other end of the phone. "Hello?" The line was crackling. "Who is it?" The reception was awful.

"It's Elliott!" a voice screamed.

"Oh, hi." I flushed and looked at Edward, who was tending his Guinness and pretending not to listen.

"Look, Elliott, now's not a good time." This was sweet justice. He wants me but he can't have me back. Did he think he could just apologize and I'd forgive him?

"I think I . . . you." He was breaking up.

My eyes widened. "This reception is terrible—I can't hear you—what, what did you just say?" I was panicked.

"I think I lo—" The line went dead. Shit! I was dying. An infinitesimal world of possibilities, a Kierkegaardian labyrinth of eithers and ors ran through my mind. I considered life spans' worth of love, heartbreak, and death in fractions of seconds. Finally I searched my heart, and I determined that even if Elliott was in love with me, I still felt the same way about him. He was a piece of shit.

The phone rang again. It was him.

"Hi."

"Yeah, hi," he seemed rushed. "I don't know what was up with that connection, but I was trying to tell you I think I left my card at your house."

I was incredulous. "Your card?"

"Yeah—my Citibank card. Can you look for it? I think we used it when we ordered burritos last Thursday."

I remembered. I remembered well enough to remember the credit card perched in front of my fake orchid on the ledge of my window, where I'd found it days ago and decided not to tell him. "I don't think I have it, but I'll look," I said, and I hung up.

Another One Bites the Dust

When I looked up from the glowing red STOP button on my cell phone, Edward was talking to another girl to his right. I couldn't get a good look at her, but she seemed attractive. I felt a stabbing in my stomach. Another battle lost. To top it off, Cassie was at the other end of the bar talking to Stuart, her bartender-suitor du jour. It didn't seem to matter that their relationship consisted mainly of heavy oral flirtation and dry humping on kegs of Corona in the stockroom. Cassie enjoyed having a boy around to flirt with.

Meanwhile, Elliott had fucked up another night and possibly my entire future. I glumly nursed my Sin Cider and kept an eye on Cassie in one corner of the mirror of the bar and Edward in the other. Half an hour later Cassie was making out with Stuart next to the bathroom at the end of the bar, so I tapped her and whispered in her ear, "I'm outtie." I was walking out the door to mourn my loss when I felt someone grab my arm. It was Edward.

"Hey," he said, looking embarrassed. I noticed his large square hand on my arm, squeezing slightly. I have a hand fetish. I adore big, boyish hands. Goosebumps bulleted down my arm and neck. He towered over me, probably about six foot three or four. I have a tall fetish, too.

"Hey," I said, trying to sound aloof.

"Listen," he said, "I'm sorry, that's someone I used to know. Someone I used to date."

"Oh." That was reassuring.

"In high school. I had planned on meeting her and her boyfriend, but he couldn't make it. We were just catching up." I let him continue. "Listen, can I call you? I'm going back to Massachusetts tomorrow, but I'd really like to see you again. Maybe you're up there sometimes visiting your parents?"

"Yeah, I visit my parents sometimes." He was winning me over. He grabbed a Heineken coaster off the bar, and I wrote my phone numbers, work and home, in a circle around the green periphery. As I walked to the F train, briskly, I said his name under my breath fifty times. Elliott was an abstract recollection, a distant dream. Edward, Edward, Edward . . .

☯ EIGHT

What an odd collection the trusted professionals are. One trusts one's lawyer, one's doctor, priest I suppose, if you are a Catholic, and now I added to the list one's private detective. A detective must find it as important as a novelist to amass his trivial material before picking out the right clue. But how difficult that picking out is—the release of the real subject. How can I disinter the human character from the heavy scene?

—GRAHAM GREENE, *THE END OF THE AFFAIR*

God Is in the Details

As a little girl, I found God. I imagined Him not as an omnipotent or sovereign character, but more like a modest puppeteer, and His provenance was the weather—specifically, snow. I prayed for it all year long, but particularly in the fall, when my birthday started to roll around in late October and the smoky fall air pointed to a potentiality that was more ripe, more *on the verge* than any other time of year.

Even as I got older, I craved the equalizing and quieting effects a snowfall had on the world around me. In high school, on one of the two snow days ever, just before heading out with Cassie to smoke Larks in a Boston alleyway called the Crevice and say "Fuck you" to the world, I fell back against the door of my room, with its Lemonheads poster and picture of Johnny Rotten and Sid relieving themselves, holding their members like battling warriors, and felt tingly from the beautiful anarchy of it all. My High Holy Days were, strictly speaking, snow days. There was no more solemn time, no state of being more deserving of reverence and awe.

The day of my boss Sol's father's funeral was a snowy day. It was three weeks into my job at the Agency. I arrived at the office a little early to find Evan holding court with a Marlboro Red hanging out of his mouth and one foot on his desk. "Hey, Gray," he said, calling me over and gesturing with his chin like a movie-made mafioso from the 1950s.

"It's freezing in here," I said to him. It couldn't have been more than forty degrees, and the whole airy space shivered as gusts snuck through cracks in the windows, holes in the floorboards, pipes in the walls.

"I know, it's pretty bad," he said. "I just wanted to tell you that the heat is busted and you can feel free to take your laptop and go work at home, 'cause it'll probably be awhile before we get this fixed—HEY, ASSMAN!" Evan called over me to Matt to deliver him the same good news. I was blissful with the prospect of a grownup snow day, a clean white layer to erase everything— my doubts, my mistrust, my hangover. I was opening the door of the office, which swung open a little too easily with the pull of the wind behind it, when Evan made an announcement: "Nobody move!"

We all gathered around his desk. Evan explained that Sol had called in and told him that his father had just died. We could use our discretion about whether or not to attend the funeral, which would be that day in Neptune City, New Jersey. They were going to rent a van to get there.

I was quietly beset. On the one hand, I was thrilled with the gift of snow, and relieved to have another day to clear my head. On the other hand, it would be an egregious slight to blow off the funeral to have a few extra hours at the Liquor Store Bar, or, even worse, shop, which my bank account couldn't sustain right now. Still, I was used to the steadfastness of massive central heating systems, like the one in the fifty-floored building, where I'd hammered out flap copy till one or two in the morning to the soothing hum of the air flowing through ten thousand tiny grates in ten thousand tiny cubicles in a hundred thousand square feet of perfectly calibrated office space heat. A broken heating system was—a gift from God! It released me, however temporarily, from another day of professional self-flagellation. A day off was painfully alluring, but attending the funeral might be the perfect way to ingratiate myself with Sol. Or he might consider it an intrusion to have me there, a new hire, witnessing one of the most intimate moments of his life. In the end, I decided to go.

Another Baptism by Fire

This funeral was actually the second time in two years that I'd started a job and been plunged into the intimacies of death and loss in the lives of my bosses. Two weeks before I graduated college, I got my first publishing job, and a week later I was in Cape Cod, with my mom for the weekend. I went into town in the morning for a hot jelly doughnut and the *Times*. When I sat down with the paper I instantly noticed a front-page article titled PULITZER WINNING WRITER DIES IN CLIMBING ACCIDENT. According to "unconfirmed sources," the writer's body had not yet been recovered, but it was believed that, while hiking a particularly difficult part of the Himalayas, he was overtaken by altitude sickness, leading him to freeze to death. His hiking partner had managed to return to a base camp and was hospitalized in critical condition, with both legs amputated. I wasn't sure it was him at first, but I remembered some particulars my new boss Gloria had revealed to me about her husband: He was a writer, and his nickname was Newlyn or Newt Ebersol. At my you've-got-the-job-lunch at La-Grenouille, she gave me the portentous warning, "Never marry a writer." When I read, at the end, "Mr. Ebersol leaves his wife, Gloria Nelson, a book editor, a son, Myer Tate Ebersol, and a daughter, Olivia Marcel Ebersol," I dropped my plate and said, "Fuck!" I left the hot raspberry jelly and torn dough in a fleshy pile on the floor.

A week and a half later, I was sitting in St. Bartholomew's Church at Park Avenue and Fiftieth Street, listening to a parade of swinging dicks of the publishing world. Princeton classmates and colleagues from *The Wall Street Journal* told clever, sometimes stirring, elegiac stories about him. Newt was a social scientist who wrote vast, assiduously researched works of social conscience. There weren't many left like him anymore. The Ebersol children, Myer and Liv, sat in the front of the crescent before the stage like dolls, with tiny porcelain grimaces. The only-outside-the-establishment speaker was a black woman who had been a subject of Newlyn's Pulitzer-winning documentary book on the Crown Heights riots. She stood up in front of the 99 percent white, 98 percent male, 97 percent Century Club audience and collapsed into hysterical sobs, wailing, "Why he got to go do that? Oh, God, why? Why he gotta do that?" It seemed like the question everyone wanted to ask but no one had dared. A wave of uncomfortable murmuring shook the otherwise stoic literati. The one-hundred-pound ivory-weave stock of the memorial programs absorbed many tears. Liv and Myer were quickly escorted by their nannies out of the auditorium. Some stiff upper lips slackened.

I spent the next year reading and talking about Newlyn, sending excerpts from his published and unpublished works to magazines and papers and speaking expertly in the hushed, sympathetic tones used to speak of the tragically dead. I, like most of the reporters I was fielding, was trying to mourn someone I'd never known. Gloria almost never talked about him, but I would hear her occasionally muted tones on the phone with friends, talking about how Newt had broken an arm on that same mountain six months earlier, and how she had forbidden him from going again, but he insisted, even going so far as to start researching an article for *Harper's* about the tradition of ice climbing. Her voice would flail up and down in a way that divulged a profound anger—anger that he would *choose* to leave his family. I wondered how he could challenge death in a way that seemed so indifferent, that even mocked the grim effect it could have on his wife and his children. I imagined Newt, sitting on that mountain in a frenzy of swirling whiteness, calmly absorbing the baptism of the snow, closing his eyes as he yielded to the cleansing, to the wiping away, of everything. Slowly, I reconstituted Newt, gathering and amplifying data and repartees and minutiae until I could almost imagine having known him.

New Jersey Girl

Two and a half years later, the van ride to Sol's father's funeral was not what I expected. Instead of being somber, everyone was joking and foul-mouthed. Vinny and I talked politics a little. "Amy

Gway! You came!" he exclaimed. I climbed in the bouncing tan Chevrolet that Evan got at a rental place for reconstituted and seized vehicles. The van was swimming with profanity. Vinny was a fourth-generation Italian-American New Yorker, and his great-uncle had been a big-time trade unionist in the twenties. Hence, Vinny explained, he believed in big labor and liberal government. Gus added "big breasts" to the list in a whisper right before we pulled into the aluminum-sided Yahrzeit Jewish Memorial Home. (Vinny called them "cans," which he saw a lot of at dance clubs out in Bay Ridge, where Giuliani's topless-only statutes weren't enforced.) I talked to Vinny about the cases a bit—he had a photographic recall of the roughly five hundred the Agency had handled since he started working there. "Oh, yeah," he'd say, "I wemember number fifteen-one-eleven, dat one was a doozy," or "Nine fifty-seven had a hundwed and seventeen lawsuits connected to it!"

When we entered the funeral home, Sol was standing in the foyer, holding his infant son. His other son, Joshua, was holding a balloon and running in figure eights around the guests, yelling "Daddy, look, I'm an airplane. Watch me Daddy, *watch me!*" The Agency people got in line to give Sol their regards, and he kissed everyone and said, "Thanks for being here." I held back, but Sol saw me and kissed me hello on the cheek, as he'd done with everyone else and said, "Thanks so much for being here, A. Gray," and I was glad I'd come.

When we sat down for the service, the baby was sitting with the nanny in front of me, crossing his eyes and staring at what appeared to be nothing at all. The rabbi made a speech and talked about how Sol's dad had worked almost up until the day he died and how he almost couldn't have imagined the successes his sons would have seen in their lives, both attending college and becoming successful, self-sufficient men in the tradition of the Rubensteins. He turned to Sol and his brother and said, "May God comfort you among all the mourners of Zion and Jerusalem." Sol's mother started crying softly in the front row, and I saw him touch her shoulder from two seats away and mouth the words "I love you."

Just then I saw a line from the baby's mouth—which was smiling widely at me—to the floor at my feet, which I realized were splattered with vomit. The nanny stood up to take the baby out of the room, and he was literally *beaming* at me as they walked away.

To my surprise, we all followed along in the van to the cemetery. Sol didn't have a lot of men in his family, and he needed pallbearers, and I almost cried when I saw Big Gus and Evan and Linus and Matt standing by the circle of black earth in the center of the snowy field in their ill-fitting blue and black blazers, looking very serious for the first time. Sol's mother threw herself on the ground and sobbed, and he and his brother pulled her up while the rest of us looked away and the boys put the casket on the webbing over the open grave. The ride back to Manhattan was subdued and by the time I headed home I barely noticed that it was way past dinnertime and all I'd had was a Big Mac at a drive-through on the way.

Filing My Way to Heaven

When I was still toiling away in publishing, one day Gloria called to say she'd be going out to the dentist and then having a meeting for Newt's memorial foundation, and I settled down in her office, which for some reason was bigger than that of my other boss, Boris, and had a beautiful view of the East River stretching below. I brought in some hundreds of pages of dreaded filing I had to do and then spaced out (for seconds, minutes?) admiring my cute patent-leather Sigerson Morrison Mary Janes crossed at the ankle on her desk. Since I'd been working for Gloria I had completely overhauled the filing systems, putting into place an intricate and aesthetically pleasing system of color-coded folders corresponding to matching shaded laser-printed courier lettering on sleek matte transparent Filofax labels. I was proud of my accomplishment, which required extra hours of work each day, not to mention whole Saturdays and Sundays.

The filing project somehow felt like more of a triumph, more *me* than the perfunctory reports I wrote about middling manuscripts and book proposals I took home each night. The books I liked got rejected anyway, even if, as only happened a few times, I actually wrote at the end—"I strongly recommend reading this. This could be the environmentally bent, biracial, gay Rick Moody," or "A strong commercial read, appealing to the market where Mary McCarthy and Irvine Welsh intersect." My reports would sit on Boris's desk for months, settling over with a fine layer of dust.

On our cleanup day, which was usually once a week, I would sit in Boris's office and take dictation while he plucked unread manuscripts off his desk and pitched them into an enormous trash can I would bring in for this purpose. He would pick up the manuscript with my report, and finally say, "I have appraised that report, which was well written, but the project is not right for me." And, with that, he would throw it in the trash, as he did with almost all the manuscripts he received, solicited or otherwise. I was constantly drafting notes to peeved agents telling them, "Please resend the proposal," "There has been some error," and "Boris never received it." "But I sent it by messenger!" they would say, exasperated.

In Gloria's office, as I filed away, I came across a picture of her and Newt posing over a Scrabble board, looking engrossed and in love for the only time in any picture I'd seen of them together. I also found a piece of paper on which she'd tried to figure out how to spell the word "fugue"; it had such variations as "fewgue" "feogwe" and "fooge." I found a note she'd written to me that said, "Amy: to do: 1) Make new Xeroxes of *all news articles* for my books and make a new Pendaflex file called 'Current Media,' 2) Help figre [sic] how to Back up my Personal Digital Assistant, 3) What is going on with Raffeter contract and why haven't you mentioned it? 4) Please type thank you letter to my mother which I will dictate." I stuffed her chickenscratch in my pocket and threw it away when I got home so she couldn't dig it out of the trash.

From the glint on my shoes on her desk, I gazed over the view, watching airplanes leaving La Guardia, rising like tiny discolorations, almost indistinguishable filaments against the bruised pale sky, and then surging up, from behind the arching girders of the Brooklyn Bridge, like tendrils rising out of the massive towers. The incoming planes followed a sweeping path to the left of the bridge, and the outgoing ones rose in a half-ellipse to the right. Together they formed a V, like the two edges of a highway meeting at a distant vanishing point.

"What are you doing in here?"

Gloria was standing, red-faced, sharp-eyed in the doorway, her language a little slurred, a cup of water in her hand. My eyes stung. I swung my feet off the desk.

"I thought you weren't coming in." She closed her eyes for a second into slits, and looked like she might pass out, then opened them up again so wide I thought they might roll out of her head. "Amy, what the hell is going on?" I geared up to explain why I was in her office—I was up all night working . . . I was getting some tea from her desk . . . "I was just in your office and I saw files in there I gave you days ago," she said. "Plus, there's a contract I haven't heard back from you about."

I threw her a bone, albeit a false one. "The Bielman contract is signed and done."

"No, no, that's not it." She paused and looked confused. "Well, I can't remember what contract it is, but I'll get back to you about it, but whatever it is, you should be coming to me and not the other way around. You have to think one step ahead of me." The one-step-ahead thing was her mantra. She was constantly telling me that. But one step ahead of her was as useless as ten steps ahead of her, since she was miles *behind* everybody else. All of her books were years behind schedule because she took months to "edit" every page, if she was doing anything at all, and 80 percent of the work I did for her was personal: organizing dinner parties, drafting thank-you notes to the socialites that seemed to be friends of hers through her dead husband, sending to-do lists to her gardener, her housekeeper, her accountant, her lawyer.

But that day, she seemed too out of it to remember to dress me down for being in her office, and instead sent me to my desk to get a pad of paper because she had something she desperately needed to get done, and by the way she'd be working late tonight and she'd need my help. I couldn't tell if she'd been crying, but she probably had. She continued to issue edicts, despite an unsteadiness and a suspect swagger when she turned corners.

That night at seven she had me follow her into the bathroom ("I'm in a huge rush—we just can't miss a *beat* here!" she said) and take dictation from her to the sound of her piss hitting the water while I scratched down a note to her mother, filling her in on who would be attending a dinner party. My empathy for her had hardened into an angry piece of coal in my stomach, which was stoked to incandescence every time I even thought about her. A week later, I quit my job.

✪ NINE

One thing is, to be a spy, you have to rely on your hunches.

—Woody Allen, "The Whore of Mensa"

If This Guy's Who He Says He Is, I'll Eat My Own Asshole

"Don't mix business with pleasure." George told me that. In the case of the Three-Ring Wedding Bandit, the two were impossible to separate.

George was doing some preliminary research for a wedding planner, the friend of a friend of a former employee. He was heard cackling across the office, "Ha! If this guy's who he says he is, I'll eat my own asshole." I'm certain none of us wanted to see that happen.

As George explained when he called me over to give me the case, he'd been doing this stuff for twelve years and he knew when he was dealing with a criminal, and this guy the wedding planner had called him about was the real thing. But even though he could tell me that and even impart his suspicions to the client, what we acted on had to be entirely based on what we *knew* in evidence, not just on what we suspected.

George had been approached by Goldie Gabriel, a grande dame in the cutthroat New York wedding industry. An hour after George debriefed me, we paid a call to Goldie. "Oh my gawd!" she exclaimed when George and I came into her office, which was upholstered in a potpourri of throw pillows, each in a different pattern and color scheme from the sofa's side cushions, as well as from the balloon curtains, with their separately upholstered valences. "Yoor adoorable! I love this—don't you love this? I love this!" She wrung her hands together with excrescent energy and kissed George and me hello, saying, "I can't believe there are real private investigators here—This is so *wild*," pointing us out to her barefoot, long-haired assistant, Paul, as if to say, "Who woulda thunkit?" Paul scratched his disarrayed, curly black tresses and shuffled around his desk, smiling at her familiar histrionics.

Goldie took us into her office, which looked like a war zone of competing English floral patterns. At the center of this cacophony of climbing roses and ranunculus on balloon curtains, envelopes, and wallpapering, Goldie held court. She explained that she'd been approached by a couple a few days before to "do an event," which she'd been doing for fifteen years, by the way, and she'd never had doubts like this before. It became clear that Goldie possessed a highly attuned cultural barometer in which the combination of a no-carat ring and a six-figure flower budget was "lunacy," forgoing the use of a private caterer in a loft space was "borderline," and a stipulation that "money is no object"—no matter how rich the client—is cause for calling the local investigator, which is just what she did.

"There is nobody, *nobody* so rich that money is no object. I don't care if you're the Sultan of Brunei; even he has a budget, and let me tell you, the richer they are, the *cheaper* they are." Goldie imparted this with the hushed tone of someone divulging a grave but certain truth. The groom-to-be and object of Goldie's misgivings was older. He looked forty-five, she said, even though he said he was only thirty-eight. The bride-to-be said she was twenty-seven, and probably was. There was no ring, and he'd said they were in such a rush that he'd given her one of those gold-plate cubic zirconium artificial Tiffany settings that you could get at any good pawnshop for $200. "That was naawt normal," Goldie declared. "I don't care how rushed you are; when I see a rich older guy like that and a young woman like that I expect a *rock* on her finger and nothing less. I'm not saying rich people won't skimp on some fronts, because they definitely will. But . . ." She threw her hands out as if to indicate all of the above was just *so* obvious, "Nawt the ring."

"Listen, I like to cut through the bull," Goldie said defiantly, "and I think I know what this guy is doing. I think they might be reporters, and they might be undercover to do an exposé about the wedding business, for, say, *Vanity Fair.* I want to know if they're going to write about *me*!" I imagined a subterranean war room of journalists and infiltrators meeting around a strategy board at the center of which was a cutout of Goldie's head, and around her an elaborate system of arrows, snapshots, stratagems, and frilly fabric swathes. Graydon Carter would sit at the head of the table in camouflage, this season's black, and imposing Lagerfeld-style sunglasses, barking, "Find her secrets out at any cost!" No, I didn't think there was a cloak-and-dagger story in the works. George looked intent, his blue eyes converged, his upper lip protruded earnestly in what seemed to be a sign that he had checked all sarcasm at the door. I tried to look serious, too, even though Goldie's *Vanity Fair* fantasy made me want to giggle. But I didn't crack a smile.

George asked lots of questions, and I wrote down things I thought might be relevant on the pad I'd brought with me. What did this guy do for a living? Goldie wasn't sure—he had a startup, or maybe it was an older company that he'd taken over—and then some foundation that he was starting for his future wife. Or maybe the foundation *was* the startup, but he also implied that he had the security of a vast family fortune. He mentioned the Willkommen family, the founder and owners of a small but profitable Austrian airline called Rheintalflug Air. They had assembled a net worth of more than $400 million doing it. Goldie thought he had also mentioned something about a family marinara-sauce business, which "raised some red flayags" in her mind. "It was very Gawdfawther."

George took a very cautious position, saying, "Listen, I'll tell you right now that I think this guy's a crook, but until we have evidence, you should be doing nothing and saying nothing to him. Just don't accept any checks from him."

"Oh," Goldie said, "Well, I guess that's another thing." The groom said they were in such a rush to book the whirlwind wedding, he'd asked her to start booking vendors immediately. But the check he'd written her for the $100,000 to cover the just-getting-started charges had bounced and she'd written checks to the vendors that were supposed to draw on this check, including a $10,000 deposit at the Waldorf and another $6,500 for the Carolina Herrera dress. The guy had apologized for the bounced check, saying it was a miscommunication with his bank. Supposedly he was wiring her the money now, although nothing had come through yet.

George and I left the meeting with about fifteen pages of notes and a Xerox of the guy's card, which read:

Garry Wilbur
Entrepreneur/Philanthropist
917-555-9899

It reminded me of a card I'd gotten from a guy who followed me all the way from the Borough Hall station in Brooklyn to my gym. He followed me for two blocks, calling, "Excuuuse me, miss!" before he said he couldn't help but notice my "beautiful spirit" and "nice booty." Saying he wanted to "portray me in paint," he handed me his card, which read: "Tyrell G. Artist, Portraits, Dancing, Business Consultant." After spending the next forty minutes hiding in the ladies' changing room of the New York Sports Club, I ran home.

The Arm-Wrestling Champion of the World

Back at the office I put Wilbur's card in the file and booted up my computer. I wanted to impress the hell out of my bosses with this case. I would eat and breathe it until I had cracked Wilbur open like a nut.

I looked up. Linus was diving across my desk. He came to rest in a classical pose and flashed me a crooked smile. "Let me ask you something."

"Okay."

His eyes flickered behind trifocal lenses. "Do you think you could outwrestle Noah?" Noah was one of the new guys who started with me, and our desks were blocked side-by-side. We barely spoke. I probably outweighed him by about fifty pounds, even though he subsisted on Ding-Dongs, Egg McMuffins, and sopping-wet pressed Cuban sandwiches from the Twenty-One deli around the corner. He was a caloric black hole.

"What kind of wrestling? Arm-wrestling or regular?"

He thought about it. "Arm."

"I think so."

Linus turned to the rest of the room triumphantly. "Okay, she's in! I'm taking bets here. Three-to-one odds for Amy!" Sol and George were laughing as Sol threw a twenty at Linus and said, "Just take it. For making this happen."

"Listen, I don't know if I want to do this." It became clear that they wanted to see Noah getting beaten by a girl. I felt embarrassed for him if I beat him, and even more embarrassed for me. What would that make me—a she-man? I wanted to be a girl whose wit allowed her to muscle out of situations and kick ass, but I didn't *actually* want to be seen as manly or otherwise mannish. But things had escalated beyond my control. Big Gus, Wendy, Evan, Otis, Morgan, Sol, George, and even Assman and Nestor were crowded around my desk. My protests of "I don't know about this, guys" were met with thumping chants of "Fight, fight! and "Let's go!" "Let's do it!" and "Kick her ass, Noah!" In an etherlike suspension between humiliation and punchiness, I rolled up my sleeves and leaned over the desk. Noah seemed shell-shocked.

I beat him in five seconds. I'm not sure he was even trying, but the roar of the crowd and the cries of "You go, Gray!" and "Aww, beaten by a girl!" told me I'd won. Noah stumbled away, dazed, and I sat down to catch my breath. We were like the two kids sent into the closet in junior high to make out, emerging from the darkness with their shared trauma having done nothing to pierce the rift between them. The whole scene harked back to a time of Benetton sweatshirts, Wham!, and constant indiscriminate humiliations.

When things settled down later, I got an instant message from Evan asking if I wanted to drink at the office that night. (This in spite of the fact that it was an even day.) He postscripted me that he had a bottle of Wild Turkey in his desk to get us started. At five-thirty, Sol was the second boss to cut out, and when the steel door slammed shut behind him, Evan lit a Camel Light and poured us all whiskey shots.

"To A. Gray, the arm-wrestling champion of the world, and to Noah, for taking getting beaten by a girl like a man!" We all drank to that. Everyone was gathered in the conference room except for Assman and Nestor. "Do you guys want to drink with us?" I asked tentatively. Nestor grunted something about how he had somewhere to be and Assman said he had to do laundry. Then he said, "But you run along and hang out with the cool kids," and then turned away from me. I flushed. I was hurt by their closeness, but said nothing.

There were some rumors circulating among the investigators about the Wilbur case. Everyone wanted to know what was going on and how I got assigned to it. "What's up, Dingleboy?" Gus said. "What's Gray doing for you that I'm not? I thought I was your 'go to' guy for this stuff."

"You were, but now I'm using your mom," Evan said.

How Can He Be So Skinny and Live So Fat?

The next day at work, George and I made a list of things for me to do. I plopped a sixteen-ounce Gatorade on my desk and a bottle of Alleve. We had in our notes an exhaustive catalog of every contact Goldie had ever had with the couple, when it was had, what information was shared by which individual, physical descriptions of both, and a list of all the other vendors that were allegedly and verifiably in contact with them. At the top of my agenda was getting in touch with the people in the eight penthouse apartments of the Sixty-second Street and Central Park West address where he claimed to be building a luxury duplex for himself and his new bride to be, Alexis Dominique Whitcomb. I called a bunch of their neighbors, saying my client was considering doing business with a man who claims to live in that building, and that I was trying to get some independent references about him.

Although nobody had heard of him, his rich alleged neighbors seemed loath to cast any doubt on him, and seemed to have a fraternal rich person's alliance with their notional neighbor. They said things like, "Well, I don't know him, but perhaps he's been leasing the place to Mrs. Haverman," or "My apartment is very well soundproofed, so I might not hear the workmen doing the renovations." I got the feeling that people in this building took pride in their collective claim to agoraphobia, a birthright to keep to themselves and protect their right to ignore one another. I imagined bony women living there for decades and walking their Lhasa apsos in hand-crocheted doggie coats past faces they saw daily and to which they never cared to attach names.

It turned out a few not-too-minor celebrities, including Rutanya Alda, who you might remember from *The Deer Hunter,* as well as the guy who played Doogie Howser, M.D., were living in the building, the Worcester. I looked up the property records for the building and got the name of the broker at Sotheby's real estate division who handled the sales on six out of the eight penthouse flats in the building. She was a chirpy Australian who seemed enthralled by the possibility of an imposter claiming to live in the building. "This is vaary serious, of course," she commiserated. "It puts all the residents there in jeopaady. This maan could be gaaining unloorful access to the propaaty." She couldn't remember if Mr. Wilbur was a client of one of her agents. I had spoken to the residents of the two units she hadn't sold, as well as four of the six owners of the other flats she transacted, and ruled them out as having any association with Mr. Wilbur. The property records for the other two listed a Mrs. Alix Von Albrecht Halle and a Ludmilla Melnikov as the owners, respectively. Mrs. Peacock, the realtor, said she'd "git baaack to me on this as soon as possible." In the meantime, I took the liberty of calling Mrs. Von Albrecht Halle, who was listed as living in Vancouver.

It turned out Mrs. Halle had passed away, but her middle-aged son Claude, in his words, "knew nothing of this Wilbur character!" I left a message for Mrs. Melnikov, and in the meantime was planning to visit the building to talk to the building manager, when I got a call back from another neighbor I'd called, who lived in the apartment directly below one of the penthouses that I thought might belong to Wilbur. The apartment was actually listed as belonging to Lani Guinier, the Clinton nominee for U.S. assistant attorney general of civil rights, but John Speakbrooks, the guy who called back, explained that he was her nephew-in-law and that she had leased the apartment to him. After he confirmed that he didn't know Mr. Wilbur, I had an inspiration. "You know, I was thinking that talking to the building manager, superintendent, or doorman might be helpful to clear this up, since I haven't had much luck with the residents."

He gave me a number for Hector, the handyman, assuring me, "Hector knows everybody in this building, and he's been here at least ten years." I called Hector, who didn't seem surprised by my call.

"Yeah, I figured I'd get a call from somebody like you at some point," Hector said.

"Really?" My pulse hurried—my mouth was cottony.

He told me that there was a guy, whose name he couldn't remember, who had been claiming to live at that address for years. "He's a real piece of work—there was a piece about him in the *Daily News* a few years back about how he planned a circus wedding in Texas and bilked some people down there out of the whole cost of the wedding." Hector didn't recognize the name Garry Wilbur, but when I mentioned that the guy I was checking out was working on another wedding scam, he seemed convinced. "That's definitely the same guy. I don't know about the name, but I know it's him, and if it is, there are guys at the Sixteenth Precinct lookin' for him. He was indicted in New York too a few years ago for an insurance scam." Hector gave me the name of a detective friend of his in the Sixteenth. I got off the phone and reported my eureka moment to George.

With his quiet, no-bullshit intensity, George let me know he was proud by telling me I'd "done good" and "hadn't fucked up." I felt triumphant.

He also had an interesting discovery to report. There was nobody, in any of our credit sources, who listed a Garry Wilbur. George told me to go back to my desk and do an extensive database search for the con artist Hector had told me about.

I plugged in some search terms: "circus" and "police" and "wedding" and "indictment" in various combinations, and, on my fourth or fifth try, I got twelve hits. The first line of the first article I clicked on read:

January 19, 1997—Dateline: Houston, Texas—Until last week Larry Willburr was living a life of luxury, staging an extravagant three-ring circus wedding—literally. Willburr and his bride, Rosemary Burney, followed up their lavish wedding, for which they paid the Houston Acrobatic Circus fifty thousand dollars in bad checks, with a two week honeymoon in Texas, also paid for with check kiting and an insurance scam for which Willburr was previously on probation in New York.

The wedding was held in a tent, where, it was reported, "the bride and groom entered on the backs of Indian elephants decorated like can-can dancers," and then exchanged their vows before the "swooping backdrop and aerial tricks of three dozen trapeze artists, tumblers, and contortionists." The picture was gravity-defying. My air passages narrowed, while my internal diagnostic scope of Wilbur's sick mind expanded to cosmic proportions. What was the point of a stolen wedding? The risk-versus-reward-ratio was a gazillion to one.

The circus wedding, I read, had no master of ceremonies. No one addressed the audience or deciphered the twisted pageantry for anyone present. This spectacle was created for an audience of two. The others present were just seat-fillers, like the time I got to go to the Emmys and had to sit in the empty seats of famous actors while they took a leak. In this case, the role of the bride and groom were played by—themselves. It was a pure display of egotism and opulence, witnessed by no one.

The article went on to explain that "Mr. Willburr" was a multiple felon with scam-related convictions in two states. It was late in the day, but George had me call Goldie and tell her to put a stop on any checks she'd written on Wilbur's behalf. She mentioned that the money he was wiring had never materialized. George and I made an appointment with Detective Louis DeSanto at the Sixteenth Precinct for the next afternoon at three.

What the World Needs Now Is Love, Sweet Love

During my first week in the office there was a constant stream of music playing daily from an old dusty Aiwa system in the center of the loft. Then our accountant complained that it sounded unprofessional to have music blaring when she called clients, and it was banned except for off-hours. Apparently, I had started working at the Agency when all our most noteworthy privileges were being rescinded. On this day, though, the clicks and creaks of the office's usual music-free soundtrack were disrupted by Linus, who started singing quietly, "What the world needs now . . . is love, sweeeet looove!" As he was chanting, he danced over to the tape deck and hit PLAY.

Evan, Wendy, Otis, and Gus and I were all looking up, spellbound by the simplicity of this sentiment, a radiant contrast to business as usual. Everyone was laughing. I jumped up and sang my way to the back of the room, where Gus and Wendy and Linus now were swaying and belting it out. I saw Sol get up from his desk, and I held my breath, at once transfixed by the incantation and scared that he'd fire our asses on the spot. But he sashayed out the door, shaking his head as if to say, "I can't believe I work with these crazy people." "What the world needs now, is love, sweet love . . . no, not just for some, but for everyone . . ."

It was stuck in my head for days, as I headed around the city and Brooklyn with love on my mind.

✪ TEN

The detective is the one who unlocks, who listens, who moves through this morass of objects and events in search of the thought, the idea that will pull all these things together and make sense of them. In effect, the writer and the detective are interchangeable.

—PAUL AUSTER, *CITY OF GLASS*

The Fake Baby

Garry Wilbur lived in a world totally disconnected from reality. He had at least seven aliases, fifteen fake Social Security numbers (several of which rightly belonged to other people), dozens of fake addresses, fake businesses, one fake bride and possibly a second, a fake baby (more on that later), a fake book, a fake career, many fake businesses, a fake family (we had checked out that he was *not* in any way related to the Willkommen family), a fake chin, hairline, cheeks, and lips (he'd had some extensive plastic surgery, as documented in the *Arizona Star*), and, in a more general sense, a fake life. Figuring out what was real about this guy was the hard part, because almost nothing about him wasn't perverted by his artifice.

There didn't seem to be anything at the core of Garry Wilbur, and it frightened me. I was alarmed by the fact that I hated his dimwitted Midwestern svelte little bride, who was about to marry a sociopath, even more than I hated him. As a spy, I had hoped to know everything. I wanted to ward off the unexpected with knowledge, and protect myself from surprise with shrewd insights. And who wouldn't rather be the duper than the duped. Except I figured that would make me more identified with this fucked-up crazy maniac than with his poor gullible girlfriend. I tried to imagine what would make someone pursue appearances to the point of total loss of self, where everything about oneself was simply to signify to others. I thought about becoming the red dot in my high school yearbook, about willing things with Elliott to be something they weren't. Could I be . . . like Garry Wilbur? I was mulling this very scary thought when Cassie called and invited me to Niagara that night. It was only ten fifty-one in the morning. Minimum of seven hours until a bibulous respite. I suggested Plant Bar. She sighed and said, "That place is sooo loud."

"Yeah." Silence. "Well, we can go to Niagara."

She brightened, "Okay!"

When I got off the phone, George motioned me over.

He was staring at his computer, chewing his cud. He always seemed to be chewing something, but he did it very deliberately and placidly, like a cow.

"What's up," I said. He kept chewing.

Five long seconds later, he looked up. "Yeah, I've got something I need you to do. I talked to Goldie a minute ago and I want you to call her, too, but basically she wants you to follow the girl, Alexis. Today, if you can." He looked at his watch. "Okay, it's eleven-thirty, just go by the house, it's in Brooklyn, right near you, I think, and I want you to see if she really lives there. Look at the buzzer and talk to the neighbors, see if they know her."

"Okay." I was thrilled. "Who should I say I am?"

"Just say you're looking for your sister, who's supposed to be staying with her. When you get there, call her number and see if anyone answers. If she's there, don't talk to the neighbors, just see if you can catch her leaving and see where she goes. I'll have you go back next week in the morning and follow her to work." Supposedly she was working as a part-time music teacher at a fancy Upper East Side conservatory, but Goldie was skeptical and Lou wanted to know if she was at all implicated in the fraud. I called Goldie's office and got a very detailed description of her from them, down to the kind of manicure she had (French-tipped) and what Goldie described as a "ratty, pilly, gross" belted sweater-slash-overcoat she'd worn to both meetings. "A real thrift-store foind," Goldie added. "Uh-huh," I said, writing. "Thanks, dawl!" she said, when we got off the phone. I packed up my coat with cigarettes, a flashlight, a small camera, and a tape recorder and made it down to Brooklyn in just twenty minutes, I was so excited.

I was wearing my trench coat, actually, and black pumps. It was raining, so I stopped by my house and picked up an umbrella.

The apartment building was near me, but in a completely different neighborhood. New York is like that. You can walk two blocks in any direction and be catapulted into another country, culturally. She lived near the loading docks and warehouses of downtown Brooklyn, across the street from a dusty lot with some melted tires and an old moving crane sitting in the middle. The building had a gray metal façade, and on the left it faced onto the waterfront across the street. This was one of the parts of the East River where sailors docked when they were in New York, and twice in the summers they'd swarm the Promenade and Montague Street and Fulton Market in their shocking white outfits and uneasy carriage.

It wasn't a very nice neighborhood, particularly for a girl slated to move into a ten-million-dollar duplex on Central Park. But stranger things have happened.

I made a phone call to her apartment on my Nextel. I blocked my phone number first and then dialed. A woman's voice answered. "Yes, is this Acme Advertising?" I tried to sound young and confused. This is what we call a "ruse" at work. It's performing, really.

"No, I think you have the wrong number—what number did you dial?"

"Oh, no, I see I did misdial. So sorry." I hung up. I went into the building's foyer, where the buzzers were, and looked for her name. It was there, in yellowed typed tape: ALEXIS D. WHITCOMB. When I'd spoken to Goldie before I left the office, she told me she'd been contacted by Alex's (this is the name she went by) sister, Marion, who said she was very concerned about Wilbur and that the family was suspicious that something was up. Meanwhile, Goldie had called up Wilbur herself, without consulting George or Lou, and said, "I know you're not who you say you are, so what's the game?" When George heard about this he was furious. "It's all about fucking *her*, isn't it! Those bitches are all the same!" I wasn't sure who "those bitches" were. "She's got a lot to learn. I'm gonna rip her a new asshole!"

I shuddered. "Yeah." I reminded myself to avoid pissing George off.

I stood in Alex's foyer for two and a half hours. At three I called in to say there had been no movement. I repeated the same into my tape recorder. George told me to stick around for another few hours and see if she left the house. He also said to check if she had a car and get her license plate. Good. An errand to do. I was dying of boredom. It was pouring out. My mascara was dripping down my face. I was turning into an unsavory-looking character.

I put up my umbrella and went around to the river side of the apartment building, where there was a parking lot with numbered spaces. I saw her car, a tiny two-door Nissan, and said the number into my recorder. I decided to stand outside for a while for a change of scenery. An hour into that, a guy came out of the building and started putting trash bins out on the street. "Hey, sweetie," he said.

"Hi." Could I make myself more conspicuous?

"Can I help you with anything?"

"No, I'm meeting my sister. She's, uh, with someone upstairs."

"Okay. Let me know if you need anything."

"Thanks." For the next couple of hours the super was skulking around the property, and every so often he'd ask me if I wanted a chair or something. Or if I knew who my sister's friend was so maybe we could buzz him, and I'd decline, and he'd smile and I'd go about my business of counting the tiles on the walls and thinking of good comebacks I should have used with Elliott and twisting my hair. I did get a kick out of knowing how incognito I was. This guy clearly had no clue who I was. At six I was back in the foyer, and I thought my legs were going to crumple. I called George and gave him the license-plate number; he ran it and it came up as hers, with nothing unusual. Her birthday was two days before mine—she was twenty-five. Just then a tall blond figure in a black-belted thigh-length sweater brushed past me down the stairs.

"Yeah, so I'll see what I can do," I said, keeping the cadence of what I was saying as natural as possible.

"Do you see her?" George asked.

"Uh-huh."

"Good. Let me know what happens."

"Great, okay. Love you too, Mom." I clicked my phone off and tore out the door. She was walking away from the building with her back to the river. She was probably heading for the subway. I quickened my pace. When I followed her into the subway, I was glad I'd heeded George's advice to stock up on tokens, magazines, and dollar bills. She leaned against a peeling green column in the station, and I breathed in the mist of urine and garbage rising warmly from the tracks.

Alexis and the Amazing Technicolor Dreamcoat

In New York, the proximity to squalor has been transformed into an aesthetic principle. This has inspired a booming industry in artificial distressing. Rich uptowners pay big money to have the butt cheeks on their jeans worn through, or to have the paint properly cracking off their armoires. They are trying to look like everyone else who has made hipster virtues of necessity.

On the subway platform, following my first subject into the underbelly of New York, I shivered happily. I have evolved so far in my love of the damaged and dirty that I get a perverse thrill out of being so near bodily emissions and refuse. I'm really doing it, I thought.

When the train pulled up and she coolly walked on, I sat at the opposite end of the car. I could see her sun-bleached hair, and when the train pulled into the station I followed her ponytail up some stairs, through the turnstiles, up some more stairs, and then onto Lexington Avenue, where she stopped in a deli. She came out, opened a pack of Silk Cut 100s, and lit one, and then continued uptown, where she turned into a storefront at Seventy-second Street. It was a Kate's Paperie. She fingered pretty silvery vellums and creamy hundred-pound envelopes, then headed to the back of the store. I closed in, clutching a lime-yellow stationery set and inkwell to the light, making like I was choosing color combinations. I kept her blond head hemmed in my line of vision by the scallop-edged papers and ink bottles.

Since I'd gotten into the store, I kept imagining jumping up and outing myself. To the soon to be Alexis Wilbur, I'd say, I'm sorry to tell you your future husband is a con artist, and you've been conned. We know about the penthouse you've never been to, the son he had with a previous girlfriend you've never met. Well, there's no penthouse, there's no child, and there will be no marriage. Your future husband is being arrested at this moment. Don't cry. Things will be much easier this way than if you had never known. At this she would collapse on the floor, crying, and I'd tell the stationer, dryly, It could happen to the best of us. Somehow it just doesn't. I couldn't bury my hostility. How could someone be so dense? The guy was a classic bullshit artist, what George called a "fucking red flag of psychopathology."

The stationer said something to her, and I heard her say, "Yes, I'm looking for wedding invitations." My stomach folded over. She smiled and blushed. There was a chair around the corner from the stationer's corner, which I quickly sat in and, whipping out a copy of *New York* magazine, put my tape recorder between the pages and clicked ON. I pretended to read the Gotham section.

"So when is the *wedding*?" The stationer was a thin, manic New Yorker type with a terrible arts-and-crafts style. She wore a quilted patchwork catastrophe of a jacket with glittery rainbow fabrics sewn next to printed text swaths with words like "dream" and "miracle." The coat combined the worst style of high school art teachers, flea-market patrons, and therapists everywhere. She also seemed to italicize the last word of every sentence.

The girl, Alexis, had a crumbly, thin-pitched voice, like a girly eleven-year-old smoker.

"Well, it's soon actually. In May."

"So *soon*." The stationer thrust out a bell-sleeved arm in excitement. The word "imagine" appeared at the inside of her elbow. "That's *terrific*. So it will be a *rush job,* if you choose to go with *us*. So how did you meet your *fiancé*?"

"Well, at a bar, actually, which is the last place I thought I'd ever meet anybody." She laughed. Yeah, me too, I thought to myself. "His name is Garry. He's the most generous, romantic, beautiful person I've ever met."

"That's great—is it your *first*?" I imagined the stationer was probably on her second or third marriage, maybe to a part-time junk collector and painter who lived on disability and an army pension, but she was used to giving lip service to the translucent-skinned, unripe brides. Even the fashion-disaster stationer in her amazing Technicolor dreamcoat seemed to be more in on the joke than this poor girl I was tracking.

"Yes. It's his first, too." Guilt overtook me. I was feeling sick. I imagined demon-eyed daredevils in tight black-and-silver latex leotards on bicycles doing figure eights through three flaming rings in my mind. "At first I thought a gorgeous, successful, brilliant thirty-eight-year-old guy like him couldn't even exist." Thirty-eight? He was fifty-two, according to our research! "Like he couldn't even be real, you know. But he proved to me that he's the real thing." I was horrified. She seemed so relieved to have found him. How could I blame her? As disturbing as the circus wedding was to me, it didn't compare with the terror it would probably inspire for this poor girl. Like any of us, like me, I thought, she just wanted to be loved.

From Kate's I followed her to Harry Winston's. At the jewelry store, she asked to see a yellow-diamond-and-platinum tennis bracelet, where each link was a yellow teardrop surrounded by a sunflowerlike crown of small white diamonds. She admired it, but didn't try it on, and then asked to see three engagement rings, each with sleek white-gold bands and between three and four carats of diamonds on them. One had an exquisite jadeite centerstone with two blue diamonds on either side The jeweler told her it matched her eyes. It cost $255,000.

"When are you getting married?" he asked her. "Well, soon, but I promised my future husband I'd look at rings and then just show him what I wanted."

"Well, that's very generous of him. You're lucky. A lot of men want to surprise their brides, and they end up with a quarter-million-dollar ring that the bride can't stand and they have to sell it back and buy another one. I think letting the bride choose is the proper way to do it."

She was still glued to the glinting baubles in front of her, sitting on a piece of velvet the jeweler had rolled out for viewing, like a tiny red carpet. "I have to bring him back with me," she said. "We live right in the neighborhood, actually."

"Really, where?" he asked, looking too interested.

"At Sixty-second and Central Park," she said. "Well, we're still building the place, we're joining two apartments, but we're moving in within the next few weeks. I think. If the contractors do their job. Which, you know, they never do."

The jeweler, shabbily genteel with a pink ascot, suddenly seemed to smell the stinking undercurrent of money oozing from her, and broke his haughty demeanor, chortling, "Isn't that the truth, honey!"

By the time she hailed a cab and told the driver she was going to Brooklyn, I felt a huge relief. It was bad enough identifying with Garry, but my contempt for Alexis had turned into sadness. Who didn't understand wanting to be wanted? I swallowed hard and told George about my discoveries.

"Nice work." He was in an effusive mood that day. I was starving, having last had a boiled hot dog from a street vendor about eight hours prior. I indulged myself with a cab home that I couldn't afford. When Abdullah, my driver, turned onto the FDR Drive toward Brooklyn, I rolled the window down and tried to wash her out of my mind with the salty wind running off the East River through my hair.

I had him drop me off at an ATM machine near my house, and I withdrew twenty dollars. I had forty-three dollars and twenty-two cents to last me through the next two weeks until I got paid again, although I would have to give all that money, minus ninety-five dollars, to my landlord. The rotary of my financial situation was driving me nuts. I was poor enough that an ad I'd read in *Allure* magazine at my dermatologist's soliciting "dreammakers" for the "true woman's gift of egg donation" gave me pause.

At home, as I passed my only mirror, I noticed that my hair was windblown and snarled into tornado shapes on top of my head. I pulled a can of Spaghetti-O's out of my cupboard. My eating habits had become a great indicator of my psychic well-being and the status of my love life. Before Elliott and I broke up, I was having oatmeal for breakfast every morning and salads for lunch. I was ironing my sheets. I even flossed. Now I was eating macaroni with tomato-flavored sauce.

The phone rang. It was Cassie.

"Hey, I'm leaving the office now. Are you coming out?"

"Yeah. Yeah." My smoke alarm went off. The Boyardee sauce was burnt and bubbling on the sides of the pot, and a thick black smoke curled off its edges. I turned off the burner. With that I opted to get the hell out of my apartment and have a comforting night of free G&Ts and girl talk.

Looking in from the Outside

Niagara's clientele represent the fragile social ecosystem of the Lower East Side. We once spotted Matt Dillon, who was flanked by two Amazonian big-breasted lesbians. We'd also met a guy who was an uncanny dead ringer for Iggy Pop, although he took great offense at my characterization ("That dude's ugly—and old!" he protested); a guy who carried around a handheld DVD player showing a grisly film he's made for PETA about ferrets, and who also claimed to have invented the "morphing" software; and a freakish barfly Cassie and I liked to call the Spider Lady, who had tattooed her entire body—face included—with a web design that makes her look like an unusually buxom smallpox victim.

When we're not trying to snag a seat or butter up the bar boys, our conversation typically concerns three central motifs: boys, guys, and men—although admittedly our actual experience is primarily with the first two.

Truth be told, our adventures at Niagara keep me coming back, too, even if I don't have the same kind of stake in the place that Cass does. Maybe it's the hope that, by some miracle, I'll have a chance meeting with the boy of my dreams here, too. But probably not.

I wanted to tell her about Garry Wilbur and my fear that I might be like him—even a little bit—but I couldn't. Not only was the case strictly confidential, but I didn't want her to think I was a total freak. I stuck to trashing Elliott. Pretty soon, two attractive guys with messy hair and Carharts approached us. They said they were record executives and named some bands they represented. The bands all sucked, but we feigned interest. The shorter one, Jake, seemed to really like Cassie, and the other one, Dino, out of de facto default, was talking to me.

"So what do you do?" he asked me.

I wanted to avoid inciting any conversation by mentioning my job. "I'm in research," I said, looking distracted.

"She's a PI!" Cassie interjected, leaning over from Jake. I groaned. Cass loved to expose this to strangers. It was a great conversation piece with people I wanted to talk to, or the worst kind of conversation snare with boring people.

Dino launched into the usual wide-eyed interrogation. "That's such a sexy job." Ugh. "Do you carry a gun?" No. "Do you ever fear for your life?" No, but I fear for yours. I found myself nodding, not listening to a word he was saying, gazing out the window of the bar with a dreamy smile on my face.

Aside from the spittle from Dino's mouth occasionally hitting my left ear, I shivered from the warm sight of the ochre-lit trees of Tompkins Square and the streetlamps on Avenue A yearning out with their warm, carroty light. Still nodding, still smiling. My eyes landed on the window to the right. There stood a homeless man who had hovered outside the windows of Niagara since the first night I remembered visiting the bar, arranged between me and the park like a scarecrow talisman. He wore an elaborate headdress of tiny thornlike Christmas bulbs over his oil-slicked hair, and he had stuck five grimy pigeon feathers in them. He beat his arms, draped in what looked like a woman's sparkly blue gossamer dress ripped down the front and donned as a cape. Still nodding, still smiling. His arms thumped against the windows like the frantic flapping wings of a bloodied bird that had flown into a window. It was as if he desperately wanted to will himself to the other side of the divide, staring in the window at the elusive world beyond. I looked out at him with corresponding panic and envy, wondering what I was doing there. Wondering how I could get out.

Then my cell phone rang, and I realized at once that Dino was looking at me like I was nuts, saying, "What's so funny about that? Why are you laughing?" and I found myself saying, "Hold on one second . . . I just need to get this call," as I groped around in my purse. I got it on the last ring.

"Hello?"

"Hey, Amy?"

"Yeah." I was looking at Dino apologetically, but I was apoplectic. The homeless guy was receding from the window like a fallen angel.

"It's Edward. I met you last week at Niagara . . ."

Everything disappeared at that point, and I was drenched in the glory that *he was actually calling.* "Of course I remember you," I said.

"So, I was thinking of coming down to visit the city soon. I have a long weekend at school coming up next week."

"Oh, really?" My hands were cold and wet, and I wanted to laugh so hard I could cry.

"I'd love to see you. Actually, I'd love to stay with you, but that might be kind of weird, so—"

I interrupted him. "No, I don't think so"— I caught myself. "Let's just see how it goes. We'll figure something out." We agreed that we'd talk in a few days, when I wasn't in the middle of a noisy bar. At the end of our conversation he said he couldn't stop thinking about me. Without thinking about it I said, "I know," and for the next three full seconds there was silence until I said, "Okay, so I'll call you tomorrow." When I turned my attention back to my surroundings, I noticed Dino and the guy in the window had both quietly slipped away.

✪ ELEVEN

The most beautiful thing we can experience is the mysterious.

—ALBERT EINSTEIN

Don't Shit in My Mouth and Call It a Sundae

George and I stopped for apple fritters on the way uptown to meet Detective DeSanto. We sat in the Dunkin' Donuts at Fifty-sixth and Second, munching away. He punctuated the quiet by telling me stories and asking me about my love life.

"So, are you still all busted up about your boyfriend dumping you?" He smiled and dropped a last piece of fritter in his mouth.

"He didn't *dump* me," I protested. "I dumped him. It was sort of mutual. We outgrew each other."

"Uh-huh." He was already looking dubious. On the way out, he started to tell me about a friend of his wife's who had gotten involved with a cardiac surgeon. I hadn't told him about Edward and was a bit freaked out by this.

The woman, Karin, had always had shady taste in men, but she fell really hard for this guy and, as George said, "the fact that he was a fancy doctor really got her going." Totally different from me and Edward, I thought to myself, although I didn't really know him well enough to *know* exactly what attracted me to him above and beyond his stunning good looks.

Right before Karin was due to marry the vet, George did a little research on the guy, just by calling up his medical school and checking on his degree. It turned out he didn't have one. He was a physician's assistant for eleven years, and had completed two years of a master's degree in nursing. He also had a $200,000 lien on his house, which was barely worth more, and two ex-wives he forgot to mention to Karin. George went to his wife, who gave the 411 to her friend, who then broke off the engagement.

"The first time I met that guy, I knew he was a fucking prick. The thing is, the next guy she met was a piece of work, too. He took out a four-hundred-thousand-dollar life insurance policy on her and tried to have her thrown off a powerboat."

"Are you serious?" I was sickened.

"Yeah, but the guy pussied out and went to the cops. Meanwhile, she let him cosign on all her bank accounts and credit lines, so he's got his grubby fucking hands on most of her assets now. The people that are attracted to these losers never change. If I out one of these guys, she'll find another. She's a loser magnet. I mean, don't shit in my mouth and call it a sundae."

This was definitely an unappetizing commentary. I thought about all the women in the world who found themselves repeatedly and inexplicably hooked up with con men, polygamists, sociopaths, felons, petty thieves, pathological liars. They distorted these men through the lens of their overwhelming desire to be loved. I hoped I wasn't one of them.

When we got to Lou DeSanto's office, Goldie was already there, and the two of them had made fast friends. She was sitting on his desk, leaning back and laughing, saying, "Lou, yawr a caaard!" He was laughing loudly enough that we'd heard him from the other end of the tiled hall as we were escorted down to meet them. He had a neat mustache and a round belly, and looked like a guy who had been around.

"Miz Gray, Mizster Neilan, have a seat." He waved us into two ancient Naugahyde-upholstered chairs in front of the desk.

"You toow would not believe . . ." Goldie drew in a breath. "Lou and I know a lot of the same people." They smiled at each other. It felt like we'd stumbled into their first date. Lou cleared his throat, "So tell me what's going on here." George talked, and asked me for backup sometimes, and I'd explain what the parole terms were for Wilbur's conviction in Texas or whatever. Lou shook his head a lot and interrupted us to take a few calls. At one point, he got a message on the intercom telling him he had a call from Frank Marispone. "Frankie!" Goldie squealed. "From security at the Plaza?"

"Holy crap," Lou said, "do you know him too?" When the call buzzed over, Goldie grabbed it and said, "Frankie, do you know who this is? I'll give you three guesses. No. No. Okay two— yeah, yeah, it's Goldie. I'm in his office right now!" After Goldie and Lou had chatted with Frankie and squared away their connections, George resumed pitching the case. When he was finished, Lou put an unlit cigar in his mouth and started chewing on it.

"I don't see a crime here—yet—except for some possible check fraud, unless Goldie had a written contract with him that he's violated by not paying her." She didn't, so Lou's idea was to try to work with the people over at the St. Regis to snare him, probably by getting him to sign a contract and then pass a bad check. Our only other hope, he said, was that Garry might be violating his probation. When we left the office, we agreed that I'd draw up a report of everything we knew about Garry for Lou that night and get it to him the next day. He'd see what he could do, he said, adding, "But without a crime our hands are tied." Even if there was a crime, if it was just a misdemeanor or if it didn't violate the probation, it was too small for the police to get involved. "This is New York, ya know, we've got bigger fish to fry." At this, Goldie made a pouty face, and Lou added, "But honey, I'll do everything I can."

George and I went out for a celebratory beer after the meeting. Over a few frothy Guinnesses, we talked about his kids. He had a cherubic, tow-headed three-year-old son, and a brand-new baby. The older one, Stuart, seemed to be totally unlike his tough-guy dad. When he came into the office, he held his dad's leg and shielded his face, sometimes bursting into tears and crying into his dad's pant leg, squealing, "I want mommy!" Stuart was the same age as Sol's son and at least three inches shorter, and his blond locks fell softly around his head, making him look more like a pretty little girl, with tiny, pinched, pouting lips.

"You just hope when your kids grow up they have the equipment to handle this world," he said, "because it's full of ugly things." And with that we left O'Hara's Tavern and headed our separate ways.

I went back to the office and worked up my report for Lou. I transcribed the whole tape I'd recorded in the field with Alexis.

Jesus was the First Jewish Carpenter

When I got back to the office, Evan seemed curious about my case. He asked me if I was enjoying playing cops and robbers. "Nailing these guys is better than sex," he observed.

"I couldn't say, I've never had it." I said dismissively. "Besides, I thought you liked girls." Cries of "Ahhh, busteeed!" escaped from Assman and Nestor's direction.

"Amy, I have a surprise for you." Linus came out of the conference room with a cat that Nestor's girlfriend had donated to us. A big, cuddly, mostly red-haired tabby. "Ohooooooooo, hi sweetie, hi, little one," I coooed. I love cats, and I'd had to give the one I had with Ben back to him as part of the division of assets. "What's her name?"

"Kitty," Linus said.

"I think I love her." Kitty was purring aggressively on my lap. Then I noticed Sol. He had started wearing enormous hands-free headphones around the office so he could do his wheeling and dealing and walk around, too. With his headset and his ungainly posture, he looked like an operator at a spina bifida telethon. He thought he looked cool. He walked over to me as he was hands-free schmoozing with a client. "Yeah, that's what I'm saying. I think we should do the searches in California and Colorado because the ex-wives are there and his credit may have been under their names. Right. So it's another G. Think about it and call me back." He left the black monster on his head.

"So, Miss Marple, you're back," he said to me.

"I'm just curious," I said. "Do you get direct TV with that portable satellite dish on your head?"

He was never one to take a compliment lying down. "I get Yiddivision—all Jews, all the time. But you wouldn't know anything about that, Miss Amy-make-like-she-came-off-the-*Mayflower*-Gray."

I hadn't been given this much shit for being a bad Jew since my cabinmates at summer camp freaked out because I didn't know what a mezuzah was.

Sol seemed ready to burst in anticipation of asking me, "Okay, A. Gray, who's the most famous Jew in the world?"

I hesitated. "Kid Rosenthal!"

"Nice. And Jesus was the first Jewish carpenter." Sol was cracking himself up. His headset hung around his neck like a stethoscope, and he was hysterical, slapping desks, the upper tones in his cackle bouncing off the back walls of the office.

❧

My report started thus: "Although the evidence contained herein is not conclusive, our research indicates that Ms. Whitcomb is unaware of her fiancé's illegal activity. Her comments indicate that she believed Mr. Wilbur is thirty-eight years old. As you'll see in Exhibit F of this report, identification sources show Garry Wilbur was born on November 6, 1947." It continued in this parched language for ten pages. I sent it to George by e-mail around nine-thirty, and he sent it back with a few changes soon after. I made a copy of the audiotape, included it as Exhibit H, and had it messengered over to the Sixteenth Precinct. It was almost ten. I was the only one in the office, except for the occasional sounds of rats scurrying along the walls, but I didn't even look up. From the strain of staring at my computer screen, it felt like two holes had been bored into my eyes with blowtorches. I rubbed them and tears of exhaustion rolled out from the corners and smudged my face.

Being the only one in the office when the phone rang, I was sure it was for me. I straightened my face and answered it. "Amy Gray speaking."

"Amy, it's Lou DeSanto."

My spine pricked up. "Lou, how are you?"

"Great. Great. Listen, that report you sent was excellent." Nice to know I'm not the only one working late.

"Oh, good."

"It was a very professional job. Very professional. I just wanted you to know that I talked to my friend Eddie, who's the head of security at the Waldorf, and it looked like Wilbur sent a kited check over there, which we can use to nail him for a parole violation."

"Great."

"We have a meeting set up tonight with him at the hotel, and some agents will be there to take him into custody. I can't guarantee anything, but at the very least we can try to extradite him to Texas."

"Really?" I hesitated. "Don't you want to prosecute him?"

"We don't have much to hold him on now, honey." I was touched by Lou's term of endearment. I imagined myself, years into my investigative career, perched on his desk, bending his ear with my stories of corrupt corporatiers and then using him to cultivate a seductive symbiosis with the police. "Let me know if you ever need any help with anything. Some cases you're working on, whatever. Give me a call."

When I got off the phone, I felt a profound sense of disappointment. All of a sudden, just as this case was getting interesting, the police were pawning him off to another state. I felt cheated. What would happen to Alexis? What other people were being manipulated by this guy right now that we knew nothing about? I called George at home and apprised him of the situation.

"Okay," he said. "Sounds good."

"So why don't we try to put together a real case against him in

New York?" I pleaded. I could hear George's lips curl into his usual smirk.

"Let it go," he said quietly.

I'm The Best Lay You've Never Had

I packed up my laptop. It was cold and misting outside. When I arrived downtown, the halogen lamps that limn Niagara's sign were haloed, giving off a dirty cartoonish yellow light against the blue. Unlike its one-of-the-wonders-of-the-world-namesake, Niagara looked ever more the set-piece for urban squalor. You couldn't get more Gotham than this. I felt a warmth emitting from inside and scurried into my shabby refuge. Cassie and my other friend Skye were sitting faithfully at the bar, sipping frothy beers.

Skye was a gorgeous six-foot-one giantess with the confidence to match. Although she and Cass were temperamental opposites, they had a kind of social symbiosis that was mutually beneficial. Cass seemed to become a little more vulgar around Skye, and Skye always seemed slightly less unhinged around Cass. We each ordered rounds of scotch-on-the-rocks and talked about our lives, and gradually unwound. Cassie, as usual, was keeping an eye on Stuart, but more important, she was contemplating an old boyfriend who was suddenly coming to town.

Jack had moved to Los Angeles after a generally smooth six-month courtship. He had seduced her with gifts (a Boston bull terrier puppy), romantic dates (picnic in the park), and sweet nothings ("baby, you are *fine*," he said, famously). When he got a dot-com programming job in the City of Angels, Cass knew she couldn't expect him to kick $100,000 a year and lots of stock options out of bed, and she agreed not to end their relationship. They said they'd "see how things go" long-distance. Two weeks later she called him and a woman answered the phone. "Who's this?" she asked.

"This is Carolyn," the girl answered.

"Really?"

Cassie heard the sorry yelps of their terrier puppy in the background.

Jack picked up the phone and confirmed that Carolyn (pronounced Cairo-LEAN) was indeed his new girl, and suggested that Cassie probably shouldn't call again. She was devastated. Cass decided that during her six months of being in indifferent-like with Jack, she had actually been in love. She rewrote their six months together with the kind of stubborn nostalgia that is unique to getting dumped.

Now, a year after Cairo-Lean, Jack was coming to New York. He had called and asked Cassie if she'd like to meet for a drink, and had expediently mentioned that he and the new Mrs. Jack were spending some time apart. Cass couldn't conceal her glee as she repeated this. She was trying to decide if she should sleep with him, tease him, or completely ignore him. I noted that sleeping with ex-boyfriends was nice, because it doesn't add to your numbers: i.e., when someone asks how many people you've slept with, the numbers don't go up. For men this is probably a drawback, but for women it's a boon.

"Totally," Cass agreed. I mean, on the one hand, I'd like to," she contemplated, "but on the other hand, I don't want to give him the idea that I'm just going to forgive him for how he treated me."

Skye and I nodded. Skye, who chewed men up and ate them for dinner, probably wouldn't know her numbers if she was asked for them, but I knew her just-get-on-with-it attitude might help tonight.

Meanwhile, as we sat mulling over the love of her life, Cass had me sit closest to the end of the bar, where I was freezing my ass off, so she could keep a better watch on Stuart's coming and goings. "Listen, before you say another word about your beloved, can we move? I'm going into hypothermic shock." We compromised when she lent me her sweater.

I maintained that she should tease him to the brink of satisfaction and then tell him that she was the best lay he'd never have. It was a line I'd got from Elliott once, and I'd been waiting for someone to use it on.

"But he has had me," Cassie protested.

"Right, but he'll never have you *again.*"

"Well, saying 'I'm the best lay you'll never have *again*' doesn't have the same kind of punch to it."

Skye threw in her two cents. She pointed to Stuart rinsing glasses at the bar sink. "Is that the bartender you dated? Forget about Jack—he's hot!" If Cassie was through with Stuart, Skye mentioned, she was happy to pick up from there. Cass declined.

I, meanwhile, was anticipating Edward coming to town. There was no way I was going to sleep with him—I was debating how to handle having him stay with me without blowing my wad when Skye pointed to my left ear and squealed, "Jimmy!" Standing behind me at the bar, holding a Molson Golden, was Jimmy Fallon, the hottie from the cast of *Saturday Night Live,* whom I'd admired long before he was asked to host the American Music Awards or pose for *Teen People* magazine.

"I'm going to talk to him," Skye said, slipping past me, and, sure enough, minutes later they were having what looked like a flirty encounter by the bar, whispering in each other's ears.

"She should bottle herself and sell it," I said glumly. Skye hadn't even known about Jimmy Fallon until I had pointed him out to her in a spread in *ID* magazine a few months earlier.

"Listen," Cassie said, "I've been wanting to talk to you about something. I need you to be Spygirl for me." Cass had been living with her roommate, a mutual friend of ours, for over a year, and the roommate had pets. But their landlord had sent them a notice the previous week saying that if they didn't get rid of the animals, he would start eviction proceedings against her. They were both on the lease. "I can't find a new roommate in time, and Julie won't leave anyway. But I don't want to look for a new apartment."

I told her I'd talk to George and Sol about it and try to find some dirt on her slumlord. The optimal approach would be to leverage whatever indignities I uncovered about him to keep him quiet, as in, "My lawyer will fight you on this, and by the way I know you're screwing your secretary." I was thrilled at the heady power to be gained. As Spygirl, I could protect my friends and rebuke my enemies. I would vanquish the innocent and make the boys love me. I would impress my bosses and win over my coworkers.

When Cassie and I finally stumbled out of the bar, Skye was whispering with Jimmy in the phone booth in the back of the bar. "Good-byyyye, blue Skyyyy," I sang.

"Been there, done that," Cassie quipped.

I arrived home at 1:45 to a message from Skye.

"Hey, Amy, it's Skye. I was just calling to say fuck you for letting me leave the bar tonight with my skirt tucked into my underwear! Yeah, I feel like a total idiot, but, anyway, I got Jimmy's number . . . and I have other news, so, uh, call me. Love you!"

Walking the Walk

On the cold, overcast Sunday morning the day after, I awoke, and surveyed the damage. I was still wearing Cass's sweater, a gorgeous fitted red cashmere cardigan with black beading of roses all over the arms and lapels. Evidently I'd slept in and vomited in this little number, a piece I'd always coveted since unsuccessfully begging her to borrow it in high school.

Looking back, as a teenager, my investigatory skills were honed on Sunday mornings in the aisles of the Garment District, a superstore thrift shop in Cambridge where my love of all things vintage was born. I cut my chops with Cassie sifting through tight seventies-style turtlenecks, and although by this time in my life (circa 1990) *Charlie's Angels* was already long in syndication, the convergence of fashion, masquerade, and surveillance was not lost on me. My falling-apart-at-the-seams oxblood steel-toe Doc Martens could allow me to slip undetected into a tangle of weary-looking punks at the downtown speed-metal den the Rat; clad in a black slip turned party dress, I could bridge the gap to a 1980s Eurotrash club scene. Farrah's impeccably coiffed hair and her slip of a frame, loosely swathed and exposed by a plunging-collared V- or ruffle-necked velvet jumpsuit, seemed not only apropos, but apt. The distillation of every hot, hapless number we'd dredged from the dollar-a-pound floor and made into masterpieces with quick hand-hemming and good machine work had led to this: the embodiment of fashion as power, the hard facts of perfect hipness at the bottom of a cold cellar.

Sunday mornings, Cass and I waded knee-deep at the dollar-a-pound thrift sale. We stood in knots of leather suits and clots of retro ties and adult-sized rubber-footed onesies. There was a lot to sort through. We practiced being discerning, discarding the contents that didn't fit our needs and nimbly closing in on what we wanted. We weren't following fashion; we were creating it.

Cass had always refused to lend me the beaded cardigan since the time I borrowed it and broke some of the fragile beading. "Borrow something you can't break," she'd say. Nine years after I last coveted that red cardigan, I took it off and laid it across my bed, and put my face down. The sweater smelled musty, like the accumulation of wearers it left behind. I breathed the lives woven into it, reassembled from the meager facts of a chipped button or a pulled stitch. It wasn't much to work with. I considered all the clues I left behind every day that no one would ever notice, and that was probably the most heartbreaking thought of all.

✪ TWELVE

Facts, not memories. That's how you investigate. [Memories] are just an interpretation, they're not a record. And they're irrelevant if you have the facts.

—Leonard, *Memento,* a film written
by Christopher Nolan

Unnatural Disasters

That night, I woke up and realized my house was on fire. I heard the menacing sirens of fire engines and realized I must have left the oven on, or the toaster with something in it, and I tried to get up and run into the kitchen. My arms seemed to be pinned. My vision was murky. As the screeches of sirens got louder—was it my smoke alarm or the fire trucks coming? Should I call the police?—I noticed a blazing light in the corner of my left eye, and my right cheek was wet. Was it blood? I finally struggled to sit up. I touched my cheek. It was slick with drool. My phone was ringing. I answered it.

"Amy?"

"Yeah."

"It's Edward."

I was trying to acclimate myself to the fact that my house wasn't on fire and I wasn't facing imminent death. I wasn't quite there yet.

"Hi. Ummm." I panicked. "Did you see any smoke?" I felt deeply embarrassed the second this escaped me. Cassie's cardigan had a brown-edged stain in the middle, where I'd had it stuck to my face.

"What did you say?"

"Sorry, nothing," I said quickly. "I got confused for a second. So! How are you?"

"I'm good."

I was trying to remember how long it had been since Edward said he'd call me. One day? Three days? A week?

"Well, so, I'm still hoping to come down to New York this weekend," he said, interrupting my uncomfortable silence. "Is it still cool if I stay with you? If you're busy, that's totally fine. I could stay somewhere else . . ."

"No, no, no. I think that will work out . . . fine." I guess that's taken care of, I thought.

We agreed to meet at the Krispy Kreme stand at Penn Station on Friday. As I hung up, the reality of Barely Knowing Edward suddenly dawned on me. I wanted to cheat the system and get on my computer and run some databases and use this intelligence to protect myself. I wanted to assemble clues and accumulate knowledge and coat myself in a protective cover of *knowing more* that could protect me. Or I could find nothing.

The memory of his gorgeous eyes and the softness of his lips and his parting words—"Okay, sweetie, I'll see you soon"—kept my laptop in its Targus home for the night, and my uncertainties at bay.

I got ready to lie down again and bask in the delicious anticipation of almost unbearable physical tension and first kisses, and I
heard what sounded like dozens of men running in the hallway
past my door to the "back house."

My apartment is on the first floor of a small three-story
brownstone, and there's a hallway that I enter through that leads
from the front of my building to the back and empties out into a
yard. Behind the yard is another house we call the back house, a
hundred-and-fifty-year-old three-story clapboard that now serves
as two duplexes for my neighbors. I picked up the blinds in my
bedroom, which faces the garden, to see at least a dozen firemen
running a hose up the front of the back house, then hoisting a ladder up the side of the house. It *was* a fire. "*Definitely* New York's
finest," I observed aloud for anyone and no one before I ran into
the yard. Small wisps of smoke were shooting out of the top floor
of the back house. I couldn't see any fire. My neighbor Miriam was
crying.

"What's going on?" I asked.

"My bathroom's on fire!" she cried, her hand over her eyes,
crouching. I knelt down and I put my arm around her.

As Miriam sobbed and my other baffled neighbors descended
on the garden, a fireman climbed up the ladder to the window and
smashed it in with an ax. Another fireman on the roof turned a
hose on the tiny bathroom window. The water had been on for
about fifteen seconds when they turned it off, came down their lad-
ders, coiled the hose back.

Miriam had accidentally used her halogen lamp as a towel-
warmer. When she got into the shower she threw it toward the
door handle and missed. Not until the towel caught fire, which
then spread to the doorframe, did she notice the "funny smell" of
burning acrylic and paint. She ran out of the house screaming,
"Help! Fire! Run!" The fire marshall told us that "if that fire had

been a little worse, we wouldn't have had a chance." That was hard to believe. They carried the damaged door to the yard, and it had a pathetic, blackened, singed corner the size of two dollar bills.

Shut Your Piehole

When people ask me what it's like working as a PI, I like to tell them that the Agency has subscriptions to four publications: *The Wall Street Journal, Crane's Business Weekly, The Daily Deal,* and *Mad* magazine. Evan was working on the new *Mad* inside fold-in picture when I approached his desk and asked for a new case. "New case . . . Okay, 'Fold Here A' and then 'Fold Here B,' " he directed himself aloud. The magazine started to slide off the desk as he maneuvered the slippery pages. It finally slapped onto the floor, leaving behind the torn triangular remains of Part B. "Fuck it!" he yelled, flustered.

"I'll do it for you," I offered.

"Forget it. You have to have a Ph.D. in fucking origami to do these things." He crumpled up Part B and threw the remaining wad in the direction of Oscar's desk. It arced high and landed inches away from Oscar's feet, rolling sluggishly a couple more inches. Oscar didn't flinch. Evan visibly recomposed. "And how can I help you, Miz Gray?"

"New case?"

"Ah."

He pulled a fat yellow folder out from under a stack on his desk and threw it into my outstretched hand. "What is it?"

"I'm not sure," he said. "George said it's another dot-com case, which means you'll find our subject does lots of coke in the company bathroom and spends his IPO money on whores." He reflected for a second. "Why don't I work at a dot-com?" It had the subject's name written on it in bloated graffiti-style lettering.

Below it in the lower right corner was the tag DOW. "Who's Dow," I asked him.

"Wally." Wally Yoo was nineteen and a computer-science undergrad at NYU. He'd been hired to do odds and ends around the office. George and Sol, never ones to kick a money-saving deal out of bed, had made him the unofficial network manager at the Agency. Wally did the work of an entire software-management company, all for about eight dollars an hour and the whole time outfitted like a Ninja. He was Korean-American and he was obsessed with Unix, a radical kind of martial arts called Ninjitsu, the cartoon-character Garfield, and a girlish Korean movie star named Bae Doo-na. He had a little stuffed Garfield pillow he kept on top of his computer with a heart-shaped pin stuck on it, and he usually had a black bandana tied around his head, with floppy spikes of his hair popping out the top.

I was fond of Wally, and in one moment of shared vulnerability I told him I'd broken up with my boyfriend, and he told me, in exchange for my candor, that he had Tourette's Syndrome. "I was, like, in this informational video about it," he said. "And they taught us how to control the tics, so I don't *present* anymore." He leaned in closer to me, his hair flopping forward over his bandana, one hand over his Garfield desk calendar. "That means I don't show any sign of the disease now."

But Wally did still *present*. Like the time when Evan asked him to organize our archives, which are all kept semi-numerically at a store locker in Long Island City, and Wally told him, "Shut your piehole!" Or the time at lunch when he yelled "Stinky fish lips!" for no reason. (He later claimed he'd said "Bring me some chips!")

I carried the file over to him. "So, is this your new tag?"

He laughed. "It means 'hungry dog' in Korean," he explained. "I like the graffiti style. I'd like to make a music video sometime with Korean-style animation." I wasn't sure how this latter sentiment related to the font he was developing.

The Phantom Phone Number

My new case seemed, at first, to be a typically boring e-commerce investigation. Probably my fifth like it since I started at the Agency. As I would soon discover in "The Case of the Swindling Spin Doctor," his crimes and his pathology were a prototype for the dot-com zeitgeist. At this time, March 1999, dot-commerce was peaking. At least a quarter of our clients were venture capital companies that were going through the motions of due diligence by hiring us to check out their newest incubation project. They were more like intubation projects. Many of these firms, we were quickly realizing, were like junkies trying to get their last fix before they overdosed, scavenging around for capital when they were tens (or hundreds) of millions of dollars in debt.

Our routine in such cases, in addition to doing our usual checks, included calling random lower-level employees of the company (mail-room staff, human-resources reps) to determine if there was any delay in their payroll. Certain kinds of guys were relieved to talk to anybody. José, the IT guy, is used to getting attention only when he's being berated by rich guys running his company because their keypad is sticking. We would ask the José's if any of their paychecks had bounced, or if they had missed any pay periods, only to discover their payrolls were six months behind schedule.

Many of our clients considered our work so rote that they had already started dishing out financing to the company they had hired us to investigate before they'd even engaged our services. Some had their suspicions raised by the dubious fate of that initial investment, as was the circumstance in the case of the Swindling

Spin Doctor, probably the most brazen con artist ever to appear across the desks of the Agency.

With a few exceptions, the guys we investigated at these companies were so young they barely had college degrees, let alone paper trails and business histories that showed anything but their ability to hold down a summer job at Vail or flip burgers. These cases could be extraordinarily boring, but George and Sol insisted on taking them because they paid well.

Joe Smith, my subject, was running an online software-developer and retail portal. Mostly there were a lot of dull press releases about the company. These releases are some of the most important clues we use, especially when they're read as propaganda, as Brown's dime-store Marxist semiotics program taught me. *PR Newswire* and *Business Wire* are about the party line. I read some mind-numbingly tedious ones: "Joe Smith was appointed president of U-Celerate.com on May 8, 1998. He is the former CFO of BusyCorps.com, which he founded, and has also worked in financial advisory positions at International Business Machines and Peat Marwick. Mr. Smith also maintains a private financial consulting business handling clients from northern Massachusetts to the Cayman Islands."

Anybody who wants to change their identity and slip into anonymity will pick the most ubiquitous first and last names they can muster. There are at least 10,000 Joe Smiths in the United States. It's harder to prove what evidence we find *isn't* about them than what is. Michael Ford. Karen O'Connor. These are all fitting names if you plan on committing identity fraud, embezzlement, tax evasion, or any other kind of crime. Not that I'm handing out advice to criminals. *Au contraire.* I'm Spygirl. I found tens of thousands of documents—bankruptcy records and corporate filings—for Joe Smiths. I found Joe (aka Joseph) Smiths who were convicted rapists, embezzlers, founders of Vanderbilt University, professional wrestlers, and a Playboy bunny (Joe, short for Joanna).

This annoyed me and supplemented my resolve. I hated being lied to. I wanted to find Joe Smith if it killed me. Like wading through the knot of neckties at the Garment District, my job is a tricky business of finding what's already there, and there's always an element of chance involved. I tried focusing my searches for information about Joe Smiths with dubious pasts.

I found two curious things. The first was a news article mentioning his business partner in their company, a Russian named Dmitry Aleksandrov, who was being investigated for possible mafia connections in Philadelphia. The second was something Gus had brought to my attention.

When we ran the Social Security number our client had provided us, it turned up invalid. No such number had ever been issued. "Call the client," George said. The client talked to Mr. Smith, who called back saying he'd mistyped the number. This was a big red flag indicating a big fat liar. The last digit was a seven, not an eight, they said. So Gus plugged it in again. This time, it was a valid number, but it was somebody else's. Although Joe Smith was listed as having used the number, it had been assigned to one Lonny Perkins. I was leaning over Gus's desk the whole time, and was getting very worked up. "Yes! That bastard is lying! Yes!" It was thrilling.

Gus, for the hell of it, started playing with the numbers in the Social, changing the last digits, and every time he did, he came up with another number it looked like Joe Smith was using—not to mention the similar names "Jack Smithe," "Joe Smyth," and "Joe Nguyen." Gus ran those names and got nineteen other Socials, all listed to other people, that Joe Smith appeared to be using.

I ran those names in some news databases and came up with

lots of nothing; then, finally, I hit something promising. It was a clip from the *New York Post,* which I think of as the crack rock of newspapers. But it tends to have more consistent and in-depth coverage of nonviolent criminals than, say, *The New York Times.*

"The *Post* has learned that a prison inmate conned a major publisher into signing him to a $50,000 contract for a book about how to avoid being bilked by financial consultants. Sources at the publisher now admit that Joe Smyth, a tax advisor and felon convicted of bilking his former investment clients out of more than $15 million, was slated to publish his book, tentatively titled *Buyer Beware: An Investor's Guide to Stock Analysis,* with them in 1998. Although the book's editor and agent declined to comment about the incident, the publisher confirmed that the book had been canceled, although it was only *weeks* away from publication. The book's author, Joe Smyth, is serving two more years of an eleven-year sentence for fraud and tax evasion."

I took the piece to George, who seemed underwhelmed. "Well, do we know it's him?" he clucked.

"I have a feeling it is." I knew as soon as I said this he would nail me for it.

"You can talk to your shrink about feelings. I want facts." This was defeating, but I thought I could use some of my connections in the publishing business to get hold of the manuscript. I called several friends at the publishers, but they said the whole scandal was very touchy and they wouldn't know where to get the book if their lives depended on it. Then I had an idea. Since it was a business book, I'd call Andrew. Even though I felt a little strange about my last encounter with him, he was my final resort. I figured he might have gotten the proposal, and, with any luck, would still have it.

I told him the situation. "Oh, *my God.* Amy, darling, is this work *safe* for you?" His intonations conveyed a hushed sense of shared peril.

"Don't be silly, Andrew. You know I'd never put myself in any serious danger."

"I do?"

He had a point. "Honestly, I'm much better-behaved now than I was in college."

"Hmmm. Well, it doesn't ring a bell, lamb chop, but I'll have my assistant check and see if we have it on file."

❊

Working at my desk, I was diverted by Sol, who was entertaining a mystery guest—a woman—at his desk. We almost never had clients to the office, and on the two occasions when we did, we all had to wear business attire and shave. (Wendy and me notwithstanding.) Evan's scruffy mug suggested something else was afoot.

That day on a smoking break I asked who she was.

"Probably our next hire," said Gus.

"I don't want them to hire her!" Linus interrupted.

Why? we asked.

"I think I'm in love with her," he confessed, looking exasperated. Our potential new hire, Renora, was Linus's female Platonic ideal: a gamine Sylvia Plath devotee who had translated Nietzsche's collected works and loved Tom Waits.

"You'd make a beautiful, tortured-looking couple," I suggested.

"No, I can never be with a woman I actually love," Linus insisted. "It would ruin the whole point of love—desire and unfulfillment."

"You need to stop reading so much Goethe," Morgan sniffed. "You all do for that matter."

"I think he just needs to do the Han Solo." Evan chuckled.

"What's that?" asked Noah. Wendy and Gus giggled.

We filed back into the office as Noah assured a glum-looking Linus that he had the *Star Wars* trilogy on DVD.

A One-Way Ticket to Disstown

I spent the rest of my day thinking about Edward and working on my case. There were several other abstracts and wire pieces about Smythe, but none that had any information that wasn't already in the *Post* article. The rest was spent alternating between downloading Blue Oyster Cult songs off Napster and running searches. At six, I was deciding whether to take off or call Andrew back again when the phone rang. Please let it be Andrew, I quietly pleaded. I hit the line.

"Boo?"

"Hey, Ben." My disappointment was audible. "How are you?" I asked, gently.

"How come you never call me anymore?"

"How about having an adult conversation like, 'Hi, Amy. So nice to hear your voice. How are you'?"

"Hi, Amy, how's your pussy doing?"

"I'm getting off now." I lowered the receiver.

"Mooooo!!! Waiiiiiit."

"What?"

"I'm sorry. That was rude."

"You're right, it was." I took a deep breath. "You know, Ben, you don't make it easy for me."

"I just don't understand why you don't call me anymore."

"Well, you're my ex-boyfriend and we're both dating other people. Plus you're obscene, you're rude, and you're nauseating."

"So we can't be friends?"

"Wait, I haven't gotten to the negatives yet. I think you should be grateful we're not enemies at this point—"

My other line beeped. "Listen," I said, "can you hold on a second?"

"No, we're having a convo." (Translation: conversation.) "Amee . . ." I clicked over.

"Hello?" *Pleeeease* let this be Andy.

"Hello?" The phone buzzed with static. "Hello? Hello?"

I clicked back to Ben. "Listen, I have to get off, I have work to do."

"Amy," he said, then paused.

"What?"

"My girlfriend broke up with me." His voice cracked. My heart gave way.

"I'm so sorry."

"Yeah. It's okay. She was a bitch anyway."

"Listen, I really want to talk to you about this. Can I call you back?"

"Forget it," he said defiantly. "You're on boycott. I'm sending you a one-way ticket to disstown."

"Wait, Ben, don't be so fucking immature—"

He hung up. I remembered the night before I moved out of our apartment together. My dad was in town, helping me move into my own place. I had told Ben that it wasn't a "breakup"; I just needed distance. My father and I got back to the old apartment late. When I opened the door, Ben was draped over the living-room table. He jerked up, pulling a crumpled copy of *The New Yorker* onto the floor. A fine white dust swirled low around the table. His pupils were dilated. His eyes seemed to sink back into his face like shiny malachite marbles into dough.

My dad made a quick exit.

"You piece of shit! I can't believe you were doing dope in front of my father!"

He denied it. "I don't know what you're talking about. Just chill the fuck out." Even though he protested, his denials were lazy and halfhearted. A line of black blood slowly drew out from his right nostril down over his lip. He didn't even seem to notice.

"You have a fucking nosebleed, you shit! How stupid do you think I am?"

"So? That doesn't mean anything!"

I was livid. I said, "Well, then let's settle this for good." I licked my right forefinger and jabbed it up his other nostril, removed it, and put it in my mouth. It had a familiar bitter taste, like earwax.

Ben was completely still. "Give me the rest of it now," I said. My heart was racing.

He went into the kitchen and reached under a frying pan. He threw something in my direction and walked into the bedroom. It was a small tin-foil ball. I grabbed it off the floor and ran into the bathroom and emptied it into the toilet to the sound of him quietly crying as I realized I had unwittingly become a spy in his life, that I had been one for a long time.

✪ THIRTEEN

Wonderfullest things are ever the unmentionable.

—HERMAN MELVILLE, *MOBY-DICK*

A Million and One Ways to Kill a Caterpillar

In 1982, my parents moved to the house where they still live in Massachusetts. It was the year of the largest natural infestation of gypsy moths in the United States since 1965. I remember walking up the flagstone path to our new house, flanked by an enormous oak tree. But what had looked like wispy Spanish moss from our Ford wagon was actually a dense tangle of spidery silk casements. Tree boughs hung sadly under the draping nets. Inside these dusty tombs, organisms bobbed against the mesh like war prisoners desperately pressing their faces against their prison bars. The caterpillar tents enfolded every angle and incline on every tree's dusty limbs.

By the time we reached the house, the caterpillars had fallen into my hair, my jumper, even twisting pathetically in my shoelaces. My dad was covered with them. My sister got one in her eye. They were fat and black with blue circles down their back and black dots inside the blue circles. Their feet were a running set of tiny suction cups, like narrowing train tracks down their bodies. When you picked one up, it would flail helplessly and curl into a ball, using its gummy feet to stick to itself, forming a perfect curlicue.

My friends and I also took note that when you stepped on one end of them, noxious yellow guts would squirt out one side. The walk up to our new house was covered in the dry, yellowy paste of caterpillar innards. As long as you didn't eat them—although my best friend, Peter Weeter, did once, on a dare—they offered infinite but twisted diversions.

All the trees everywhere in the neighborhood had special double-sided tape around them at one-foot intervals, and they were greased with insecticidal jelly. The tape, after a few weeks, would acquire a brownish, gooey texture, and would be crowded with bugs in various stages of gestation. Here was a male adult, half its body severed. Here was a baby one, just four days hatched, here was a blue sliver from the shell of a robin's egg, here was some sap from a maple tree. The tape caught lots of things it wasn't supposed to.

On Friday, as I sat plugging "Joe Smith" in innumerable permutations with the words "felon," "indictment," "criminal," and "misconduct" into my databases, I thought about the caterpillars, which had seemed perfectly normal to me as a six-year-old. The caterpillars, which had crystallized in my mind, like the many extraordinary things that children see and assume, must be ordinary. Like gruesome clues, the caterpillars were always there for the finding. Once I read that all the bacteria and single-celled organisms living beneath the earth's surface are equal in mass to ten times that of plant and animal matter. It was a vile statistic. Now this wasn't just "the way things are." It was sickening, encroaching on me with the claustrophobic immensity of an infestation.

It was six-ten. I leaned against a pillar at Penn Station, across from the doughnut store, and breathed in the familiar stink of frying fat, cigarettes, and piss. When Edward finally appeared at seven twenty-five, I held on for dear life.

"It's good to see you too, baby," he cooed.

For dinner, I decided on a steamy little Korean restaurant in the East Village called Dok Suni. It was dark, so we leaned in over the tiny table over steamy platters of kim-chee and bikimbob.

Figuring this was my chance to corral information about Edward, I asked him everything, and he answered with the self-confidence of the genuine article.

He was the captain of his rugby team in college. This gave me a thrill. Rugby was quaint but European. Roguish yet sophisticated. We talked about how he came to be in medical school. His dad was a surgeon, and Edward had worshipped him. "I used to go to work with him when I was little. They'd give me a little white coat and I'd follow my dad around and take the pulse of chair legs and nurses and stuff. Plus I love to help people. This last Hallmark Sentiment made me simultaneously cringe and thaw a little. I smiled and focused on his good looks. "You have the most gorgeous eyes," I murmured. I felt like melting into him.

But Edward was distracted. "Do you hear that noise?"

"I just said I like your eyes."

"No." He started rifling through his pockets. "It sounds like a cell phone."

"Oh." I grabbed my purse. It was *my* phone.

"Hello?"

It was Cassie. "Where have you been? I've tried you earlier today and your phone was fucked up or something."

"I'm with Edward. Remember?"

"I need your help."

"Okay, hold on." She was a dead woman. I excused myself to go to the bathroom.

Edward smiled sweetly. "Is everything cool?"

"Oh, yeah," I assured him. "I'll be right back."

I slammed the bathroom door behind me. There was a lonely blue lightbulb hanging from the ceiling and Asian graffiti written all over the walls. There was no toilet seat. "This better be a big fucking emergency," I panted. Jack was in town, and she was calling me from Niagara. He was in the bathroom.

"He's like, all over me. I think he wants to come home with me, but I feel weird about it. We haven't even talked about what happened between us."

"Don't do it."

"But here's the other thing. He looks so hot tonight. I don't know. I'm torn."

"Fine, then fuck his brains out." It was impossible to give her advice, and I was neglecting my stunningly handsome new boyfriend.

"Uh-oh, he's coming this way. I'll call you later."

I returned to Edward. "Hey, sweetie," he said, pulling me onto his lap. "I missed you." Next we went to Decibel, a sake bar, where we soaked up warm rice wine and held hands for the first time. I was alit by his beauty. I looked around and noticed the other women in the room stealing glances at Edward behind their dates. He reached out across the table. "I'm so happy to be here," he said.

We went to a few more bars—the Boxcar Lounge, then Luca Lounge, then I don't even remember where. On the way to Luca, I know I started to pull him across Avenue B, and he pulled me back close to him and yelled "No!" and a yellow cab swerved away from me.

"Oh, my God. You saved my life!" I said, laughing.

"Careful, baby!" he admonished, and I looked into his eyes and thought to myself, Yes, this is how it's supposed to be. By the time we got back to my house, and he squeezed me and whispered, "You're beautiful," I shivered and almost believed it.

❧

The next morning, Edward and I were awoken at ten by a call from Cass. The first thing she said was: "I'm over him!"

I was worried. "What happened?"

"No, it's not bad like it sounds. I mean it's bad, but—not for me! I'm so happy I could scream!"

"So?"

"So he came back to my house, and we were kissing, nothing major, and then he was trying to push things further, so finally I just said, I don't want to do this when we haven't even talked about what happened. He just totally dropped it and was like, okay."

"Uh-huh." I had been ready for the punch line to this story the day before.

"So then I was pissed that he'd changed his mind. He'd been after me all night, so I was like, 'So now you don't want to sleep with me?' And he finally turned to me and said, 'I have herpes!' "

"No!"

"Yes! And the best part is, guess who gave it to him?"

"Cairo-Lean?"

"Yes! Ha-ha-ha! Can you believe it? Ha-ha-ha!" That night Cassie was completely cured of Jack, and, in a moment of perfect karmic symmetry, now he was the one who was afflicted.

Professor Best

On Monday morning, my weekend with Edward seemed like an exquisite dream. I pressed my face into the pillow that had held his perfect head and inhaled his aura and the smell of his cologne. My last boyfriend who'd worn cologne was in the ninth grade. I made a note to myself to go to Sephora and douse my personal effects with his magic elixir, Escape by Calvin Klein.

I walked into the office, dreamy and smiling.

"A. Gray," Evan said when I got back. "How was your weekend?"

"Amaazing." I hummed.

"Yeah? Did you meet someone?"

"Not *some*one. *The* one. I think I'm in love."

Evan was fascinated with other people's love lives. Since he'd broken up with his girlfriend of six years, he was obsessed by matters of the heart, particularly new and steamy relationships. He was an emotional voyeur. "What's his name?"

I was only half listening to him, remembering snuggling with Edward, kissing Edward, falling asleep next to him, with him spooning me and whispering, "I'll miss you."

"He's the *best*." I said dreamily.

"Mr. Best?"

"No. He's a doctor."

"Nice. So he's Dr. Best?"

"Yep. He's Professor Best. He's a doctor of bestology."

"Cool," Evan said, looking slightly pained. "Can I get a lesson from this guy?"

"Sorry, love, you have to be *born* the best. And it doesn't hurt to be six foot three and *stunning*. But don't worry." I put my hand on his shoulder. "There can only be one Dr. Best, but there's a lot of room in the better category, and believe me, you're better than most." I pinched his cheek and he blushed.

"Awww, you're just saying that."

I turned away and called back, "You're right, I am."

He laughed and looked embarrassed. "Thanks, Gray."

"A. Gray, phone call," Wally Yoo trumpeted.

I'll Show You Mine If You Show Me Yours

I hit the line.

"Sweet cheeks?"

"Hi, Andrew." He was a master of flattery.

"Who was that raging bull answering your phones? And more importantly, is he single?"

"He's nineteen."

"Even better." He sighed. "I had my assistant check for the proposal, and of course you know I don't usually keep those things more than three months, and this was two and a half years ago."

"Uh-huh."

"But I do keep a log on my computer—or my assistant Molly, does, actually—of all the submissions I get, and I saw the title for it—didn't you say it was called *Buyer Beware*?" I said yes. "Right, so I have it here, it looks like we got it in on January 11, 1997. The agent was Claudia Perroni."

I gagged audibly. Claudia was a Jersey girl who had rebirthed herself as a lifelong Upper East Side girl with the requisite Kate Spade handbag and split ends from overprocessing. She did low-end-to-middlebrow-type books—self-help for fat girls, quick-and-easy diet books, stories about weddings with happily-ever-after endings. She'd essentially set up an homage to *The Rules* and its requisite reading culture—girls like herself. "That's interesting," I said.

"Yeah, I know," Andrew said conspiratorially. "Have you seen her recently? She's completely ballooned. Hef City!" That Andrew could turn around and ridicule me to someone else for an improperly plucked brow line, or for having yucky yellow perspiration stains on a sleeveless shirt, was part of his charm. He could just as easily turn his unforgiving vision on himself—he was as self-hating as anyone worth knowing, but when he was letting you in on it, you felt illuminated, like the only special girl in the room. "So, I had Molly go check for the proposal, and of course it wasn't there."

"Oh." Disappointment flooded me.

"And then I remembered that Bill Graves"—the editor in chief of Andrew's imprint—"keeps a general submission file from all the proposals we discuss in editorial meetings. So Molly checked in there, but it wasn't there because apparently I rejected it before bringing it up to the editorial committee. Ha-ha!"

"Well, that bites, Andrew. I'm sure Claudia Perroni won't be able to help me." She'd left the business to marry a doctor whose book, *A Feminine Touch: Bringing Compassion into the Operating Room,* she'd represented. Plus, she was notoriously self-serving and I had nothing to give her, except perhaps more embarrassment about having represented this guy, anyway.

"Not so fast, sugarlips. I'm not done with my story." He sounded exasperated. "So I mentioned your little problem to Bill and he said that Thom Sanger keeps copies of all the submissions that are sent around for review. Bill called me ten minutes ago and said that I'd sent him the proposal with a note that said, 'I think I'm going to pass on this. Am I missing something, blah, blah, blah?' He wrote back with a note that said, 'There's something off with this guy. He seems to have come out of nowhere.' Isn't that wild? That he *knew* that?"

"That *is* wild. So do you have a copy there?"

"Yes ma'am."

"Is there a biography attached?"

"Hmm, let me see. No, no, no, no, no . . . hmmm. No—oh, wait, yes. Yes! Here it is. 'About the Author. Joe N. Smyth is a prominent tax advisor currently in private practice, advising clients in Massachusetts and the Cayman Islands. He formerly held financial positions at International Business Machines and Peat Marwick.'"

"Holy shit. It's him."

"Well, slap my momma silly, I can't believe this."

"Andrew, I have to run. I'm sending a messenger over for the proposal. You're a doll."

I ran over to George with a copy of the article about the book and showed it to him. He told me to call the prison and get his real Social Security number, and get a copy of the transcript of the trial. George said he would call the clients and make sure they put a stop order on any payments to Smyth.

***

The corrections officer at the Attica Correctional Facility in western New York was functionally illiterate. I resorted to having him spell the names of the prisoners on the files he'd pulled, which I'm sure violated some sort of prison confidentiality policy. Finally, he said, "I think I got it here, but it's S-M-Y-T-H-E," and I said, "That's our guy."

He read to me from the file. His real name was John Nguyen Smythe. He was born on June 18, 1961. His Social Security number was issued in South Dakota. His mother was identified as African-American and the father as "Asian-slash-Other." I got the name of the arresting officer. From his arresting officer, a reformed beatnik living in Rochester, New York, who called himself Detective Sammy, I was able to secure a copy of Smythe's case file. According to the file, he'd lived in Ridgewood, New Jersey; Tulsa, Oklahoma;

and Auburn, Alabama. I found incorporation records in Tulsa for a Joe's Laundry, a shell company he used to funnel money from his "consulting practice," which consisted of selling phony shares in a telecommunications company he had invented.

George had spoken to the client, who was a bit shell-shocked by the news. They'd already wired $180,000 to Smythe. The first few interviews were interesting. A few class-action suits had been filed against Smythe, which were consolidated and later handled in bankruptcy court. None of Smythe's victims had seen a dime, but they described him as "brilliant, seductive" and "a genius at spin." "He could have sold a dime for a dollar," one woman told me.

Smythe had been in prison for the last eleven years. That meant that, aside from his unlicensed accounting in the eighties in New York, his entire history was forged by words and symbols. He sent missives electronically, passing e-mails to his lawyer to copy to his computer; he made collect telephone calls on designated days from the correctional facility, and typed newswire releases and let-ters to his editors on an old Olivetti typewriter he kept under his bed. He grasped the function of spin and PR beyond most pundits and politicians. He had erected a true paper moon, invented from the cloistered distance of a prison cell.

"Hey, Dinglebrother!" Among the steady clicks of fingers gracing laptops, Sol's explosion gave us a brief shock. Of course, we were used to it. Sol was the loud one, George had a gentle, soft-spoken temperament, although his Irish-Catholic intensity sur-faced occasionally. For example, in bar fights (I've heard), or when someone really fucks up at work, or sometimes on the phone with his wife. I had a math teacher in the fifth grade who used to sneeze so loudly that the entire class would scream and gasp afterward, and one pale little girl, Miranda, actually had a seizure after one of his sneezes. So I preferred Sol's way. I can hear it coming.

"Can you get Pavlov's dogs over there to get me the case file for Rotenfeld?" he continued vexingly. "Pavlov's dogs" was Sol's pet name for verifications officers. Wally Yoo probably should have been in charge of the verification department, considering his responsibility and seniority, but he was too impulsive. Next in line was Archie Jefferson, a seventeen-year-old kid with an astonishing 350-pound, six-foot frame. He was a native East New Yorker, half black, half Orthodox Jewish. Temperamentally he was most unlike his appearance, a true gentle giant and a peaceful counterpoint to Wally's hummingbird mania. Archie tried to catch and set free the rats and mice that overran the office rather than letting them suffer the swift and cruel fate of George's broom or Gus's shoe. He would set them out the window with the bidding, "Okay, little guy, go!" He wanted to get his Ph.D. in history.

The biggest difficulty for Archie was that people expected him to be mean. When I walked down the street with him, the sidewalk would part like the Red Sea dividing before Moses. Tough New York City kids tried not to look him in the eye. The world interpreted him as mean thug: a professional wrestler, a gangsta rapper, a fullback for the New York Jets, a hitman. Taxis wouldn't pull over when he hailed. So Archie, somewhat unwittingly, got used to the fact that he was terrifying. When we had big office parties, he was the bodyguard. We always imagined that if a gun-toting subject happened to rush the fourth floor to exact revenge on the people that had ruined his life, Archie would be there to at least look like he could protect us. All he had to do was stand there, impassively, and the running-away would happen around him.

Archie took particular offense to the Pavlov's-dogs epithet. But Linus's e-mail calling the verifications officers "office lackeys" sent Archie over the edge. He dashed off a scathing missive, complaining that Linus had no respect for the hardworking men and women who keep the Agency afloat. (This was, actually, true.) George and Sol thought this was hilarious, and took it as an opportunity to put an extra effort into lampooning Archie. Archie shrugged and shuffled over to his desk to look for the Rotenfeld case. There is a strange law of perception that the more you look at something, the more it disappears. Sometimes, for Archie's sake, I wished people could see less of him.

How to Pick Locks and Not Set Off Alarms

I wandered out to the fire escape and found a note on the door that said, "To the tenants of 254 East 21st Street. It has come to management's attention that occupants of the fourth floor have been using this fire escape landing for smoking. This is strictly prohibited. Lit cigarettes have been thrown down the grate and have set fire to the tarred roofing below, despite repeated warnings, causing the fire department to be called to this site on several occasions to put out small fires. This exit will be locked from now on. If anyone is caught tampering with this fire exit or in any way attempting to tamper with this exit, eviction proceedings will be initiated against this tenant."

I sucked my breath in, leaned my back against the door, and slid down until I was sitting, slumped with my head slung over my stomach, defeated. Going downstairs to smoke seemed like an unbearable chore.

I heard voices coming down the hallway. "Yeah, dude, I almost got it in a turquoise velour. But my boyfriend liked it better this way." It was Wendy and Assman. Assman said hi to me and turned right into the men's room. Wendy was wearing a rainbow velour, butterfly-style boatneck dress and white cowboy boots. She had a gold charm around her neck that said her name in thick, diamond-studded, ghetto-style script.

"Hey, chiquita." She looked at the door behind me. "What's going on?"

"They locked us out of the fucking fire escape." Wendy put her wrist to her forehead in horror.

"No fucking way!"

"Way," I deadpanned. Renora, the new girl, emerged behind her. She'd assimilated quietly, although during her second week at the office Evan had us each chip in fifty cents for a bottle of Maker's Mark on her birthday, which seemed like more than the usual show of goodwill toward a new colleague. Hormones seemed to be palpably raging since her arrival. She was wearing one of her two indie-girl outfits, a cotton skirt that looked like it had gone from black to a blotchy gray after years of washing, and a tight black V-neck long-sleeve T-shirt. (Her other outfit was the same skirt with a blue long-sleeve shirt.) She also had on a tiny pair of men's shoes that she told me she'd gotten from her friend Randy, who was a stripper she met in England. Randy had gotten them from a guy who was in love with her whose flat she and Renora both stayed in. They were ancient-looking shoes with hand stitching that looked like typical civilian wear in circa-1820 London.

"Hey," Renora said, halting awkwardly before me as Wendy slumped in front of the door.

"Hi," we said in unison.

"What's going on with the fire escape?" she asked softly.

"They locked us out," I said.

"Really?" she said, looking panicky. This was the first time the three of us girls had ever hung out together, I observed to myself.

There was also a new glossy red sign posted on the door, warning that an alarm would sound if the door was opened.

"I don't think they actually put an alarm on the door yet," Renora said. "There isn't a new handle. Usually when they install these things, they put a handle that pushes in and trips the alarm."

"Really?" Wendy asked.

"Yeah. Look." She turned the knob on the door, which was locked, but the alarm didn't go off. "If it was going to go off, it would have done it already."

"Huh," Wendy said, looking dubious.

"No, really," Renora said. She put a shaky hand in her pocket and pulled out her license. "When I lived in London my friend Randy taught me how to pick locks and not set off alarms. There were a few weeks where we had nowhere to live, and we borrowed a few places at night in Brixton."

Wendy and I both sprung up to witness her maneuvering the card. She clipped it in between the doorframe and the edge of the lock plate. I noticed that her tapered fingers were yellowed at the ends, probably stained from two packs of American Spirits' worth of nicotine a day. Her hands shook slightly. "I just need to find the clip," she whispered, looking harried, when finally we heard a click and the door swung free.

"Yippee!" Wendy screamed, and we stepped onto the fire escape. Renora smiled and looked pleased with her transgression.

"So, how are you guys liking it here?" Wendy asked.

"I like it," Renora said. "It's the best job I've had since I moved to New York. Other than my plant-watering job." She had spent six months watering plants for rich clients in Park Slope. She'd been working with a company called Feeding Flora, but after she started sleeping with and then broke up with the married owner, she had to leave. "That gave me lots of practice working on locks."

Wendy and I exchanged glances. "Why?" I ventured.

"I had no job—I needed a place to stay." She shrugged. "There was one place on St. Marks with a swimming pool and a solarium I used to crash in," she recalled nostalgically.

Wendy started to tell us about how things were when she was the only girl there. She was actually the second woman that had been hired. The first, Diana Flynn, was a curvy cheesecake who, it was rumored, had been nailed by many of the dicks in the office. Her supposed dalliances included one with the former investigator of thrown-stapler fame on the fire escape during the company Halloween party. Wendy filled us in on the sleazy details of their tryst, which led me and Renora to get up from our perch. "I'll just *lean* against this step from now on," Renora said. "How did they even—" I wasn't sure how to word this inoffensively—"keep their balance?"

"Honestly," Wendy continued, apparently tired of polite chatter, "when they first hired you guys, I was kind of ambivalent about it. I told them not to hire either of you." Taken aback by her admission, Renora and I quickly sucked on our respective nicotine-delivery systems. We didn't want to let on to our shock, just so she'd tell us more.

"The guys were worried about having to think about how they looked around the office, and I just didn't want to deal with things changing, I guess. But you're both cool." After the initial trauma of her candor abated, Wendy's declaration had an air-clearing effect. Minutes later we were laughing—Renora about her two-week-old fling with a Brooklyn bar owner who was a lot older than her (forty-three), Wendy about her boyfriend, Rocco, of three years. "I was single for, like, ever before I met Rocco," Wendy said wistfully, making the kind of pitch that girls with boyfriends make to their deaf-eared and loveless friends. "I was like *the* single girl. And it was fun." I confessed that I feared Elliott had forever polluted the way I see men. "Oh, come on," Wendy said, "You'll be over him in a few weeks."

"Nope. I'm on the wagon. Only eunuchs and hermaphrodites for me."

"That's disturbing," Renora said. "Maybe you should go back to jerks."

I told them that when Skye's last boyfriend was diagnosed with a heart condition, her mother asked her why she couldn't get a healthy boyfriend and she screamed back at her, "Mom, at least there's medicine he can take for his heart condition, but there's no cure for being an *asshole*!"

"Actually," I said, blushing a little, "I met a great guy recently. He's . . . the best."

"Is he sweet?" Wendy asked.

"Yeah." Getting redder. I didn't want to jinx things by talking about them this early, but . . .

"Is he hot?" Renora asked.

"Completely. So, so hot." They giggled.

Wendy told us that Sol had once bragged that he had the hottest women working for him of any company in New York. "Well, that's not hard to do, when you only have three women working for you," observed Renora.

"Yeah, but I think he's right," Wendy giggled.

"Yeah!" I cheered, and we held our fists in a circle, à la Wonder Woman. "To the hottest dicks in New York City!" We all high-fived, some missing, some hitting.

✿ FOURTEEN

The mystery in how little we know of other people is no greater than the mystery of how much.

—EUDORA WELTY, *THE OPTIMIST'S DAUGHTER*

Fake It Till You Make It

New York is the home of con artists. It's also the home of the self-invented, the fulfillers of the American dream. But, in New York, cons and success stories are impossible to tell apart, depending on how you look at them, or when. Everyone is working it, fronting, faking it, so much so that there's an assumption of inauthenticity about everyone. People who seem to be born-and-bred New Yorkers usually are from Jersey. Williamsburg is full of hipster artist/DJ/clothing designers remade from MIT math geeks. Society girls ditch their prep-school vestments to spend summers panhandling and sleeping on benches in Tompkins Square Park. Most enviable is the ability to replace history with a more auspicious façade—take a drug addiction, a failed hedge fund, a series of failed acting bids, and start anew: a political career, new debt-consolidation company, a hit movie. Not only is there nothing perceived to be wrong with making this jump, but we prefer our stars to be fallen. Like a glittery, Gucci-clad Phoenix rising from the ashes, the prodigal idol in New York is better than a perfect pedigree.

As much as we were all astonished by the Swindling Spin Doctor's tenacity, we reluctantly admired his enterprise. As George said, "You've got to have balls of steel to pull this shit off." But our clients were now panicked about their involvement with him. I was pulling together everything we found into my report, and doing some final searches with the information we had from the book galleys, the newspaper clips we'd found, and prison records.

I kept smelling my shirt, which I'd worn on Friday night with Edward. It was a low-V, pink-and-blue-striped cashmere sweater, and I thought it smelled like dirty metal, cigarettes, and the faintest hint of Edward's cologne. I closed my eyes and let his imprinted odor flood my memory. If only we could smell clues . . . I drifted into sweet nostalgia.

My reverie was interrupted by another, competing odor. It smelled rotten, like roadkill. I checked under my desk for an errant piece of salami. A quick sift through my trash revealed only a moldy apple core, which smelled, but not that badly. It actually smelled like a skunk had unloaded itself on Twenty-first Street. Do they have skunks in New York? It's possible, I suppose. I envisioned a mob of tough inner-city skunks huddling in alleyways and scavenging from restaurant Dumpsters. It seemed implausible. But the smell seemed to balloon the more I thought about it. I swiveled around in my chair. "Hey, Assman! Nestor!" They were both facing me, nodding in different sequences to the throbbing in their headphones. I called to them again, but they each continued determinedly rocking out. I pulled a tiny audiotape out of my desk drawer and pitched it at Nestor. It hit him in the head. He clutched his head and looked at me.

"What the fuck?"

"Nestor, does it smell weird in here?"

He sniffed. "Yeah, kinda." He slugged Assman, who took off his headset and concurred. "It smells like *ass*." How apropos.

A crowd quickly gathered around my desk, where everyone played scent detectives. "It could be a dead rat," Otis mused. He started tracing the walls, checking the sticky-glue traps for recent catch. Renora looked around the piles of crap surrounding George's desk, which could have easily hidden a small colony of skunks. Linus had been keeping a cat in the conference room for a couple of months before she mysteriously disappeared on a weekend when Morgan was working alone at the office. "I hate cats, but not enough to kill one," he sniffed.

"Has anybody heard anything in the walls here?" Gus wondered aloud.

I wandered over to Noah's desk. He was typically oblivious to the commotion gathering right next to him. I sniffed the air around him. A swell of skunky air blasted me. "Ewww!" I fake-gagged. "Noah, you reek."

As everyone encircled his desk, Noah looked anxious. He finally took off his headphones and looked around nervously. "Shhh," he hissed.

"Are you hiding your ex-girlfriend in your desk?" "Take a shower recently, dude?" Reddening, Noah shushed us and pulled a small Ziploc bag out of his Manhattan portage bag. He handed it to me. The bag held four neat buds of marijuana. I held it to my nose. "Ugggghh." Noah's scag redefined skunky.

"Alright, but I don't want to get arrested. Can you guys just leave me alone, please?" Eventually Noah conceded that he'd better evacuate his weed if he didn't want to get arrested, have George smoke it, or both.

This Ain't No Party

After the office was restored to its usual smell of cigarettes and soggy newspapers, I drifted into reminiscences about my weekend with Edward. On Saturday we woke up late and had a sleepy breakfast in Brooklyn of fried eggs and cheese grits and ham and hot chocolate. We ate at the counter on swiveling stools instead of waiting for a table and sat, locked together, my knees cupped by his legs.

We went home and spent two more hours in bed, just kissing, and then went to the Promenade and took in the salty air and the mist-laden view of lower Manhattan from across the East River. That night I wore a sun dress and an apron and made him dinner. While I was cooking, he grabbed me from behind, around my greasy, soggy apron. When I turned around to kiss him, I saw us together in the five-by-nine mirror I put in the kitchen just to torture myself. In the movie of us, I was thinking, we could play ourselves. I was giddy with the thought of him.

On Sunday, we went to P.S.1, an art-exhibition space that commissions a "beach" installation every summer. We sat next to a reflecting-pool surf and a beach of Astroturf and plastic rocks and cuddled. We looked out over a sea of hipsters, ebbing and receding like a real tide.

"This is a weird place," he said.

"Ummm. I know." I was spaced-out from the sun and beer.

"It reminds me of the set on *The Real World*."

Nausea tightened my esophagus after Edward said this, but I concentrated my vision on the sun. I imagined tiny pickaxes deploying from my hips, like something Emma Peel might have, spinning through the cold outer atmosphere to pitch me weight-lessly toward the light and heat. I wanted to anchor myself to its fiery surface. I was melting away, until the sun in my vision was eclipsed, and my eyelids pulsed with red heat, but Edward was still talking.

"The worst thing about being twenty-six is I know I'd never get onto that show. I'd love to do that."

I felt my eyes widen until the sun made me wince. "I can't tell if you're joking," I said, sounding small.

"About what? *The Real World*? I seriously think it would be awesome."

"Really? I think it would be like a living hell."

Edward seemed to consider this carefully. "Yeah, I know what you mean." He paused. "I'm fascinated by celebrity," he said with-out a hint of irony. "I'd love to date a celebrity." He was quiet for a second, and then reanimated when he said, "I could be the cardi-ologist to the stars. Maybe I can have a TV show or something. Like, *Lifestyles of the Doctors of the Rich and Famous*. Or some-thing."

House of Mirrors

I was determined to soften my critical edges, to subvert my instinct to judge swiftly and cruelly, to sustain my disbelief. Yet my natural instinct would certainly have urged me to look at Edward twice before this resolve. I probably would have looked at him a *dozen* times. So what if he wasn't part of the arty, self-hating, I-wouldn't-want-to-be-a-member-of-any-club-that-would-have-me set I was used to? I also realized that I loved being *seen* with Ed-ward almost more than *being* with him. Which reminded me. I wanted to try to meet up with some Brown friends and show him off. I had left my friend Jeremy a message and called my land line to see if he had called back.

There was a message from Cassie, wondering if she could get herpes subcutaneously, and there was also a message from Jeremy. "Hey Amy, it's Jeremy calling. I'm heading to a show tonight from that band Clinic that performs all their shows with surgical masks on. The opener is this chick electroclash band called Ladytron who had glitter guns onstage at their last show and took all their tops off. I'm sure you're already going, but if not, call me. Miss you. Bye." Jeremy was always inviting me to events with naked women so he could feel less perverted about going alone. This time, Jeremy was going to have to endure surgery without me. (It was hard to imagine Edward, or me, for that matter, suffering the arty Williamsburg performance art/electronica scene of bad music and hardcore hipster pageantry.)

Jeremy was one of my closest and most loyal friends from college. We'd met on my third day of freshman year. Our meeting was chance and providential, although, because of the other people we knew at school, our eventual introduction was not a matter of if but when. The inevitable came to pass in September 1992, when an old girlfriend of his came to surprise him, and she asked me and my roommate if we knew a Jeremy Blumstein. "Jeremy—isn't he on our floor?" I asked Sarah. Sarah was much better with names, faces, and social climbing generally than I was. "Yeah, I think he's the one that sold Sammy a dimebag of buds yesterday.

"Yeah," Sarah asserted, "he's the guy." We had sort of ripped him off, but, nonetheless, we took his chickie, Kit, to Jeremy's room and knocked on the door.

A curl of smoke rushed out of the room as he opened the door. He exhaled a sweaty blast of hot smoky bong breath. We pushed our way in. One bed was strewn with CDs, presumably

Jeremy's, and on the other, lying back with his arms folded over his head and his eyes narrowed into little almonds in his doughy face, was Elliott, wearing his usual look of self-satisfaction, the first time I had ever laid eyes on him. "Hey," he said, with obvious contempt. "Jeremy!" Kit squealed, throwing her arms around his neck and wrapping her legs around his waist. Sarah and I sat on Jeremy's bed and giggled and smoked until it was clear Kit and Jeremy were way too excited to see each other. We excused ourselves just as Kit had taken off her tube top and was holding her generous bosom up to Jeremy's face, cooing, "Boo-hoo, Kitty missed you!"

During junior year at college we spent a weekend at Jeremy's family home in Riverdale. The entire house was covered in mirrors: the floors, the countertops, the cabinet cover on the kitchen, the headboards on the beds. Ben and my other friends took the opportunity to do coke off every surface in the house. I remember sitting on the toilet, my feet grazing the mirrored eternity below, looking at a million reflections of myself to infinity in every direction. Extended in every direction was just more of the same, an infinity of humdrum sameness. In my reflection six levels deep in the walls, my eyes turned beady and black. Each generation of reflections was a poorer copy of the first, until I wasted into a fuzzy collection of light and dark with no particular form. Under the P.S.1 hot sun, with Edward's square hand glued to my thigh, I dreamed of myself in the mirrored room, refracted in all directions. I was desperately trying to find the real me. Just when I thought I had found the source, the authentic being at the center of the glassy vortex, I touched the image, only to feel shock and another cold, unforgiving mirrored pane, another bad copy.

"Maybe I could be a celebrity cardiologist, with a book series, too. The first one could be called *My Heart Belongs to Maya*." Edward's voice shocked me out of my daydreaming. His Doberman's name, Maya, was short for Amaya. Her namesake was the "hot but sort of chunky girl on Hawaii *Real World*." Maya—the dog, not the person—had been auditioning for commercials.

"Sweetie," I said, aghast, "let's make out." So we spent the rest of our time on the asphalt upper level of the imitation beach, watching everyone else watching us.

When I got home, Jeremy had left me a message saying that he was sorry I couldn't make it out, and that, true to Williamsburg hipster form, the show was "full of punk girls wearing clothes that looked like they used to be other clothes." This is just what Jeremy likes, by the way, and I should call him for details.

There weren't any other Edward incidents that weekend. That conversation and the nagging echoes of his voice saying, "I thought Puck was cool," aside, things went well. I submerged my queasiness, and when we held hands, the whole time I was thinking how perfect we must have looked together. Something felt wrong with that, but something about it felt right, too. But why was I thinking about how we looked while I was living my life— instead of just living it? There was something about being with someone so exquisite—they became entirely surface. I wasn't sure if I was emptying Edward or it really *was* him, if he was really that blank. Or if it mattered. Like Joe Smythe, like Jeremy's bathroom: surface, surface everywhere.

✪ FIFTEEN

The truth is out there.

—FROM THE OPENING OF *THE X-FILES*

Like Water off a Duck's Back

Edward hadn't called me yet since our blissful weekend. I picked up the receiver when I got home from work, hoping to hear the familiar stuttering dial tone of the voicemail. No luck. My stomach twisted. I stretched out on the bed. Call him. Don't call him. Call him. Don't. Do. Don't.

A few minutes later, the phone rang.

It was him. "Hey, baby," he cooed.

"Hi," I said, thawing at once. "Wow. It's so good to hear from you."

"I know. I miss you." He had finished a thirty-four-hour rotation and called me before he went to bed. We talked about seeing the Sex Pistols documentary *The Filth and the Fury* together, and the whole time I wondered what I'd made all the fuss about. He was so funny. So laid-back. My second-guessing was ancient history. I had all but forgotten my unease.

⚛

By the end of the week, our shell-shocked clients on the Swindling Spin Doctor case were hysterical. George wanted to wrap it up. The clients had engaged a law firm, hoping to file civil charges, and were also working on getting the district attorney in New York to reconsider criminal charges. I had to send a copy of our report to our clients' civil lawyers as well as their bankruptcy lawyers (their misjudgments had put them in some financial trouble), the top executives of the client company, and its board members. George said their chances of getting money back were about equal to Hillary Clinton's chances of getting elected to Congress. To him, that meant a probability of little to none. Lou DeSanto had also made some calls at George's request, and he reported back that New York wasn't interested in going after Smythe again. He was already in jail, they said. They'd worry about it when he was eligible for parole—in six years. They did, however, seize some of the implements of his trade from his cell: a typewriter, paper, pens, a toothbrush, some chalk, some lipstick. I suspected he could figure out a way to run an international con ring with a pair of nail clippers and cinder blocks.

"Mr. John Nguyen Smythe was born on June 18, 1961. For a comprehensive list of his aliases, please see Exhibit E of this report." As I wrote up my memo to the client, I ran a few of Smythe's more unusual aliases in some Internet search engines. Unlike our database research, unless you're in law enforcement or the FBI, we don't have specialized search engines for locating material on the web. But trial and error had led us to a number of sites and search engines that were intermittently helpful. Finally, up popped a Flash site on my screen and text started running across it, along with a voice-over accompaniment in bombastic radio-announcer style.

"This is not just another day. This is a day in the life of John N. Smith." The text faded out and a picture appeared on the screen of a stout, dark-skinned man in a suit surrounded by surgically endowed women in small bathing suits, all grabbing the leis falling across his leisure suit. Another photo faded in on Mr. Smythe standing next to a 1965 Rolls-Royce, his hands on his hips. It looked yellowed, like it was taken in the seventies. Then came a picture of him in an empty boardroom, wearing a suit and silk ascot, then on the beach with two curvy escorts. "Enter the world of John N. Smith, international financial expert, and international socialite." I must have been laughing out loud, because Vinny and Evan came running over. "Nice cans," Vinny commented.

"So is this your boyfriend, Dr. Best?" Evan asked me.

"No, this is the guy your mom was with last night."

At the end of the Flash presentation, there was a short paragraph about the Swindling Spin Doctor, how he has "lived in Paraguay, Thailand, France, and the United States, where he was a financial advisor to important international investors." Right. "Mr. Smith's book *Buyer Beware*, a guide for stockholders to avoid poor investment strategists and unethical brokers, is forthcoming." Uh-huh. Forthcoming.

I felt like Alice having fallen down the virtual rabbit hole into his demented world. I forwarded the URL to George with the subject line "Mr. Smith's shrine to the self he's always wanted." He wrote me back saying, "A. Gray: Did you see the links on that website? I think you might have missed something."

I was so embarrassed. George wouldn't look at me, which

wasn't anything new. But I was worried I'd fucked up big-time and missed something critical.

Pulling up the site again, I noticed that there was a page at the end with links to "Smith" 's favorite websites. "John N. Smith, Entrepreneur, Inventor, Consultant, World Traveler." Demented sociopath. Narcissist. Liar. The links were mostly travel and shopping portals. But here was one, "CopsforCops.com," that looked interesting. It was roughly designed, with flashing Vegas-style lettering that enticed police officers with any number of opportunities: "Employment Help!" "Get Tips on Exams!" "Great Online Investments & Banks Tips!" "Free Online Law Library!" "Get Connected to Police Fraternal Organizations!" "Stress Management and Counseling!" "Order Your Calendar Now: Sexy Ladies of Law Enforcement!" There was even a message board offering "Stress Relief!" and a chance to "consort" with fellow officers. "Consorting" sounded like cop-speak for "sure."

I clicked on the message board, but an error message came up, saying, "This site cannot be found." The online library said the same thing. None of the features advertised actually functioned. There was one thing, however: a link to a "domain manager." The e-mail address was the same one listed on Smythe's personal website. My self-promoting Sociopathic Spin Doctor was spinning an online web support site for cops from prison.

✤

On Wednesday I sucked up my pride and called Edward. The first thing he said was, "Thank God it's you." When we rang off, two and a half hours later, my cheeks hurt from laughing. "I miss you," he said at the end. "I know," I echoed. We made a plan that he would meet me at the Dunkin' Donuts in South Station in Boston on Friday night. It was a hint of things to come.

I stuffed the last piece of hot blueberry-filled dough into my mouth when Edward appeared in front of me at the train station. "Umm, dough-nutty," he said when we kissed. Later, in the car, he pulled a package out of the glove compartment. "I have a present for you," he said.

"I looove presents," I cooed.

"Wait. I don't want you to open it now. I'm giving it to you now. But I want you to wait until you're home and you miss me to open it."

It looked liked a lumpy wrapped sponge. Or a purply sack of new potatoes.

"Oh, I can't wait! Please, please, please let me open it." I thrust out my lower lip and bounced girlishly in the passenger seat in mock impatience. This wasn't hard to feign, since I'm chronically challenged in the area of gratification-deferral.

"Good things come to girls who wait," he admonished.

Suffering Fools Gladly

The town of Amherst, Massachusetts, is about an hour and a half outside of Boston at a good clip. Edward didn't live in Amherst, however. He lived two towns away. As we started to near his house, I noticed a mile of abandoned clam shacks, auto graveyards, and strip malls passing by. "Where are we going to have dinner?" I asked.

"Oh, you haven't eaten yet?" He seemed surprised.

"Well, I had pretzels on the train, but I'd still love a pack of nuts."

"Ha-ha. Well, I got me some of those," he said, winking as he squeezed my knee. That's my boy, I thought to myself.

As it turned out, I didn't think much about being hungry, because as soon as we got to his house, we started kissing, and we didn't stop until four the next morning. The last thing I remember before I fell asleep was resting my head on his chest (yes, it was everything his tight T-shirt that first night implied, and more) and seeing a pair of snowflakes fall across the triangle of light from a streetlamp.

Waking up at Edward's was like arriving there for the first time. His apartment was big, if a little antiseptic. There was a huge kitchen, a living room, a bedroom, and a study. Excluding a dartboard, empty beer bottles, a bed, and a synthetic couch embossed to look like lizard skin, it was pretty empty, except for his dog, Maya. She was a hundred-pound supermodel of a dog. Despite her bulk, Amaya was delicately proportioned and graceful, and she was guaranteed to get any attention to be had when he walked her, which, granted, wasn't much in rural Massachusetts.

"Dat's daddy's baby girl. Oooooh yeaaah," he cooed. Maya's tongue was all over his face, slapping away, and his was licking her back. For a split second, I felt jealous of Edward's dog. I reminded myself aloud, "She's a *dog*."

We didn't get up until eleven. Edward didn't have any breakfast food in the house, so he took me out. "I don't usually eat breakfast," he shrugged. There were five inches of fresh snow on the ground, which would have thrilled me if I didn't have the blood-sugar level of a goldfish. We brushed off the front and rear windows of his coupé and he navigated the strip of superstores. "This must be the last place in the world without a Starbucks. It's like the Old West of coffee," I cracked. He took me to Dunkin' Donuts, which was pathetically familiar to us now.

There isn't much to do in Edward's town, so he took me to his school to show me the grounds. Then we stopped by the veterinary school. The newborn lambs were in an open-sided barn under big heatlamps. They bounded around the barn, swathed in a warm, pinkish light that contrasted with the blue clouds made by their exhalations. *"Baaayyy! Baaayyy!"*

"I love them!"

"Do you want to hold one?"

"Yes!"

He cupped his left hand under the front legs of one of the tiniest ones close to us, and the others ran away, crying, *"Baaayyyy!"* The lamb yawned and nuzzled its little nubby white head in my chest. "I'm in love!" Edward put his hand under my chin and pulled me toward him.

"So am I." He said it in a way that was frighteningly serious. I was speechless.

By the time we got home it was three. Edward had said he was going to cook me dinner. He made me watch TV in the living room while he cooked, because he wanted to "surprise" me, and I was too hungry to do anything but lounge anyway. Two and a half hours later, we sat down to a plate of rice pilaf and a mystery meat.

I didn't want to be rude, so I cut into it really slowly. Then I relished it like it was filet mignon. "Ummm," I said. "Chicken?"

"Nope," he said, smiling.

"Oh. Is it—" I was grasping—"turkey?"

"Nope." This was getting a little annoying. "It's emu." My revulsion must have been evident, because he quickly added, "It's really good. Lots of athletes eat it because it's low in fat and very high in protein."

"Really?" Now that I had lost the bliss of ignorance, I was fixating on the knowledge that this meat wasn't native to this hemisphere. I noticed that it was foul-smelling and weirdly colored. Purplish.

"You know, there are so many meats out there that people don't even know about." Do I want to be having this conversation—ever? I was wondering. "I like to take care of my body, so I read, you know, a lot about this stuff. My feeling is, my body's my temple."

"Right."

"I take care of myself, and it's worth it. I mean, look at me." He made right angles with his biceps and gave me a creepy body-builder smile.

"So . . ." I was scared to ask, "Where do you get this stuff?"

"I mail-order from bodybuilders' catalogs. Ostrich is another good one that people underrate. I should make that for you next time—"

"No!"

After Edward ate all my emu and I ate both of our rice portions, he took me to Subway for another dinner. How appropriate that I was out of New York City in barren middle-American hell eating at a place called Subway. Nothing else was open at eleven on a weekend.

Before bed, I noticed that Edward brushed his teeth for twenty minutes and took a thirty-minute shower. He also wouldn't let me wear shoes in his bedroom or sit on his bed unless my clothes were off because his bed and bedroom were "temples," too. I sat naked on his bed, except for my socks, which I always wear to bed, come hell or high water.

"Nope, can't break the rule," he admonished.

"C'mon, I always wear them. It's a security blanket."

"You have to leave your security blanket behind." What's up with this creepy bedtime voodoo, I wondered. I felt like I was sleeping with Jim Morrison.

"Please, I really"—I was exasperated—"want them."

"You can't have your present until you take them off." The

socks came flying off. Aside from wanting my swag, I thought maybe he was right, maybe I needed to lose this hang-up. They're only socks, after all. Then the lights went out.

"Ahhh!" I screamed. Edward was standing in front of me with a candle held near his upper thigh, where a new Asian character was carved. My "present" was apparently a new tattoo near his crotch, some scrawl inside the prongs of a wishbone. What the hell kind of a gift is this? I thought.

"What does it mean?" I asked, darkly.

"I choose life."

"What made you decide on that?" I croaked. Just as I was beginning to ask all kinds of questions I had no answers to—like why was this a present for me? in what fiendish twilight zone did I inspire men to tattoo their thighs? what was up with that aphorism "I choose life"? and why me?—he gave me one.

"You did, baby," he said, sweeping me onto the bed, bare feet and all, and reminding me silently why I'd chosen him. Yes, I recall thinking, I remember now. Looking back, I envision myself picking clues to fit a crime, choosing to ignore the evidence at hand to get what I really wanted. Like so many of our clients, I had explained our findings to close the deal. It never led to good partnerships.

When we were saying good-bye to each other the next day, even after listening to him talk about how he had thought about faking his driver's license to get on *TRW* (his acronym, not mine), and about his daily beauty routine, and I was just about to throw in the towel, I looked into his spectacular eyes and thought, He's perfect—looking. On the Delta shuttle home to New York, I pushed my nose against the oval pane to see the sun still catching the clouds like a burr on cotton. I collected my uncertainties, sweeping them away like little cumulus clouds from an otherwise perfect horizon at 15,000 feet.

✥

I was lonely and drunk. I called Edward. He wasn't home. I left him a message that went something like, "Hi, it's me again. I guess you're not home. I miss you so fucking much . . ." And on and on like that for about fifteen minutes. I don't remember that it was that long, but that's what he said when he finally called me back two days later. By then I'd left him five messages. That same night.

"Hi!" I tried not to sound too excited and surprised when I answered the phone. "How are you? I mean, where have you been? I've been trying to reach you. I guess you knew that."

"Yeah." I guessed I'd blown the subtlety plan. He didn't *say* anything.

"So . . . I'm sorry about all those messages I left you."

"Yeah." Another silence.

"Edward—"

"Amy."

"You first," I said.

"No, you."

"Okay." I wasn't sure what to say. "I'm sorry about all those messages the other night. I hope I didn't freak you out." *Another* silence.

"I think we need to slow down with this," he said.

I breathed. Hard. "What?"

"I think we're moving too fast, and I need to be focusing on my schoolwork right now."

I breathed. Hard.

"I just think we have different priorities and I really need to concentrate on mine."

"Are you breaking up with me?"

"Let me finish. I think you're just more into this relationship than I am. You're like the debtor and I'm like the creditor."

When we got off the phone I had a horrifying and stomach-turning thought. I'd never opened Edward's present. Panicked, I raced to my suitcase and flung it open, exposing the squishy purple paper. I grabbed it, ripping and ripping, until all that was left in my hand was an edifying relic of our demise: a stuffed Mickey Mouse, holding a heart that said MY SWEETIE. A half smile gathered over my wet face.

Four hours later, I was at Niagara, screaming at Cassie, "I overlooked the fact that he spelled 'crazy' in his e-mails with a 'k'!"

She nodded her head in sympathy for the hundredth time. I was not to be succoured.

"Winslow Homer was his favorite painter. And *he* broke up with *me*!"

She was agreeing with everything I was saying, but her attention span was shot. Her hand was paused in midair, ready to hail the next bartender or cab that came her way, whichever turned up first.

"How are the two foxiest girls in the East Village to-*nite*?" I squinted in the glare of Stuart's shiny bald head, beating down right next to me.

"Shitty." Stuart must have sensed that I was not to be reckoned with because he was *never* that nice to me. Are there tears on my face? I wondered. Is there a tattoo on my forehead that says, DON'T KICK ME, I'M ALREADY DOWN FOR THE COUNT?

Cassie air-kissed him. "Stu, bring this girl another tequila shot." She patted me on the back. "And me too, while you're at it."

❧

There are certain kinds of pain that I can't imagine feeling. I can't imagine what it feels like to have a sick liver. What does a liver feel like? I can feel my arm, for example, or my knee, but if someone hadn't already told me I had a liver, I'd never know better. Pituitary gland, gallbladder, ovary, duodenum, these are the humble workhorses, the unsung sentinels of the body. Three Cuervos later, I held my hand to my chest. This must be what a heart feels like, I thought to myself.

✪ SIXTEEN

In another moment down went Alice after it, never once considering
how in the world she was to get out again.

—LEWIS CARROLL, *ALICE IN WONDERLAND*

The One You Left Behind

For regular subway riders in the morning, there is a certain
steadfastness and comfort in being so familiar with your surroundings, particularly when they're as urine-stinking and oppres-
sive as the New York City underground. In July, the summer draws
every hidden stench out of winter's dormancy, and the subways
become a repository for every punishing odor. It's *my* stinking
subway car, they're *my* belligerent, schizophrenic winos with me
every day. Time passes. Attachments develop. I see the same people daily, and I keep a running mental log of their evolution. I remember reading Harriet the Spy's impressions of the New York

City subway: "I don't think I'd like to live where any of these people live or do the things they do. I bet that little boy is sad and cries a lot. I bet that lady with the cross-eye looks in the mirror and feels just terrible." Of course, I'm somewhat more evolved than Harriet was at nine years old. I noticed a sign one day in the stairway leading downstairs into Bergen Street, my stop on the F train. It read:

Who are you? It was yesterday afternoon on the subway. We were stalled between Delancey Street and Second Avenue (or was it East Broadway and York?). I was astonished to have met such a sweet, generous, spirited person. Plus you liked Beck. Stumble back into my path. Coffee maybe? E-mail me at theoneyouleftbehind.com.

This is the kind of John Hughes story that I dreamed up on mornings when I got enough sleep to be cognizant. Eyeing cute boys, I could create elaborate narratives of our meeting. On a July morning, I was at Broadway-Lafayette when I felt someone tap me on the shoulder.

I swung around, poised for war, and a cute blondish guy with a guitar strapped on his back was smiling at me.

"Hey," he said. "Were you at that Built to Spill show last week?"

I thought about it. "No." But wait, I *was* at that show. Wasn't I? Not having had my coffee yet, I was in my usual morning stupor, racking my brain to remember. He looked puzzled.

"It's okay," he said, raising his hand as he painfully coped with my rejection. "You're probably, like, 'Why is this weird guy bothering me at eight-thirty in the morning?' "

"Yeah," I said, unwittingly. He started to turn away.

"No—wait. I'm just confused."

"About talking to me?"

"No, about the show. Honestly, I'm not a morning person. I'm totally out of it."

"Well, that makes one of us." He put out his hand. "I'm Dan." I shook it.

"Amy."

"I'm pretty sure I remember you from that show. At Maxwell's. Last Friday."

It came back to me like a slap in the face. What an idiot. "You're right. I was totally there. Sorry about that. I'm really only semiconscious until I have my iced grande skim half-caf no-foam latte."

"Wow. You don't have any problem saying that."

"Years of practice. Ask me what my middle name is before noon, and I'd say iced grande skim half-caf no-foam latte." We chuckled a little. He was an art director for a new dot-com start-up. We talked about how much we liked Built to Spill. As we pulled into Twenty-third Street, I shuffled my bag around to alert him that I was getting off.

"Well . . . it was nice to meet you." It seemed like as soon as I'd said that the subway doors were opening and I was spilling mindlessly onto the platform. "Nice meeting ya," his voice trailed after me, as I turned around with a thousand other semiconscious people, none of whom knew I'd just blown my opportunity with what seemed like a nice guy and forgotten to give him my number. "Fuck!" I yelled to myself, drawing irksome looks from the straphangers swarming past me. The train pulled away, leaving only a rush of wind and the memory of my blunder.

He'd Be Hot if He Weren't Heavy

Renora and I had become regular smoking buddies. Although our friendship was forged out of convenience—Linus, Gus, and Wendy had decided they were all quitting—they were all back off the wagon and Renora and I were actually becoming friends. Plus it was a gossip-fest.

"Any budding romances you know about around the office?" I asked her. The only in-office action I had known about had gone down—*literally*—years prior between Diana Flynn and the infamous stapler-thrower.

"No." We were yearning for some secret tryst to spice up the office life. Never mind that there was a serious dearth of women to participate in said dalliances, or that by recusing ourselves we eliminated 70 percent of the possibilities for further entertainment.

"I think Linus is kind of cute."

"Yeah," I said mindlessly. "Wait, Linus? Seriously?"

Though she was already red-faced, it still wasn't hard to detect some embarrassment from Renora. "Yeah, well, he's smart. It's just his personality, I guess, that's cute. Whatever."

I thought about them together. It was too weird to contemplate, but they did have similar coloring. Pale-skinned, Germanic, high-cheekboned features mixed with a little rosiness around the cheeks from hard drinking. "You guys would look cute together," I offered.

"Okay," Renora said, pulling a fresh American Spirit out from behind her ear. "So, if you had to sleep with anybody in the office, who would it be?"

"Ugh. That's not a choice, it's a curse."

"That's why it's so fun."

I went through the checklist in my mind. No, no no, no no, no. "So?"

"I can't pick."

"C'mon. You have to."

I wanted my choice to be original, and saying "Evan" would have been obvious, and the thought of him in any amorous light was disturbing.

"Okay. I have it. But my pick is conditional."

"On what?"

"On the person losing fifty pounds."

She looked stumped. "Is it Adrienne?"

"Ha-ha. No, it's a man. Or a boy, at least."

"I have no idea."

"It's Assman."

"Whaaaaaaatttttt???!" Her scream made my eyes water. "Are you joking? Assman? Ha! Ha-ha-ha!" Renora was laughing and coughing, with her cigarette hand cupping her mouth. "Ha! Assman!"

I was protective. "He used to be an athlete. He was the captain of his high school football team. He'd be hot if he weren't heavy," I protested. "He's a diamond in the rough!" But the cork was out of the bottle. She danced in the hallway back into the office, quietly singing "Amy and Assman, sittin' in a tree, K-I-S-S-I-N-G . . ."

Speak of the Devil

It was mid-July. I sensed the onset of emotional gangrene. Numbness set in. It was alarming but predictable, considering my symptomatically dormant love life. When one doesn't use a limb, it starts to die. But I was also due for a new case, and it was possible I was just bored.

Evan was trying hard to look like he was working. Eyes squinted. Lips parted. I walked around behind his desk and leaned over and whispered in a gravelly voice, "Whatcha doin'?" He nearly ejected from his seat.

"Uh, nuthin'." He slammed his laptop closed. Now I was embarrassed.

"Sorry to sneak up on you, Ev. I just wanted a new case."

He sighed. "Okay, okay." He opened his computer again and appeared to shudder at the barely distant memory of me freaking him out. "Gray, don't sneak up on me again."

"Now that I know you're gathering intel on the teen-porn industry, I won't tell a soul."

"Ha-ha," he erupted, expressionless. "Nah, I was downloading Napster shit."

"I haven't gotten into that yet," I confessed.

"Dude," he protested. "It's insane. Check this out." He opened his computer screen and pulled up a window with songs written down it. "Okay, I have the entire Bob Dylan Basement Tapes." He scrolled down. "The new Built to Spill album, every Yo La Tengo album ever, the AC/DC song TNT, a bunch of ELO . . ." He suddenly eyed the room nervously as Sol plodded past him, and slammed his computer shut. "Just don't let Sol see you doing it, he's onto us. He told Assman the other day that if he caught him again he'd cut him loose."

"Believe me, I won't."

He handed me a folder. "So it's two guys. Niels Norrsken and his son Nars." He put his hand to his mouth to indicate he was divulging top-secret intelligence. "They're father and son."

"Thanks, dickwad. I figured."

"Hey," he admonished, "you're insulting dickwads everywhere."

The subjects, Evan explained, were Swedes, but had lived in Paris, Prague, and Berlin, which made finding information on them somewhat more difficult. European countries have different laws about public information, and often it's not available through our databases. But the son, Nars, had married and divorced an American girl, and both of them had done some business in the U.S. They ran a massive publishing empire headquartered in Sweden, and the father, Niels Norrsken, had recently retired and put the son in charge of their company. The client was a wealthy New York hedge-fund manager considering about $20 million of diversification in their company's publishing wing. The Norrskens' company was called KNUT, which gave the perenially gutter-minded Evan and me a good chuckle.

I went back to my desk and started working on the case. The Norrskens had assembled their filthy publishing fortune managing a group of trashy tabloids and soft-porn publications sold all over Europe. In the new technology-based economy, the Norrskens and their smutty rags were practically throwbacks. There was something almost charming about these robber barons making their living printing actual newspapers and magazines. *Piddle Paddle, The Daily Rear, Granny Fanny:* These formed the foundation of the ill-gotten Norrsken fortune.

Their American presence was appropriately immoderate. When in New York they were socialites of the order that attended events hosted by Puff Daddy. The father, once a dashing playboy, now looked more like a pastier version of the aging Siegfried and Roy. (Either one, really; I can't tell them apart.) The skin on his face appeared partially collapsed after facelift surgeries. Pulled tightly across his mouth and over his eyes, it showed effects of hard living and age in the corners of his eyes and neck, where he had a suspended purse of tissue like a chicken's gizzard.

There were a number of defamation lawsuits against their company, KNUT Enterprises, and the umbrella company KNUT Publishing. Lawsuits aren't necessarily a red flag, however. In fact, so rarely do we investigate a company that has no lawsuits against it that finding *nothing* would probably be a red flag. Such lawsuits were considered routine, and they usually were, since they rarely went to trial and were typically settled out of court. But the moral implications of the flagrant lies they printed were considered incidental. The subject of many stories featuring infidelity, sex addiction, or other disgraces were expected to suck it up. Unless the financial awards were huge and threatened the sine qua non, no one cared.

Just then I got an e-mail from George, who was sending me their newest press release, just put out that day: "A. Gray, to be reviewed, sincerely, George."

KNUT Enterprises had made a net profit of $4.9 million in 1999 on gross revenue of $38 million. In case you're wondering, that's good. The company was clearly very profitable, but these figures were way down from the previous year, when they had made $19 million on $59 million. Most of the losses were for the final quarter of the year, when they had acquired a papermill in Canada and a bunch of real estate investments. The release warned about possible net losses in the next quarter, but insisted these were "largely resulting from recent acquisitions," and, they insisted, "were not to be taken as an indicator of the financial results of the company." It didn't seem to be coincidental that this release had just been made available, long after most companies had already published their earnings for that quarter.

The company's CFO had resigned only weeks before, according to wire reports, and he was the fifth individual with that job in the past twelve months. Also, I noticed KNUT had changed its American accounting firm only a few weeks prior as well. Something seemed afoot, and I was ready to trip them up.

❧

At lunch that day, Sol sauntered in and began picking pieces of Swiss from the waxed paper under my ham-and-cheese.

"Hey, how about, Can I have your cheese?" I said. "Or thank you?"

Sol, smiled, chewing. "I don't have to ask. It's the lunch tariff. It's written into your contract." He grabbed some of Otis's supersize fries and chomped with satisfaction. George was laughing.

"What you've got to do is have a decoy lunch," Gus advised.

"I keep a stash of Doritos on me at all times," Linus added.

Sol's pilfering meant that we all had to mooch off one another. It was a vicious cycle of graft. I stole a couple of bites off Evan's meatball sub, who took Otis's bag of salt-n-vinegar chips, while he pilfered Wendy's pickle and the crusts from a homemade peanut-butter sandwich, and so on. Wendy even purloined a bite of Wally Yoo's potato chips, promptly spit it back out on a napkin, and said, "What the hell is this?"

"They're crispy dried shrimp," Wally said, smacking his lips together with satisfaction, popping in some more freeze-dried crustaceans.

That was the last time anybody tied to steal from Wally. Sol bid me adieu, saying, "See ya, Graystein." And with that he left me in the conference room, joined only by old Zinger wrappers and the lonely remnants of Otis's foot-long egg-salad-and-hot-pastrami hero.

An Upside-Down Snow Day

I closed my laptop for the day at 6:45 and breathed in the steamy air. It was eighty-four degrees, and we hadn't even hit the weeklong heat wave that was supposed to slog New York. Hot air was rushing in through the three open front windows looking over Twenty-first Street and swirling through the office, blowing loose documents into lifting helixes. Then I realized it was snowing. I pointed out the window.

"You guys! It's snowing. In July!" There were only a handful of us left in the office. Evan, sitting closest to me, yelled, "What the fuck?" and we all ran to the end of the office. Sure enough, mirroring the swirl of paper near the window, outside there was a torrent of flakes, rising up toward the rooftops of New York buildings, like a fun-house mirror image. "It's snowing upside down!" I said, and we were wide-eyed and delighted when Wendy said, "Wait a minute—I *caught* one."

There in her sweaty palm, framed by her glistening green-polished nails, was a perfect unmelted crystal. When we looked outside again, the storm had subsided enough to reveal a New York City Sanitation truck, parked on Twenty-first Street about one hundred yards west, from which was soaring like a covey of tiny birds the equivalent of a hundred old pillows' worth of feathers. When I looked back at Wendy's hand, I saw the feather, still pristine and unchanged. It was almost better than the real thing, I thought to myself.

⚡ SEVENTEEN

In the age of transparency, the allure of the secret remains stronger than ever.

—LUC SANTE

Stan Lee Is Not Dead

Less than a week after my fateless meeting with Cute Subway Boy, I was riding to work in the morning, pining for my Starbucks fix. Usually when I got on the train, I tried to position myself standing in front of people I thought would be getting off before me. There were a few I recognized as getting off at Jay Street, the stop after mine, and I'd always position myself to the far side of the door I thought they'd use. That way, when they got up I wouldn't be blocking their way, and I could jump in their seats as soon as they stood. Usually there was an equally ambitious person on their other side who tried to grab the seat, too, but I always won out with my away-from-the-door strategy.

Today I had strategically placed myself in front of a mother and son. Child-parent groups were usually a good bet because most parents in Brooklyn didn't take their kids into midtown for school, so they'd likely be getting off before me. It worked, and I was practically falling asleep when I heard a subway panhandler asking for my attention.

The world of subway hustlers is a microcosmic universe unto itself, with the requisite bottom-feeders and high-rollers. Usually, the panhandlers' scripts are humdrum: "Ladies and gentlemen, My name is ———, I'm homeless, I don't drink or do drugs, any money you can give me would be appreciated, God bless." There were a few talented performing-artist regulars: the doo-wop groups, the guys who did old-school breakdancing and a two-man cartwheel down the length of the car, and the balloon artist I'd seen only once, on the R train.

But this guy, this guy was different, and I had seen him before. "My name is John Wilder. I'm a comic-book artist and I used to work at DC comics, where I was a protégé of Stan Lee. He died and I was left custody of his two daughters. I need money to support these girls, so I'm selling off my DC comic-book collection to support them." The weird thing about this guy was that he was nothing like any other panhandler I'd ever seen on the subway. He was wearing a tweed jacket and matching vest underneath. He looked like someone I'd know, like a grungy Williamsburg boy, a skinny-tie-wearing member of the Strokes meets an 1850s English schoolboy. The familiarity of him tugged at me, and I figured at the very least I could acquire a comic in the process. Several people on the subway held up dollar bills, and Tragic Comic Guy tried my patience by spending eons talking to two giggly teenage girls.

"What do you guys like to read?" he asked.

"I don't know," they laughed nervously.

"Well, you look like White Lotus types. She's a really cool

character, actually. She's a chick and she's beautiful. . . , See, look at her—but she also kicks butt. See, in this one, she's in the Supermen of America team." The girls were exchanging glances and giggling. I kept crumpling my bill and smoothing it out again, undecided if I still felt so sorry for him. He seemed to be getting plenty of money and action without me.

By the time he got to me, he seemed tired and eager to get off our car.

"Sorry." He looked at me and then looked away. "Did, did you want one?" Feigned caution, self-effacement: classic manifestation of a well-oiled shyster.

"I dunno." Now I played disinterested and distracted. "Do you have any White Lotus?"

He checked through his messenger bag. "Actually, I'm out of those. Here—this is Crazy Jane." I looked down. Crazy Jane wasn't beautiful and ass-kicking like White Lotus. She was a scarred blue-haired girl who, the cover boasted, "has multiple personality disorder after a gene bomb explosion."

"Thanks," I said.

I was reading about Crazy Jane's ability to channel sixty-four distinct personalities from Scarlet Harlot to Hangman's Daughter—ugh—when I heard on the subway-car P.A.:

"Ladies and gentlemen, due to an incident at West Fourth Street, this train is being held. Please be patient and we'll be moving shortly." Boos and sighs echoed across the subway car, and the cartoon guy, seemingly spooked about hanging around, crossed over to another car. We were between East Broadway and Delancey Street.

Stuck underground with nothing to read except for my crappy comic, I tried to read the *Post* off the guy next to me until he caught on and double-folded it. Bastard. At least I figured I'd done a mitzvah, a good deed, as my mother would have said.

"Which one did you get?" I heard coming from above me.

Looking up, I saw Dan standing over me. He was clutching his comic book—from the Tragic Comic Guy, too. Just like that, Mr. Maybe-Right had resurfaced in my life. I was euphoric.

"Where did you come from?" I asked, smiling.

"I was over there"—he pointed to the far opposite side of the train car.

"Wow. This is a nice coincidence." I blushed.

"A very very lucky one," he added.

Embarrassed, I asked him, "So, which one did you get?"

"Some shitty piece of crap."

"Well done."

"Yeah, well, I only bought it because I was curious about the guy and I was gonna ask him some questions. But I didn't get a chance. When the train stopped, he split."

"Why? Is Stan Lee alive and well?" I joked.

"Yeah, he is, actually." Dan, it turned out was more than an amateur comic-book fan. "I knew he was lying, the second he said he worked at DC—Stan Lee is and always was at Marvel. But his spiel was so cogent. You've got to admire that ambitious capitalist spirit. Even if it is misguided and fraudulent."

"Really? So you think he was really lying?" I catch people in lies every day. It's my *job*. But the Tragic Comic Guy had put me in a state of cognitive dissonance. I couldn't square his nice White Guy looks with the very desperation and debasedness of his scam. How could someone like him—like me—panhandle in the subway? It made me angry at myself and all the other guilty liberals who saw ourselves in him and wasted a dollar on his crappy comics.

"I just saw a profile of Stan Lee on the E! channel the other day," Dan added. "I'm pretty sure that, as of last week, he was still kicking it." We agreed that I would check him out at work that afternoon.

As we pulled away from Fourteenth Street, Dan dug into his pocket and pulled out a small spiral notebook.

"So, can we make it more official this time? Can I have your e-mail or something?"

"Sure," I said, smiling as I recited the letters like my well-versed commands to the Starbucks counter guy.

Society for Ersatz Intellectuals

I walked into the conference room at lunch, with a roast-beef-on-rye sandwich and a Twinkie for Sol and a copy of the *Post*.

Vinny lit into me immediately for my choice of reading material. *"Amy Gway."* He always called me Amy Gway. His accent fell in some lonely place in the voice-continuum where Rain Man meets Elmer Fudd.

"Whadayadoin' weeding da *Post*! Dat's fascist, wight-wing cwap." Vinny was a classic man of the people, working-class, labor-union, liberal.

"I know, Vinny. I *like* it because it's crap."

"Murdoch, Jewriani—day're da wurst! Yeah, dese people, dey don't want gun contwol so dey kin wun awound in dare backyawds and shoot squawels. How can you use a huntin wifle in New Yawk? It's wadiculous!"

Vinny's passion with the cause of old-time labor liberalism was charming. But I wanted him to shut up.

"You know that truism, Vinny—keep your friends close and your enemies closer. That's why I read the *Post*."

Otis laughed. "That's bullshit if I ever heard it, man."

"Actually, Amy, now that you mention it, maybe I should move over and sit next to you," Linus said with a chuckle.

"Linus, I'm proud to be the enemy of anybody with your

fashion sense." Linus was acting a little strange that day. First of all, he was wearing a suit. He normally wore scruffy cords and a T-shirt, and today he was wearing a mildewy herringbone three-piece suit with corduroy patches on the elbows and his usual duct-taped shoes and his hair slicked back. He looked like an erstwhile professor who'd been fired for consorting with his students. I told him as much.

"Yeah, man, you do sort of look like a demented middle manager," Otis chimed in.

"Okay, everyone, leave Amy alone so I can eat her lunch," Sol chastised, chomping on somebody's else's hot wings.

"Not this time," I said, pleased with myself. "I brought you a bone." I threw the Twinkie in Sol's direction. "Anyway, where's our token Republican to defend me when I need him? I looked at Morgan, who, despite his claims of being an off-the-map Libertarian, was trying to fly under the radar as he perused *The New York Times*. "Help me out here, Morgan," I pleaded.

"I'm simply an idle aristocrat fallen on hard times," Morgan scoffed. "My allegiance is to no one."

"What about when we elect our new president this fall?"

"I'll be out of here before then. Thank God." A look of repugnance eclipsed his face.

That Rat Bastard

Later at work that day, I got inspired to call DC Comics and check out my Tragic Comic friend. I called the publicity department and spoke to a senior publicity staffer and explained the situation. "I used to work in publishing," I said, "so I know the truth is sometimes stranger than fiction, and frankly I just had to know if he was for real. Plus, I think you should know about it, too."

The publicist laughed. "You're not the first person who's called about this. Stan Lee works at Marvel, first of all. As far as I know, he's alive and well. You can call the Marvel people about this, but I know this guy's a total scam artist."

"Really?"

It was strange to me that the Tragic Comic Guy would go to such elaborate lengths with his scam and still get his facts so clearly wrong, almost as if he wanted to be found out by the right kind of amateur detective.

❖

Back at my desk, I heard the familiar bleep indicating new mail. There was a message from Dan already in my in-box with the subject line "F Train." It read: "Amy, I can't wait to take the F train again. Maybe we could try to run into each other on purpose sometime? Dan."

I screamed. "Everything okay, Miz Gray?" Sol said. He was wearing a canny smirk. I bit my hand in embarrassment.

"Sorry about that." I opened a reply and drafted a response with the subject line "Stan Lee Is Not Dead." In the message I typed Y-e-s, taking a deep breath and then hitting the SEND button.

❖

I was making calls on my Case of the Eurotrash Pulp-Peddlers. My number-one target was Anna Vinka, the recently departed CFO of the publishing division. I called her at home. She was brusque and uncomfortable.

"I can't talk about it."

"Ms. Vinka, our client is considering a major investment with the Norrskens, and frankly, I would like to know if there is any reason they might not be a safe investment. I think you're in an ideal position to help our client—"

"Miss Gray," she interrupted. "I worked at KNUT for three weeks, and I signed a confidentiality agreement not to talk about it."

"I understand," I said hesitantly. These are tricky situations. "Let me ask you if there are any of your predecessors I might contact who would have more . . . flexibility about speaking about KNUT."

She paused. "Tord Ostgaard left about three months ago. He's working at Lloyd's of London now. Ring him. He might be more helpful."

I did some preliminary research on Ostgaard. He also had been at KNUT for less than a month. Before he started there, however, he had been a trustee of another Norrsken-owned business, a property-management arm called Pickwick Property Management. There were literally thousands of KNUT-controlled companies, shelters, and trusts. I'd seen Pickwick's business filings, but hadn't done news or litigation searches for all of the thousands of KNUT affiliates, excepting the ones that were directly related to the KNUT Publishing division. Even more disconcerting, I discovered a recent article that said Ostgaard was under investigation by the Swedish regulatory arm called the Financial Intelligence Unit (FIU) for "misappropriation of pension funds for Pickwick."

I called Mr. Ostgaard, and he, like Ms. Vinka, was unhelpful.

"I can't talk about this," he barked, and as it sounded like he was about to hang up on me, I yelled into the phone, "Mr. Ostgaard, I am trying to protect my client from getting fucked over by these people." I didn't know what I meant by that, even as I said it, but he paused.

"I understand you don't want to talk about Pickwick," I said, trying to sound soothing, "but can we talk about KNUT?"

"That's the problem. You can't separate them."

"What do you mean?"

"Miss Gray, tell your client to stay as far away from KNUT, the Norrskens, and any of their business as possible."

"I will."

"Now that's all I can say."

＊

I e-mailed Sol and George right after the calls and wrote the whole thing up. I also did some more news searches, looking for KNUT-related entities and any kind of pension fraud. In fact, the pension managers and several trustees of four other KNUT-owned companies were being investigated for fraud. I sent my bosses everything. The database searches I was doing were long and grueling. With thousands of related company names, the potential search for material was almost endless. Before I knew it, it was eight-thirty, and Gus was the only one left in the office with me. No e-mails from Dan.

Gus came by my desk.

"Wassup?" He poked me in the head.

"This case is giving me a headache."

"Well, it can wait until tomorrow," he said.

"I know."

"But this Wild Turkey can't." He pulled a bottle out of his pocket and we sat and swigged it until 11 P.M. I told him all about Dan. And Edward. And Elliott. And Ben. He laughed and said, "Shit, just ain't the same as when I was datin'."

"Gus, you're only thirty-two."

He laughed. "Yes, I guess it's not that different."

Getting Lucky

It was eleven-thirty and I didn't trust my tipsy self on the subway, so I decided to call a car home. Since I moved to New York I've been using Lucky Car Service. I don't take cars often, usually at night or when I'm incredibly late.

I called them. Mussah, the owner, answered, "Hellooo, Ameee. Of course, my loveleee. No problem." I packed up my laptop and walked down the back stairs (the elevator was stuck in the basement—again) and sat on the small concrete fleur-de-lis pedestal curling along the stoop.

Originally, when I first went to Lucky, it was run by a guy named Mustafah, and one night he followed me home, calling after me, "Let me take you out on a date. Come on! Let me take you for dinner, meese. Let's go!" I told him I had a boyfriend and he stopped and looked dejected. "He a lucky guy, this boyfriend, eh?" Then he brightened. "We don't have to tell him, eh?"

I still had to walk past the Lucky Car Service every day on the way to the subway, and he'd give me creepy, dark stares. Months later, I walked down the block to get a car and saw a dozen cop cars in front of Lucky and what looked like forty guys on the ground with their hands behind their heads, including Mustafah, a pained look on his face, his flabby arms twisted back into metal cuffs. He was wailing. I felt a swelling in my throat. I ran back in the other direction.

The storefront was boarded-over that night and the company reopened two months later, a block closer to me, with a whole new set of guys running it: Mussah (a former Iranian army general), Moez (who was Tunisian), Sammeh (Lebanese), Muhammed (Egyptian), Mumar (Iraqi), Nasir (Turkish). "What's up with these 'M' names?" I asked them once when I was waiting in the dispatch room for a car to the Lower East Side.

"I dunno. We are Muslims. There are a lot of Muslim names that start with 'M,' you know?" Mussah told me, "You don't have Jewish name—why not?" I reddened.

"That's true, Amy isn't a Jewish name. How do you know I'm Jewish?" I asked.

"Oh, c'mon!" He laughed, clapping his hands together. "That is what all the guys at the base calls you. You are the nice-looking Jewish girl." I remembered once telling one of the drivers I was Jewish after he asked if I was Swedish. I laughed.

"Nope. Wrong, wrong, wrong."

"You are Christian?" he asked.

"Nope, Jewish."

"Ah, Jewish," he said, pausing. "But I like you. You see: Muslims and Jews can be friends, see." Evidently, word spreads fast.

I would arrive at the base to get a car and I was always in a major rush. "Ameee!!! My loveleee!!" Mussah would sing.

There was one driver, Moez, on whom I had a little crush. I'd go into the dispatcher's office and Mussah would smile and say, "I go call Moez. He is off now, but he will come back for you." Or he'd say, "He's on a call now, but I know he like you to wait for him." When he finally returned to the office, all the other guys would say things to him in Arabic and slap his back, and he'd look embarrassed and sheepishly wave to me before he quickly prayed.

Now, sitting on the stoop at work, I saw Moez pull up in a cream-colored 1989 Lincoln. (He drove a vast rotation of long out-of-repair Town Cars.) I tried to pull open the back door. He rolled the back window down. "Is stuck. Hold on." He reached back from inside and released the door.

"Good safety measures," I joked.

"Piece of shitty car," he conceded.

We sat in silence for a while. I relished staring at the back of his neck. He was tall, probably six-two, with strong, large hands and a ropy, thick soccer player's build.

I studied the mirror image of Moez's eyes. Frontalis muscles tensed. Mastoid muscles relaxed. Indicating anxiety. Insecurity. Puzzlement.

When he pulled back onto the road again, I tried to memorize his face. I hoped to be able to decipher this particular arrangement of signs in the future. I saw his mouth framed in the reflection of the interior rearview mirror, and a tiny smile crept onto either side of his mouth. We were right at the center of the Brooklyn Bridge, and he seemed to be laughing to himself.

"Why are you laughing?" I asked him, thinking that I'd done something to embarrass myself.

"I am happy," he said. I reddened. "To be with you."

✪ EIGHTEEN

He who fights monsters should look into it that he himself does not become a monster. When you gaze long into the Abyss, the Abyss also gazes into you.

—Friedrich Nietzsche, *Horror*

Worth the Price of Admission

"Hey, Sol, did you get what I sent you last night?" I asked.

"You mean that abortion job you call a case?" He looked up, his headset cocking, his mouth twisted into an on-the-verge-of-hysterics half-smile. "Yeah, there have been some complaints about your performance. You're really slacking off here, A. Gray."

He waved me over to discuss the case some more.

"The client is really happy with the calls you got, and I think they have a pretty good sense that they're not going to touch anything those Norrsken slugs have their grimy little hands in."

"Okay."

"I think, to close this up, they'd like to see something that links KNUT Publishing to these incidents. Otherwise, they won't be totally comfortable that this impacts their investment, and I'm telling them it will."

"How do you know that?" I asked him.

"I don't. I just have a feeling here, and that's what people pay me for. I have a feeling, and then I prove it's right."

"Well, none of those people are going to talk to me. I think they all had termination agreements that had confidentiality clauses."

"Here's what I want you to do. There are two people I want you to get in touch with. One is the former lawyer for the indicted pension-fund manager at KNUT Trust V." The lawyer had sued for nonpayment, which meant that he didn't legally have to honor the attorney-client privilege. The other call was to Nars Norrsken's former parents-in-law.

"Norrsken and his American wife, Anne Wallinghurst, divorced six months ago. Call his former in-laws and find out if they'll talk about him."

"Why would they?"

"The divorce was sealed, but the dockets show her parents testified on her behalf. I have a feeling that he might have alienated them."

"Why wouldn't we just call the wife?"

"They've been spotted together in the last couple months, and there's some speculation that they've rekindled the marriage."

The plan was to call the in-laws, be very laid-back, ask about their son-in-law, pretend like we didn't know about the divorce. With these kinds of situations we take a slow approach, and ask something like, "Is there anything you know about Mr. Norrsken's character that our clients should know about before they engage him in business?" It's important, I'd learned in my time at the Agency, to let the interviewee lead the conversation. If they seem to be reluctant, lead them gradually to negatives. If they're bursting with bad information, be sympathetic and encourage them to spill it. If they're anxious and don't seem willing to talk, let it go. The situation we most wanted to avoid was Norrsken finding out about the work we were doing.

I located the parents, who were living in New York, just off Central Park in the Eighties. Sol told me to call them and try to get an interview. Mr. Wallinghurst answered the phone. When I asked about Nars, he said, "Well, you know, he and my daughter are separated."

"No, I'm sorry, I didn't realize that," I said quickly.

"Well, maybe I'm not the best person to ask about him," he continued. "I'm not his biggest fan."

"No, Mr. Wallinghurst," I said, my pulse quickening, "I think you could be extremely helpful." He agreed to meet, and we set up a rendezvous for Friday.

When I got off the phone, I screamed in triumph.

"Try to keep it under control, Gray," George warned.

"Okay boss," I said, and I screamed again for good measure.

Nicotine Redux

At eleven, I went out for a ciggie break. The fire escape had been dead-bolted, and now the alarm really worked. (We tried it.) Renora was walking out of the office at the same time, an American Spirit squished between her two small yellowed fingers.

"How are you?" I asked.

"Shitty," she replied. Renora was doing the Atkins diet. Although she was already the embodiment of the waiflike heroin-chic Manhattan ethos, she was hoping to be emancipated from the tofu-and-kale diet she'd been maintaining since adolescence.

"I just want some bloody, bloody steak and some fucking

fatty milk," she asserted wistfully. I, who hadn't discovered wheat bread or 1 percent milk until I'd moved to New York, still sympathized with her need to break free from her shackled existence in a city where thinness is tantamount to godliness.

I told her she seemed more relaxed than her usual phobic, twitchy self. I asked her how she was feeling.

"Terrible. I'm exhausted. I have no energy."

"Well, maybe that's a good thing. For you."

"This is like the *Through the Looking-Glass* diet. I'm eating things I haven't eaten since I was, like, twelve. Some of them I've never eaten before, like whipped cream, and I'm not allowed to have any fruit. I'm craving a peach, or a banana."

"Can't you eat cheese?"

"Cheese, eggs, meat. I'm eating everything I've fantasized about eating for my entire adult life, and all I want is a goddamn banana. Plus I think I might actually be getting *fatter*." She was a week into the two-week "induction" period in the diet, and the restrictions during this period were the most rigorous. She explained that further along into the process she could have berries and certain kinds of fruit again.

"But no banana."

"No. I can never have another banana." As we both sat there, contemplating life without bananas, two restless souls alone in the world but for their desperate clinging to New York mores of beauty, a guy walked over to the two of us and looked like he was about to say something.

Renora rolled her eyes and continued to talk to me, while the guy, youngish, with brown hair and not particularly attractive, just stood there blankly. Finally she turned to him.

"Can we help you?"

"Sorry." He seemed nervous. "I work across the street from you guys and we've always wondered what you do for a living."

"Really?" she bit back, totally uninterested. "Why is that?"

"Because you're always out here having cigarettes." Renora and I traded amused glances. The guy, who finally told us his name, said that they had taken bets on what we do.

This interested Renora, who would never kick easy money out of bed. She asked him if he had a ten, and she took it and held it between her thumb and forefinger, flicking it, saying, "Okay, guess. Tell us what you guessed."

"I said it was a dating service."

We laughed. "And the other people?" Renora asked.

"One guy thought you were running a chatline. Or a travel agency."

"Wrong, wrong, and wrong," she said, stubbing out her cigarette under her weatherbeaten men's shoes and turning around.

"Tell me what you do, though. Guys, wait!" He called after us. When we got to the fourth floor, we burst into hysterics.

"I can't believe they've been watching us out the window!" I cried.

"I know, we've got to tell everyone about this!" She was laughing, her banana-withdrawal seemingly quelled by the distraction. We gathered a group of interested parties in the window right behind Sol's desk. He was unamused when he came out of the conference room to find his desk encircled by idle investigators.

"Outta here," he said.

"Look, look over there!" Evan yelled, pointing excitedly across the street at the building to our right.

There, in the window, were about fifteen guys, standing around a hand-lettered sign written on computer paper. It said, CALL US 212-555-8888. Below it, they had written AMY and WENORA (sic) in smaller letters. Shrieks rose from the ranks. Even supercilious Morgan was amused despite himself, muttering, "This is not my life. This is *not* my life."

"Did they ask Vinny how to spell her name? *Wenora? Wenora?*" Sol wondered aloud.

"They're right," George chuckled. "We *are* running a fucking dating service here."

Let's Rock This Joint in the Old-School Way

Dan and I e-mailed all week. They were all charming, inconsequential little missives. We made plans to see a Japanese movie he suggested on Wednesday. I was happy to be realizing two top priorities in my life's to-do list: something culturally ambitious that makes good dinner-party conversation *and* dating with the potential for a little action.

I met him at the East Village Cinema on Twelfth Street, a hole-in-the-wall art-film theater that I'd never been to before. He had shaved his dark hair since Monday, and his chin looked a little less defined without the dark scruff. But still cute.

"I brought you a present," he told me. His sincerity was a little embarrassing. He fished something out of his backpack and put both his hands behind his back. "Pick a hand." It was a mixed tape, and along the spine he'd written "From Yer Friend Dan."

"Awww. That's so sweet." Maybe too sweet. I shrugged off my any-club-that-will-have-me-isn't-worth-belonging-to pangs. He seemed pleased with himself. While we were waiting in line, he leaned over to me and said, "Look, it's Ad-Rock, from the Beastie Boys." There he was, two people in front of us, in line with his hot Asian girlfriend, looking well ripened since his *Paul's Boutique* days.

The movie was awful. When we stepped out of the darkened theater, I heard Ad-Rock in front of us tell his girlfriend that the movie "rocked."

"Wha'd you think?" Dan asked me.

"It rocked," I said, hoping Adam Horovitz wouldn't lead me down the path of ill-repute.

"Really? I thought it was pretty shitty."

"Me, too," I recovered. "I said it wasn't pretty."

"Right."

We took the subway back to Brooklyn, and the ride home seemed to soothe my prickliness. When we got off the subway and he took my hand, I didn't pull away.

We got to my apartment, and I led him out the back door to the garden. Everything was shaded in smoky indigo and black. We spread an old sheet on the ground and lay down. Flashes of green-yellow light shone unsteadily across the lawn. Fireflies were our secret indulgence in Brooklyn. Could anyone imagine how, on summer nights, beneath its austere skyline the city was ablaze with a different kind of light from the artificial glare of Times Square? Out of the starkness of the city, a fragile ecosystem blossoms. Delicate nettle, wisteria, and morning glories wound through labyrinthine concrete gardens.

We sat on the grass. I put my hand out and let a firefly wander on to my palm. I cupped my other hand around it and held it up to my eyes, opening a small space between my thumbs to peek in and see the lines of my hands effervesce, and then fade again.

"Look, violets," he said, plucking a tiny petal amid the climbing ivy and brush covering the brickface along the length of the garden. He crushed the flower between his thumb and forefinger and held it to my nose, letting me smell the perfume, and then, in one motion, brushing my cheek and pulling my face closer to his. I was too busy enjoying the smell of the flower and the feeling of his smooth skin to notice the garden humming around me.

✪ NINETEEN

But the world is neither meaningful nor absurd. It quite simply *is*. And that, in any case, is what is most remarkable about it.

— ALAIN ROBBE-GRILLET

Heir to the Throne

On my way to my interview with Mr. Wallinghurst, I copped a latte at Lexington and Eighty-seventh. His building was a grand town house, the kind that runs from eleven to twenty-five million green ones. Nice work if you can get it. The door was answered by an Indian manservant who introduced himself as Mr. Singh.

"I will get Meester Wallinghurst for you, Meese Amy," he said, winking, and strutted away. He wore traditional Indian dress, a colorful turban and a sherwani of green silk with matching shoes that curled at the toe.

When Mr. Wallinghurst came out and introduced himself, I was surprised by how frail he seemed. He looked like he was probably in his early eighties, and it was hard to connect this elderly man with the effete voice I'd spoken to.

"It's a pleasure," I said, grasping his hand, which shook as I held it. I took a seat at his desk, which was framed by a bay window. The walls around us were covered with dark oak bookshelves, housing, among others, *The New York Law Journal* from the last forty years. I realized I wasn't sure what Mr. Wallinghurst did, although it seemed fairly clear at this point that he was retired.

"I must say, when you contacted me, I wasn't sure if I should talk to you." He, like George, tended to talk to a me just over my left shoulder and fifty yards behind me. He also rubbed his eyes a lot, keeping his hands in loose fists near his face should he need them. "My son-in-law has a glitzy life and there are a lot of hangers-ons and paparazzi that come sniffing around." I nodded sympathetically.

"I suppose when you said you want to protect someone else, I understood that. I think enough people have been swindled by Nars." Wallinghurst handed me a folder from his desk. The first document inside it was a copy of a promissory note Nars had written him, signed in 1993. Wallinghurst had lent him $400,000 over three years for various KNUT-related schemes. He showed me canceled checks, more promissory notes, and letters from Nars, some apologizing for "trying" Wallinghurst's "goodwill," and others angrily demanding more money.

This presentation took more than twenty minutes. The documents, which he had Xeroxed and given to me, were methodically organized and listed.

"Mr. Wallinghurst, I hope you don't mind my asking, but why did Nars ask you for so much money when his own father was one of the wealthiest men in Europe?"

"Niels cut him off years ago. Nars desperately wanted to prove to him that he could start and run profitable businesses, so

Niels slowly let Nars take over some small KNUT offshoots that tickled his fancy."

"From what I've read, Nars has become very active in the KNUT publishing arm, which is the division our client's deal concerns."

"That's true." He paused and brought a shaky, liver-spotted hand up to wipe his glistening brow. "He's done nothing but hurt it in the long run, though."

"How do you mean?"

"KNUT has experienced serious losses over the last few years due to natural attrition in the publishing business and with the success of Internet publishing. Nars basically siphoned the money off his other businesses to stop the hemorrhaging at KNUT Publishing and the other showcase businesses in the KNUT Group, and his father let him do it."

"Do you have any evidence that he embezzled money from KNUT pension funds?"

"No," he conceded. "I can tell you, it's out there. The SFA in London is shaking them down. That's why these pension managers at KNUT companies are being investigated for mishandling the funds. Nars is on the board at every one of those companies, and he was using pensions at his other companies to pump up the numbers at KNUT Publishing."

"He was defrauding his own employees to keep the numbers looking good at KNUT?"

"That's correct," Mr. Wallinghurst said. "My daughter and he were married for seven years; they have two children. I don't want to press charges against him, but the Swedish authorities are going after him now, and so is the Financial Action Task Force."

"They are?"

"All of these pension indictments are going to be used to assist in ultimately arresting and charging Nars."

"Really?" I felt ill at this point. KNUT was a major player in international business, although a lot of the tech companies in the U.S. seemed to be run by European expatriates. The repercussions of KNUT's demise could be another kick in the groin to the "technology economy." We had all noticed a lot of our clients' technology companies faltering in the last six months. The high life of dot-com-sponsored open bars and the stampede of buying property in the Hamptons had gone from a downpour to a slow drip. I couldn't count on ten hands how many businesses we'd seen go under since I'd been at the Agency, and it added to the general sense of unease.

"Have they contacted you?" I asked him.

"They have, and if I'm asked to testify at the trial, I will. This will all be coming out soon."

"Do you know what the schedule is for bringing charges?"

"I don't, but with the pension indictments over the last several weeks, I think they're moving quickly."

"Do you think Nars knows they're coming after him?"

"I believe he does." I looked down at the yellow legal pad where I'd been taking my notes. The paper was warped from sweat, and ink stains dotted my palms. I looked at Wallinghurst's hands, clutching each other, shaking, and then at mine, poised for more work, also shaking violently. We spoke some more. I thanked him, then he called Mr. Singh to come and see me out. "I had always hoped Anne would meet a wonderful man." He seemed to be fighting tears. "I feel betrayed, Miss Gray. I hope you can protect your client from that feeling. It is truly awful."

As Mr. Singh led me downstairs and out the gilded doors at the entrance, I thanked him and on my way out added, "Please take care of Mr. Wallinghurst."

"Yes, Meese Amy, of course. I will indeed."

Let Them Eat Cake

Back at the office, I e-mailed Sol my report, and ten minutes later he called me.

"A. Gray?"

"Yep."

"Excellent work. I just spoke to the client. They're spooked, but I explained that Nars Norrsken might not know about the investigation in Sweden, so they won't be mentioning it."

"Good. I know Wallinghurst doesn't want to be the one taking Nars down. He wants the information we have to go *just* to the client, and to let the Swedish authorities take care of the rest."

"Okay, Gray." Sol smacked his lips together. "You did a great job."

"Thanks!"

"But don't let it go to your head."

"Right."

I went back to my desk to finish writing up the case. The knowledge of KNUT's betrayals felt weighty, cumbersome. I imagined how many thousands of their employees had lost their retirements, a lifetime of promises shattered. The worst part was, most of them didn't even know it yet. My stomach was taut and I wanted to cry. I flipped through my mental Rolodex, wondering who could cheer me up. Dan, maybe. I wrote him and waited to hear back. Then the phone rang.

"Amy Gray!"

"Jeremy! Almost the boy I was just hoping to hear from."

"So I'm the runner-up to the cute indie-boy rock star you've been seeing. I can live with that. He can do things I can't."

"Who told you about Dan, anyway?"

"Ben."

"Ben? He doesn't know *anything.*" I wondered where the hell Ben got off telling my friends who I was dating when Jeremy cut to the chase.

"Aim, I have a huge favor to ask you. And you can totally say no. But I think you might like it. But if you don't want to that's totally cool—"

"Jeremy? Spit it out!" It turned out Jeremy was blowing his load to go to this party that boys could only get into if they were with a girl.

"That sounds like every club in New York."

"No, this is different. It's a club created to promote women's sexuality, so they have lots of chicks in lingerie or underwear, and vibrators for sale, and men being treated like pieces of meat."

"Sounds like your wet dream."

"Exactly." Jeremy was a living oxymoron, a highly educated denizen of low culture. The sexy soirée was sponsored by Cake; the all-girl club promised to wave the $20-per-person cover charge if you filled out the membership application: "To me, sexy is ———." "The most erotic place on my body is ———." "The most outrageous place I ever had sex was ———."

"Can I answer these questions by saying 'no comment'?" I asked. "This stuff is kinda personal, and I can't get it up to answer them."

"No, you have to write something really outrageous, or else they might not accept your application."

"What? They're *judging* my answer? Forget it." I got Jeremy to agree to do the nasty deed for me and then I would send it in. But, I protested, wasn't a horny artsy guy going there for chicken-choking fodder spoiling the point of this girlie love-in? Jeremy pointed out that he hadn't gotten laid in months.

"Puuleeease do this for me," he begged. "I haven't had sex in sixteen months."

"Stop! This information doesn't fall into the need-to-know category."

"I'm the guy who joined a lesbian Riot Grrl rally in college because I wanted some threefer action. I'm incorrigible."

"Hey!" I was indignant. "You took me to one of those meetings. I thought you were a real militant feminist radical! So I guess being secretary of the ISO was just a ruse, too?"

"Ilana Richards, the vice president, had the cutest little rack."

"Jeremy!"

He sounded sheepish. "What can I say? I'm a pervert."

"You're sick."

"I'm desperate."

"Okay." Hopefully, this evening of gurl-on-gurl action would have a mollifying effect on Jeremy. Furthermore, I hoped my adventurer's spirit would pay off in the karma department. This might actually be just what I needed. It's so wrong, it's right.

"Hey, the invite says to wear something 'hot 'n' tasty.' "

"Jeremy, honey," I warned. "You're already getting lucky. Stop while you're ahead."

The Leading Economic Indicator of "My Moms"

Dan asked me to go to a show with him on Thursday, but he had to cancel the day before to "Help my Moms move." His divorced parents both lived in Manhattan, and his mother was moving in with her boyfriend of ten years.

We ended up seeing each other on Saturday. "You wanna see amazing rock?" he asked me (we were talking only on the phone by this point.) We went to go see a band called Old Prince. They were great, but then we stayed for the second band, which was loud and performance-based. The lead singer sang all the songs like a rabid Goth evangelist on crack. They even had the accoutrements of religious fanatics and freak shows, including a flaming crucifix and a caged python onstage. "And He's gonna get you, and when He does, you're gonna burn in heeelllll!" he railed. When we walked out of the piss-'n'-beer-stained Brownie's, I was experiencing my usual post-show syndrome, a kind of shell-shocked dream state I also get after leaving movie theaters. We shuffled our way, dazed, onto Avenue A.

"Actually, that second band used to play a different kind of stuff."

Dan started skipping and hopping his way down the block. "But dude," he marveled, "I just can't believe I got to see Old Prince with Jack Press drumming on that last track. That was so awesome." He continued telling me how this guy used to be the drummer for this other band, and that whole riff they did on that track totally reminded him of that other band, and how "that totally rocked." As he said this, he was air-drumming heavily. His face contorted in alarming and disfiguring ways as he strained to his imaginary cymbals. "Aww!" He gave a Mick Jaggeresque yelp.

"Ummm." How could I respond to that? As we ambled down First Avenue to his practice space, Dan was slamming the hell out of his imaginary drums and humming another unidentified tune.

In fact, it sickeningly dawned on me, the whole night I'd been listening to him expound on the musical histories of every member of the band. How the drummer was once on a chain gang in Detroit, how the bassist went to Yale and dropped out to start a mink farm before he joined the band. On our last date, I had winced several times when Dan kept quoting the lyrics to songs on the B sides of limited-release EPs by now-defunct bands. But I'd brushed it off. Chalked it up. Overlooked it. The problem was, I wasn't sure what to talk to him about if it wasn't music.

"I love the sounds of the city," I offered, immediately realizing I'd ruined my opportunity for a reprieve.

"Dude!" he burst forth, "I was just thinking that. This totally reminds me of this Gene Loves Jezebel Song." Then he started singing. "Nah, nah, nah, Take it over the bow, Window-dressing sow." Or something like that. Not that I knew the words or the song. This was probably the fifth time he'd spontaneously broken into song since we had our first Brooklyn Lagers five hours earlier.

"Hey," I snapped, "my name is not 'dude'." Don't be mean, a little voice inside me warned. But at the same time, another voice countered the whisper with a scream: Be mean! I struggled against the urge to lash out. But he was so . . . annoying.

Dan looked surprised. "Sorry."

"It's fine. Just don't call me 'dude.' " He looked sullen. We walked silently. Dan sent an empty Red Bull can traversing across the street.

Mr. Indier-Than-Thou was a pristine example of a hobby become an obsession. There are many of these in New York, it seems. New York is not about being well rounded. It's all sharp edges. Like a bumbling Kafkaesque examiner, he was bogged down by the volume of facts, but the crime perpetually evaded him. He would be a terrible investigator, and I, on the other hand, didn't want to be with someone I could sum up in a two-page report.

He invited me back to his place. It was a couple blocks away and I thought, at the very least, I might avoid the long haul back to Brooklyn. Plus I really wanted to be kissed.

At the fifth floor of his walkup, I plopped down in front of his door.

"How . . . can . . . you do this. . . . every day?" I panted. "It's hell."

"Actually, I'm one more floor up."

His apartment door opened onto a long, skinny hallway off of which was a tiny kitchen upholstered in yellow linoleum, then his roommate Zac's room. Then there was his other roommate Oliver's room, then a living room that fit a small couch, a TV set, and about

2,000 records and 4,000 CDs, and finally his room. It was a classic railroad tenement. The place smelled like fish and chips.

His bedroom had guitars slung around and the walls were plastered with Devo posters. The Devo thing was part of a back-to-your-rock-roots movement, targeting bands that were previously seen to have little or no intrinsic musical talent. Now they were "fucking geniuses," in Dan's words. I sat on his bed and he kept jumping up to play music for me. "You've gotta hear this!" and the music was really beautiful. He made us rice and beans—he was designing for a dot-com, after all, not running one—and we drank beers and the music was enchanting. He came back into the room after putting on the Palace Brothers, and instead of giving me the liner notes, he touched my hand. His index finger, which was smooth and callused from playing guitar, slid over my hand. I closed my eyes, smiling, and then I felt him reach over my wrist, my arm, my shoulder. And then the next thing I knew, I felt the warmth of his face near mine, his nose near my neck, and he whispered, "No more talking." And then there was silence.

Taking the Fall

On Monday morning, not only weren't there any seats on the F, but I had to wait for two trains to pass me by before I could even get on, never mind actually sitting.

Clinging to the overhead bar, I held my daily fix of the *Post*. I usually skip to Page Six and leave it on the train for the next weary traveler. A headline on page three caught my attention: EURO PORN BRASS FALLS TO DEATH. I gasped audibly. "The heir to the Norrsken publishing fortune plunged to his death yesterday in what is believed to be a suicide. His death comes just a week after revelations that several division managers in his family empire had been misappropriating pension funds to offset losses. It is believed that

Norrsken was soon to be indicted for his alleged role masterminding the fraud." I looked up. Two older women sitting in front of me must have seen me look strange or heard a couple of muted yelps, because they offered me their seats. It wasn't until I got off the train and started walking to work that I realized that the tears falling from my face had turned most of the page into a damp smudge.

I imagined Nars Norrsken, sitting shirtless in his gilded suite in the Grand Hotel in Stockholm, feeling crushed by the knowledge of his exposure. A stifling, stiffening dread overtakes him, as numbers and data in the wake of his crimes sickeningly converged, like snowflakes mounting into suffocating drifts. I imagined him, in the final moments, like Newt Ebersol in his snowy sepulchre, relinquishing calmly to the chaos with stillness, falling into the cool open air.

Sol was already in the office, and I walked straight to his desk, dropped the article, and said, "Read it." He did. "Holy shit" was the only thing that escaped his mouth for a while, and then he stood up and hugged me. "This is not your fault," he said. "This is not your fault." Not much was said after, either. He told me to take the morning off, but I didn't want to go all the way back to Brooklyn, so I took a nap on the yellow threadbare brocade couch in the conference room. Sol put a note on the door that said, "If you enter this room and wake Gray up, you're fired.—The Management."

❖

When I woke up and got back to work, I started to think about Dan more. Our best times together were when he wasn't talking. Or singing. Or dancing.

Thinking about him all last week, I'd felt dreamy. Now I was homicidal. Dan was of a breed, actually. This breed particularly likes to assemble in New York, where there's a plethora of highly specialized record stores catering to the said overeducated audiophiles, as well as *The Onion* distributed free, and plenty of dot-com jobs to get hired for and then fired from, so they could collect unemployment and spend more time going to rock shows. I like this kind of guy. Still, I was a little miffed that Dan had said he would call me on Sunday, but he didn't, and now it was Monday and there was no sign of him.

I went out for a cigarette and found Renora and Linus in our usual spot out in front.

"Hey, Amy." Renora seemed a little uncomfortable, as did Linus. I wondered if they didn't know how to talk to me about my subject throwing himself out of a fifteen-story building to his death. I shuddered.

"Not my best day," I confessed.

"Yeah, I'm off Atkins."

"Really, why?"

"Because I was so sick of meat and cheese and fat I didn't want to eat anymore, and I was drinking just straight vodka because it's low in sugar and has no carbs, like beer. All of these factors led to a sort of alcoholic haze over the last forty-eight hours."

"I'm sorry," I said.

"So, what's going on with your rocker boyfriend?" she asked.

"Oh, I don't know, I think he's a little too one-note for me."

"That's funny. He's too one-note. Good comedy," Linus offered, slapping me on the back. I whacked his hand.

"He was supposed to call me last night, but he didn't, which I guess I was sort of glad about, although now I'm a bit annoyed. He spends every Sunday at O'Connor's." O'Connor's was a shabby locals' bar in lower Park Slope that had been co-opted by younger hipsters thanks to its cheap beer and ass-kicking jukebox.

"I was at O'Connor's last night, actually," Renora said, excited.

"Really?" I said. "Do you remember a blondish-haired guy, tall, maybe six foot three . . ."

"Honestly, as I was saying, my memory isn't so good now, but—"

"He probably would have been wearing skating sneakers, and his friend Jeb would have been there, too."

Renora paused. "Jeb. Jeb sounds familiar. I think I spoke to a guy named Jeb who had a friend." She seemed embarrassed as she recalled being there with her friend Beth and having two guys start talking to them about their band.

I blanched.

"But it might have been Jeb more than Dan doing it," Renora added hopefully.

"Ha!" Linus cackled, bending over from the strain of his own busting gut. "Wouldn't it be funny if Amy didn't hear from her boyfriend this weekend because he was off hitting on Renora? Ha-ha-ha." I wanted to get out of there. Fast.

"Here—" Renora was fishing in her pocket for something—a flyer for their show they'd given her. When she handed it to me, I wanted to drop it and run. But I knew it was the one. How many red flyers cut out to look like an old train boarding pass were circulating Brooklyn? I saw the flash of red in her shaking hand and I heard her saying, "Is that it?" as I turned back into the hallway.

"I—I'm not sure. I'm not sure what the band is called." I ran down the hall, down the stairs past the elegy for "broke-ass bitches," and around the block to Twenty-first Street, just to calm down. Everything was falling apart.

Dan e-mailed me later that day. I didn't write him back. He asked if I was angry with him. I didn't respond to that, either. Nor did I respond to several phone messages. I busted him for hitting on Renora, on a night when we were supposed to see each other.

Plus he annoyed me anyway. At least I had my Cake party to look forward to and distract me from the daily front-page articles in *The New York Times, The Wall Street Journal,* and yes, even the *Post* and the *Daily News* about the Norrsken death. Every time I thought about it, my heart skipped a beat.

Take It Off

Before meeting Jeremy, I went back to Brooklyn to change. There was a message from Dan. "Amy, is everything okay? I feel like you're blowing me off. Sad. Dan." I felt a momentary pull of guilt. Then I got religion and deleted it.

Sometimes I would have to wait for the car while my driver prayed. "He is praying," Mussah would tell me. "Just wait one minute." At the back of the tiny storefront was a door leading out to the rear with four strips of cloth partly covering the door. I could see Moez and some other drivers, side-by-side, kneeling, their heads touching the ground, only to raise them and bring them back down to the ground again. Their lips moved quickly.

Afterward, on the car ride, I talked to Moez. I had my standard questions. "So, where are you from?"

"Tunisia. Casablanca."

"Wow. Like *A Night in Tunisia.*"

"I don't understand."

"You know, Miles Davis."

"Meles Davees?"

"Oh, it was a stupid thing I said. So, what's it like there?"

"It is beautiful. It is a peaceful way of life. I live very well there. My family live very well. We have many property, you know, one on the sea. I go to the beach every day, with my friend, you know. We have a house in the country. It is a beautiful country, not like New York. New York is great in some way, you know, but it is not easy way of life. My country is beautiful." He told me he was born to a French mother and an Italian father. His parents were artists and wanted to raise their children somewhere remote and magical.

The first five minutes in the car were usually awkward. Then I'd ask him questions and he'd talk the rest of the way: about how his mother wanted him to move back home, how his sister was getting married and wanted him to come for the wedding but he didn't know if he could afford it. Clinton Fresh Food, my destination, was appositely on Clinton Street, a former bastion of heroin-dealing that was now a trendy refuge. He pulled a Polaroid out of the glove compartment and handed it to me. "It is new," he said. "I bought today. Automatic, you know."

"Cool. Take my picture," I said, handing him back the camera and squishing myself back into the corner of the car, smiling. He fumbled with it. The flash detonated, making me wince. Then he held the picture and I leaned over the front seat and we watched. The gray rectangle turned into an oozy orange and yellow-gray. A humanlike form emerged, and finally there appeared a picture of me, leaning back awkwardly, something akin to a Mona Lisa smile across my face. Moez was grinning, too, as he handed me the snapshot.

"You can keep it," I said, getting my money out to pay him.

"No, no," he said, pushing my money away. He looked at me intently and insisted, "No money. This picture is enough." There was an awkward moment when I handed him the photo back. My thumb was still on the picture when he put his finger over the far corner. I briefly imagined his scruffy cheek brushing mine. Then, seeing Jeremy waiting for me out the window, I turned away, opening the door. "Bye, Moez. See you soon."

◁▷

After dinner (I told Jeremy I needed to get *something* out of the deal), we got to the Cake party around eleven. It was at Spy.

The place was teeming. It was like the nerd version of the Playboy Mansion. Boys looked overwrought and scrawny. The girls, in their requisite tube tops and the occasional bustier, still had the emaciated A-cup New York look. Crowded into a sunken bar space facing the entrance, hundreds of people were watching the stage, where we could see unclad figures moving in front of a silvery scrim hung around the back of the stage. A woman in a pink-and-white French maid's outfit and a purple wig danced around with a sign that read, SEE THE ANNUAL CAKE STRIPTEASEATHON.

Jeremy seemed entranced. "Let's go check this out." He grabbed my hand and guided me through bumping and grinding girls and ogling boys to the front of the stage, where I was practically kissing the toes of a heavyset Asian girl swinging her bra over her head to the tune of "I Shook You All Night Long."

"She's got balls," I whispered to Jeremy.

"Maybe that's why she's still wearing the rest of her outfit," he retorted. "Take it all off!" he screamed at the stage, cupping his hands around his mouth for an extra-blunt effect. Soon the whole crowd was chanting, "Take it off! Take it off!" The girl pulled off her skirt to reveal huge white underpants, which she threw into the crowd. After she got offstage, other nervous amateurs took turns pseudo-pole-dancing and taking off their shirts and the occasional bra. Nobody else took took it all off, despite Jeremy's not-so-subtle entreaties. After half an hour, Jeremy, bored with the exposure level, went to get us scotch-and-sodas, and the emcee came out to announce that it was time to let the boys have their turn. The lights onstage went out and a black light showed a fluorescent blue male figure in a white suit with no shirt and no shoes. Girls were whistling and catcalling like construction workers. "Yeah, baby, take that shit awfff!" "You know it! Show us what you got!" Under the white suit he was wearing a zebra-striped G-string. Even still, I was sort of enjoying this segment of the show. The white stripes expanded and shrunk as the mystery guy squatted and swung his butt around in front of the crowd. Just when the soundtrack, Journey's "Lovin', Touchin', Squeezin'," kicked into the raucous guitar riff, he turned around and the stagelights sprung on him.

"Holy shit!" I screamed, just as I felt Jeremy squeezing my elbow. It was Evan, looking pleased with himself and snapping the banana hammock like it was way too close to coming off. "Let's get out of here," I commanded Jeremy, grabbing my scotch and downing it in seconds.

When we got outside, I gulped the fresh air, hoping it would clear my mind of the memory.

"Are you sure it was him?" Jeremy asked.

"I see the guy every day. Believe me, I would rather *not* have recognized him." I would have done anything, anything to erase the memory of Evan in his zebra schlong sling from my mind.

◑ TWENTY

To spy, to watch, to scrutinize oneself and others, to be nothing but a big, slightly vitreous, somewhat bloodshot, unblinking eye.

—VLADIMIR NABOKOV, *THE EYE*

The Opposite of Fun

On a windy day in late September, I walked out of the office to get my lunch with Wendy at the early hour of eleven. She and I had been getting hungry earlier and earlier. "Sometimes I think, to myself, fuck lunch by noon, I want to start dinner by then and just keep on eating," she confessed.

"I know," I said, nodding in sympathy. But when we got to the Twenty-One deli, there were a dozen people who apparently had the same idea, along with unforgiving stomachs and sharp elbows.

"Fuck this," Wendy said. "I can't wait this long." She left to get a gyro from a food cart on the corner of Twenty-fourth, and I waited. And waited. And waited. The construction crews in the area were going into our deli and ordering meals for their whole crews. They read out scribbled shorthand clutched in meaty black fists. "Dat's two eggs sandwich, one with lettuce, one without, an everything bagel with ham, turkey, Muenster, pickles, onions . . ." The other people in line groaned, spat, and yelled at the deli guys, "Ey! Let's move!" Then they stepped up and read *their* laundry lists. I pulled a bag of Funyuns off the rack and ate them while I was waiting. I read the *Post*. I took a Mr. Goodbar for dessert. I was blinded by hunger, shoplifting snacks with a low-blood-sugar-induced lack of inhibition. Just when I was about to give up on my hot pastrami with caramelized onions, Russian dressing, tomatoes, cheddar, and hot peppers, it was my turn. In between the deli counter and the cash register I inhaled my whole sandwich.

I didn't want to go back to the office yet, so I walked around to the Flatiron Building and sat in the park where Broadway and Fifth Avenue intersect. My paychecks, $1,000 every two weeks—veritable riches compared to my publishing salary—seemed to vanish just as quickly every month. I now spent an entire paycheck just on rent, versus the $500 I had shelled out on monthly living with my druggie ex, Ben. Utilities, plus food, plus the newly intro-duced supposedly money-saving Metrocard, plus day after day of Starbucks indulgences mysteriously sucked another $600 monthly. That left me a mere $400 a month for "entertainment." Buying bot-tled water on the corner all summer, no matter how healthy, had added up. So did five-dollar drinks, and those were the cheap ones. Cass and I tried to spend more time at Niagara. In the interest of free liquor, we suffered unwanted attempted pickups from loser boys and craved, fruitlessly, a successful and attractive suitor to take us off Stuart's dole. Still, I had been abstinent—unkissed—since Dan.

The single beacon of free will in the hamster wheel of my life was fulfilled by one thing—my discovery of Napster. After a shallow early-learning curve, I'd downloaded more than five hundred songs onto my computer. Unlike my financial status, love life, and profession, Napster represented wish-fulfillment in its most extreme form. I could satisfy my every musical desire; I could decide I wanted to hear Cyndi Lauper's theme to *Goonies* and, minutes later, I was transported into memories of fifth-grade crushes and eighties kitsch. The recipe was simple—identify a craving, no matter how oblique (a live "Wire" cover by My Bloody Valentine) and, moments later, *boom*. I was rocking out motionlessly at my desk.

Still, morale at the Agency was at an all-time low. Sol and George no longer seemed to relish our foul humor. Sol, the eternal pessimist, had lost his caustic wit. His lovably morbid punch lines—like "If I live until tomorrow . . . but who knows?" he'd say, or "halfway to the PI playground in the sky—finally, I'll get a day off"—had turned into burdensome silence. He didn't call us names anymore. George, already stoic, spent most of his days in the office, never breaking a smile.

The technology market that had had analysts champing at the bit just six months before was in an alarming decline. Our dot-com work, which had constituted more than a third of our business at the beginning of the year, had slowed to a mere trickle. Business was down overall, for that matter, but none of us knew how much.

My last four cases were either total duds—boring background checks that yielded little pleasure—or grist for the scandal mill, and then, on top of that, one that was amusing in its absurdity but that I'd fucked up royally. Our client was investigating a potential executive for their manufacturing company. I found a lawsuit involving an export company the subject had run in Boca Raton called Hol-E-Wood Imports, which sold adult-size costumes modeled after famous Disney characters. The only problem was, the subject hadn't applied for the licensing from Disney, and the company was sued for $40 million. The case was appended by thousands of supporting exhibits, all showing photographs of creepy men in full-size costumes named "Ronald Duck" and "Quickie Mouse," with illustrative lines drawn to them from text saying, "Note the similarity of 'Ronald Duck's' blue vest to that of the plaintiff's copyrighted Donald, as demonstrated in Exhbit D 259-328." There was something seriously demented about the whole thing. So it wasn't suprising that one of the court diagrams made the rounds at the office and one ended up on the front of the refrigerator in the conference room, with new pointers drawn to Ronald Duck's crotch saying "small penis" and the word "Nestor" written across the top. Nestor then scratched this out and wrote "Sol's mom" on top before it was snatched precipitously off the fridge, never to be seen again. Only after the case was about to be sent to the client did George notice that Hol-E-Wood was funded by a Jason A. Burtlebaum, not Jason S. Burtlebaum. It wasn't even our guy. So as rumors of impending plans to "ax" people grew rampant over the next few weeks, I hoped it wouldn't be me. But I thought it probably would.

Sitting on the park bench, a squall at my feet lifted a pile of leaves into the air, at first slowly, looking like they were floating, and then whipping them higher and higher. The gray sky above me was flecked with brown shards. I pulled my collar shut and shivered. The swell had become a tempest, at the center of which thousands of leaves multiplied like a staggering swirl of facts.

From Bad to Worse

At lunch, the humor moratorium continued. It was depressing. Everyone was chewing quietly when Wendy ran in from the hallway with tears streaming down her face. George saw her first. I had never seen him look so serious. His face slackened, his insouciant grimace lost like the orange that fell out of his hands and rolled under the table.

Everyone stood up. George was over near his desk and ran back with the bloody broom in his hand he used to eliminate rats. Renora had her hands to her face, her mouth shaped in a big O. It was frightening. Tears were gathering in my eyes, and I didn't even know why yet. Wendy was just saying, "He grabbed me. This guy grabbed me," but I could barely hear her. I just stared at her usually perfect go-go girl hair, going in every direction, a string of spit over her hand, strands of it coming out of her mouth, and I couldn't help myself from bawling.

I heard Gus yelling, "Go get him!" Then someone, maybe Evan, sputtered, "Motherfucker!" For the first time ever, Archie held himself as menacing as he looked; then he tore out the door, his huge frame thudding past us. Within seconds, all the guys were running down the stairs in a thunder of feet hitting creaky wood. And then it was silent, except for Wendy crying and me consoling her. "Shhhh," I said. "It's okay. It'll be okay." But what did I know?

Wally and Noah were still standing awkwardly in the room. Noah came over with some water for Wendy. Wally tried to ask Wendy a question, but then he started to stutter, "Wha . . . wha . . ." And then he just barked out, "Motherlover!" His tics had come back.

Noah stayed nervously upstairs, along with Wally, and ten minutes later the guys all came trudging back, dropping their ad hoc weapons—a broom, a Wiffle bat, a bicycle chain, a pocketknife— defeatedly as they reassembled around the table.

Wendy eventually told us her story, crying, with the guys swearing and punching the already dirty conference room walls in rage. She had gotten her lunch and then gone to the gym. On her way back, she was waiting for the elevator, sluggish on its best days, and a small man knocked on the door of the building, indicating he wanted to be let in. She regretted it as soon as she walked over to the glass and saw that the man at the door, troll-like and twitchy, was wearing grimy, dirty clothes, that he had greasy white hair and a bulbous, hairy nose flecked with blood. When they got in the elevator, she pressed four. He didn't press anything. The doors had just closed when he lunged at her, grabbed her chest, and pulled her shirt up. She screamed. He started to pull her pants down. But the elevator, whose movements we've always speculated were controlled by some phantom specter of a long-dead passenger, opened on three, where Wendy kicked him in the nuts and ran out into an insurance office. Her ghoulish assailant, apparently scared off, disappeared down the stairwell.

The guys ran miles up and down the blocks surrounding our office looking for him. They must have looked like some throwback to the days of New York streetfighting gangs, an unkempt roving mass of mismatched sizes and girths. They didn't find him, but the thought that they'd left the building with no intention other than to beat him to a pulp and defend Wendy put a lump in my throat.

Just Close Your Eyes and Think of Little Bunnies

By the end of that day my head was spinning. My whole body ached. I wanted to call someone and vent. I knew I could call Cassie and get some pity, but then I'd eventually complain about being lonely and she'd tell me I had no reason to be upset because I just got out of something and she's been waiting *two years,* so she's way overdue.

The night before, I'd seen Janeane Garofalo on television

complaining about how unfair it is that everyone expects women to have a man. Men who sleep around and don't need women are pigs, she said. They can't settle down because they're assholes and don't have stick-to-it-ness. I wasn't arguing with that. But I wanted to know: When did it become politically incorrect to be lonely?

I felt weak and guilty and pathetic for being forlorn, even though I saw all my other coworkers, white-faced at their desks, whispering the day's events to their significant others in shaky voices. I thought about who I could call and pretend to be okay.

"Ben?"

"Mu?"

"What's up?" His voice was disappointing the second I heard it.

"You're on boycott, remember?" Then my resolve to act like everything was okay crumbled like a hollow Trojan horse. I started crying, and his tone softened.

"What's the matter, honey?"

"Oh, I don't know. This girl in my office got assaulted today, and I don't know if I'm even good at my job anymore, or if I even like it, and I think I might get fired and—" My other words dissolved into sobs.

"It's okay, sweetie."

"No it's not!" I wailed.

"Yes it is. It just doesn't feel like it is. I prom." (Another of our baby words, short for "promise.") "What do you love?" he asked me.

"Whaaaat dddoo you meaaaan?" I bawled.

"Just think of something nice."

"Like what?"

"Unicorns. Little bunnies."

"I like bunnies," I sniffled.

"Okay, then think of little bunnies. Hundreds of them. They're cute little bunnies, all hopping happily across pretty green fields. See? It works. You know you're smiling now." I was, actually. But it was also sad that the only one who could make me laugh like this was Ben.

❦

I'd been having weird body sensations all day since the incident—whenever I touched my hand to my face, it felt like someone else's. It was like reverse phantom limb syndrome. My limb was there, but the rest of my body wasn't. It was a sort of radical disembodiment.

I was trying to explain it to Nestor, who was never in too bad a mood to rile me. "You know that feeling, when you feel like your hand isn't your hand?" It was exasperating trying to explain it. A mischievous grin crept across his face. "Yeah, I think I know what you mean."

"You do?" I was desperate to be understood. I would almost have settled for patent lies and duplicity just to be commiserated with. "Yeah, like when you get this kind of tickly electric feeling in your body."

"Yes, yes!" I cried.

"Yeah, and your hand feels like it isn't your hand."

I was getting excited.

"Oh, my God—totally!"

"And you touch your face with that hand and you're looking in the mirror and you realize it really isn't your hand, it's an *alien* hand, except it *is,* because *you're an alien*—"

"Fuck off!!" Clearly pleased with his ability to make me feel like a paranoid asshole, Nestor was cracking up and calling Assman over to tell him about his coup. But I *was* paranoid, so it didn't take much. I sat down at my desk and became aware of the blood pumping through my body in short, ineffective electric bursts. I couldn't shake the feeling of numbness. It was a feeling of not feeling, a nothingness where something should have been.

You Have to Wait Your Turn

At three o'clock, Sol told us "jerkoffs" to go home, so Renora and I took the subway back to Brooklyn together. The bars weren't open yet, so we went to Tea Too, a Park Slope coffeehouse that during normal working hours became a hotbed of out-of-work dot-commers and new-mommy playgroups. While Renora got us Chais, I plopped wearily onto a threadbare love seat that looked like it was lifted from a 1940s brothel. The whooshing air from my movements sent a pamphlet on the table next to me airborne, swinging near the ear of a close-by baby. Fifteen bohemian mommies at the next table glared at me.

"Sorry," I said. Park Slope mommies are some of the nastiest in New York.

As Renora and I walked up to Prospect Park I asked her why it seemed like all new mothers suddenly saw their childless peers as the root of all evil.

"Because we're having sex."

"No we're *not*," I protested.

"Well, that's true, but we *look* like we are."

I used to love babies. Now I hate them. They're like little albatrosses—chubby beacons of foulness afoot.

Here's how it happens. I see a cute baby. We make eye contact. The baby smiles. I "goo" or "ga," and then some mommy comes over and moves the stroller with its back to me and says, "Tyler, would you like to play with mommy now," and swoops my new friend off the floor. I tried to stop smiling at babies on the subway back when a toddler shot me a wet, toothless grin.

There are some days in New York when the city turns from its usual gritty glamour to just plain sinister. What was breathtaking and awesome a moment before begins to feel like it's encroaching, dizzying. The beautiful chaos of it is now a suffocating sepulchre. I felt like Renora and I and every twenty-something girl were embattled, stuck between two kinds of indentured servitude. First, to being lonely and single and never finding somebody, and second, to married life and motherhood. In either case, I thought, looking at the mommy group, we were damned to cling to these scraps of human connection with all the desperation of a convict on the run.

❂ TWENTY-ONE

Oedipa wondered whether at the end of this (if it were supposed to end), she too might not be left with only compiled memories of clues, announcements, intimations, but never the central truth itself, which must somehow each time be too bright for her memory to hold; which must always blaze out, destroying its own message irreversibly, leaving an overexposed blank when the ordinary world came back.

—THOMAS PYNCHON,
THE CRYING OF LOT 49

Who's Your Daddy?

Since the Cake debacle, I was stung by my memories of Evan. They'd faded into grainy, low-resolution obscurity until a day in early October when I went over to his desk to get a case file, trying not to look him in the eye. It all came flooding back. Oh, the horror!

"Hey," I said, trying to focus on anything but his eyes.

"Miz Gray. How are you?" He leaned back in his chair and folded his arms behind his head. "Did you do anything fun this weekend?" Shit! Don't look in his eyes. I kept thinking of zebra stripes and the echoing sound of his voice onstage asking the audience, "Who's your daddy? I said, who's your daddy?"

My eyes widened. "Nope, not really." Long pause.

"And you?"

"Not really," he said, leaning back into his desk. "I got laid, though."

All I could think was, play along and run. "So. Any new cases for me?"

"In fact I do have something," he said. "I think it's a good one. Can you handle it?"

I rolled my eyes. "What do you think?"

"Nope. Well, that's too bad, I didn't think so."

"C'mon, Pringle, tell me about the case!"

"Actually, it's pretty nasty, but Gray, you can handle it." Egg-licious, my subject company, was the largest manufacturer of nondairy imitation egg products in the Northwest. Gag me. The Case of the Rotten Egghead was under way.

Brushed with Fame

The phone rang in time to save me from the eggy monotony of my case. I picked it up. "Hello? Hello?" I said. But the line was dead. "Fuck this phone system," I said, cursing audibly. A minute later the message light was flashing. "Hi, hon, it's Skye. You won't believe what happened to me! Call me! Now!"

When I called her back, she sounded breathless. "I'm being stalked by David Blaine."

I was racking my brain. "The—magician?"

"Yes!" Skye was a magnet for weirdos. She was a magnet, pe-riod. She was the perfect mix of gorgeous and totally wacko. Even though she was six feet tall, she had been doing ballet since the age of three and, we joked, subsisted on peaches, tomatoes, water, and flower petals, so she was slender and lithe. Once she went on a date with Chuck Scarborough, the 5:00 news anchor on the local NBC station in New York, who was thirty-one years her senior. She also had a fling with a famous Israeli actor when she was visiting a friend in Tel Aviv, at a Jewish camp for guilty Jewish Americans. She had dated innumerable cute boys in college, too, but this was her first mega-celebrity, as much as a magician can be a celebrity, even if he did have a prime-time special on Fox.

"I was walking down the street and I heard some guy calling, 'Hey baby,' and so of course I just kept walking, and he said it a few more times and I ignored it." For women living in New York, catcalling is a part of the fabric of the daily soundscape that we ignore, along with the screams of children on the subway, the moaning of panhandlers and drunks, the booming soapbox preachers, the squealing teenagers and boomboxes and sirens and honking and car alarms and buses braking and fenders crunching and rubber burning. So when Skye said this, I completely understood. In many neighborhoods, my neighborhood in Brooklyn included, the catcalling is so pervasive that any acknowledgment might leave the door open for further harassment. We steel ourselves, and try to look bored and mean, while still trying to stay attractive and well dressed for the guys we really want to notice us, the guys who would never ever call to us on the subway. "How come the only guys that tell me I'm beautiful are construction workers?" a friend of mine once whined.

"So finally this guy runs up to me and he says, 'Stop, I want to show you something, it's magic,' so of course I stopped." She was hooked. He pulled a deck of cards out of his pocket, asked her to think of one, and pulled it out of the deck, to her wide-eyed shock. He did two more tricks and asked her for her phone number (she gave him the one for her cell phone). He then put her in a taxi and give the driver $20.

"He said, 'Take her wherever she wants to go,' " she said, giggling.

"To the driver?"

"Yep."

"That's wild." I thought for a minute. "What if you'd been going to New Jersey?"

"Well, I told him I was just going to West Fourth, so . . ."

She went uptown to her parents' house on the West Side, and when she got home there were already two logged calls on her cell phone from him, but no messages. Twenty minutes later the phone rang, and he was begging to see her that night.

" 'Please, please, please,' " she repeated. "I said I was busy."

"You did?"

"Yeah, but he asked what I was doing and I said I had a meeting so he said call me after your meeting and I said I would. But I didn't, and then he called me at one-thirty in the morning."

"No!"

"Yes! And all he said was, 'Hey sexy, what are you wearing?' "

"Eeewww. That's so pathetic."

"I know. I said I was sleeping and to call me later, and so he called me at nine-thirty in the morning."

"What?"

"And he said, 'You've been a very bad girl because I wanted to see you yesterday and I didn't get to and now you have to make it up to me.' "

"Jesus. What a nut job."

"I know. He's called me ten times. But luckily he's leaving tonight for a monthlong European tour, so I won't have to worry about it anymore."

"Yeah," I said. Only in Skye's universe is this business as usual. "So, are you gonna see him?"

"I wanted to do a profile of him in my book, but it seems like that's not really what he's interested in, which is too bad."

She agreed to call me back again if he hassled her any more.

Which Comes First?

I read some summary news and gleaned a sense of what Egglicious was about, how they were funded, who their clients were. The case seemed pretty clean, to my chagrin. It was probably a one-pager. I was both disappointed and loaded for bear. I was blood-hungry. I wanted burnt CEO for dinner. So I gave it one more look before I handed the case in; I went over all my notes and a few articles I had only skimmed before.

I was almost ready to present the case to George when I came across a news item that pricked my interest: Mr. Egghead had moved to Kansas for a while in the late eighties and worked at a computer-consulting firm, something that was missing from every other biography of him I'd read so far. I took the article to George, who was working at his desk.

"What?" George doesn't like to look at people. Especially his employees. It's a callous but effective mind game that weeds out the bullshit, which is exactly what he wants. Unfortunately, it still made me nervous, so I stuttered a bit and generally sounded stammering and unintelligible. I think I even called him "Sir" at the end, and I noticed a kind of bemused flicker pass over his face. All the while he continued typing on his computer, staring directly at the screen in front of him and maintaining the most astonishing composure, registering nothing of what I was saying. "So, I think we should do court searches in Kansas as well?"

George pulled his usual duck-and-dodge, not even acknowledging my presence by looking at me. He deadpanned, "Are you telling me or asking me?" I wasn't sure. I wanted to be doing whatever he wanted me to be doing. Telling you, asking you. My mother, my sister.

"I'm, um, asking you?" I realized as I was doing it that I was *asking him* if I was asking him. "Why the fuck are you asking me?"

One strike. "If you think we should do it, tell me why. You have to make the case to *me,* one way or the other. *I* get to listen." The issue, I gathered, was money. Some court records were available for a limited period of time online or in databases, but the rest of the searches had to be done manually, by court record researches we farmed out, and they were very expensive. We only did manual searches in areas where we knew our subjects had lived.

Choking the Chicken

I pleaded my case that Egghead hadn't been anywhere near Kansas, according to any published reports supplied by our client or found by us, and that, with the case as clean as it appeared to be, this was at the very least an opportunity to show our commitment to diligence on the matter. I got the green light.

I had to solicit Vinny's help getting the litigation. "Hiya, Amy. What kan I dew you fawr?"

"Vinny, can you help me out with the network setup?" Gus had snuck up behind us, and he winked at me and whispered, "You gotta just tell him to shut up." An hour later, Vinny dropped the goods off on my desk, with a note that said, "Would you like to get a steak dinner at Luger sometime?" Ugh.

❧

That night I took a sleeping pill, had a bath, and put on my softest jammies. I was dozing off in bed when the phone rang. Terror-stricken, I sat up in my bed.

"Hello?"

"Amy, it's Skye."

"Hi."

"Okay, I really need your help. DeeBee is leaving tonight at one for London, but he wants to get a drink, and I was thinking if

I could just sketch him and use it for the book, it would be really cool."

"Wait—what? Who?"

"DeeBee—it's David Blaine's nickname."

"Okay, Little Miss Insider."

"So he says, 'Please, come meet me.' But I don't want to go alone, and he said he'd bringing his friend Leo."

"Do you think it's . . . Leonardo?"

"I think so, but I'm not sure. But you have to come with me. Please. They're meeting at the bar at Spy in an hour."

"I don't even think Leonardo is cute."

"I know. Me neither. It's a business thing. I need you for moral support and/or protection."

"Okay, but I have to get dressed, and it'll take a while to get there on the subway."

"You're the best ever."

"I know I am."

Now, fully awake, I was faced with a crisis about what to wear to our double date with DeeBee and Leo. I knew they were probably assholes anyway, and I would be the baby-sitting, less-desirable chaperone, but I couldn't help at least wanting to *try* to look attractive.

A Crime in Four Movements

Skye and I met at Barmacy, a dive about five blocks north of Niagara and equally seedy. It was an old pharmacy space (hence the name) and the owners had kept old medical-equipment boxes and dusty bottled serums and medicines along the perimeter of the bar.

"Whaduyya want?" the bartender asked.

Behind the glass there was one cough syrup that Skye and

I had always coveted. Belladonna was now an illegal over-the-counter syrup that had been a cure-all in the fifties and was loaded with morphine. My dad's parents would give it to him as a little boy.

"How about a swig of the old belladonna?" I asked.

The bartender, Vic, who was pierced in six places on his face, just stared at me, unamused. I noticed that he had two tattooed vines running up his neck that turned into spitting snakes by his ear. "Two Vicious Vaccines," Skye said, leaning in front of me. He grunted something and walked away.

What does Vicious Vic have up his ass? I wondered.

Luckily, the special house concoction was served in syringes and administered by waitresses whose too-tight nurse uniforms glittered starkly against their Betty Page bobs. If I never saw Vic's punctured face again it would be too soon. We shot up and sat at the bar for an hour, suffering the occasional dead glare from Vic. After an hour, Skye's hyperactive babble slowed to an occasional mutter, and then silence.

She tried DeeBee's cell phone seven times, but to no avail. The less likely they were to come, the more Vic seemed to sneer. The only thing worse than basking in his glare, I thought, would be sitting here so long that Vic actually started to like us.

"At least being stood up by two hot celebrities is cooler than just being stood up by *some guy*." But I knew Skye had never been stood up before in her life, and she seemed to have trouble getting her head around it.

"Hey! Let's take some photo-booth pictures," Skye suggested, springing back to life. Barmacy had a grimy photo machine in the back that we'd tumbled into on various drunken nights. When Skye pulled the curtain back, there was a primly dressed woman sitting there, except for her blouse, which was completely unbuttoned and her breasts fully exposed.

"Oops! Sorry!" Skye looked at me, mouth covered in horror and amusement as she pushed the curtain closed.

"What the *fuck* was that?"

"I. Don't. Know." Then the curtain was swished open again and the woman smiled broadly at us. Her boobs were now concealed under a loose silk peasant blouse.

"Sorry about that, guys!" she said lightly, leaning out.

"That's okay," Skye squeezed out, still stricken. She mouthed "Whooooa!" to me.

"I love to come here and take my picture." The woman had a thick New York accent and mascara flaking onto her dusted cheeks.

"Yeah," I said, nodding like I really knew what she meant. The Photo Booth Porn Star Lady opened a book on her lap, to reveal hundreds of photo-booth shots of her torso, her makeup better arranged in some than in others. "I come heya once a week. I've been takin' booth photographs for seventeen years." She giggled. "I like to see how my body changes. My boobs have started to sag, ya know what I mean?"

Unfortunately, we did. She may have noticed we were a little freaked, because she flipped through her photographic growth chart cursorily and excused herself after giving us some tips on lighting. "The uppa left bulb is out. They just put a new orange background in—whateva you do, don't wear blue. You'll look dead."

We thanked her and piled into the booth. "Holy shit. Did that just happen?" Skye said, cradling her temples.

"I feel like we should wipe this down with Windex first," I lamented.

"I know." The pictures came out funny. In the first one we both looked like we were just slapped, and in the last three there are tears running down our faces from laughing, our mascara crumbling down our cheeks just like that lady's, a record of a crime in progress, in four parts.

A Bad Egg

It turned out that even though Egghead had left no credit trails in Kansas, he was named as the plaintiff in a lawsuit in Johnson County District Court in Kansas during the time period we were looking for. He was the plaintiff, and the case was filed against a processed-cheese manufacturer that owned a company he had worked at before developing his billion-dollar-revenue-producing mock egg batter with no required refrigeration and an appetite-killer shelf life of two years. The catch? The courthouse had physically lost the complaint. All it contained was a dismissal order showing that the matter, which was coded as "contract-related," was dismissed four months after the first filing. I called several executives at the Icky Cheese company, who were tight-lipped, but I finally happened on a sweet and slightly surprised HR representative named Lois who, at the very least, didn't tell me to go kiss off.

"Oh, you're calling about Mr. Caruso," she said, in a tone that indicated sweetness masking familiarity masking suspicion. "I'll be honest with you, Lois," I said, adopting a hushed manner of shared secrecy. "My clients are concerned about this situation. They know he didn't part on good terms with your company, and, frankly, they don't know why. They are on the verge of a major deal with Caruso, but it would put their minds very much at ease if they could find out what happened here, Lois." Repeating a person's name was a Sol technique, one he really pushed. I noticed he did it around the office, too, except he had pet names for people, like "Fuck Stick" or "Chump Change" or "Dick Squad." I wasn't sure if I was doing it too much. It also reeked of Dale Carnegie to me. But I wanted to win friends.

Lois was waffling. "Well, you know we have a policy here of not speaking about former employees, and of course I can't violate that . . ." (I heard Sol's words to us that morning: "Let people speak. They want to. This is that HR lackey's chance to shine—for the first time, someone gives a shit what *they* think about what's going on.") "Um-huh." I bit my lower lip.

"But I can tell you that he didn't leave of his own volition."

Booyah!

I tried to play it cool. "I see. Now, Lois, if I were to draw conclusions from that, I might assume that his job performance was sub-par, perhaps."

"Well," Lois let drop, "I suppose I could also say that he was hired about two months before he was supposed to start, and he never did start. He was fired before he started, basically."

What the fuck did that mean? I was trying to think about instances when friends of mine had lost jobs before they even *started* them. I knew Ben was once fired from a job at a local Providence television station when, about an hour after hiring him, the supervisor reread his résumé and noticed that there was an unfortunate embellishment on it. He had already listed himself as having worked there.

"Was he dishonest about his working past, Lois?"

"No, not really. But let's say all new employees are subject to a company orientation, and Mr. Caruso was found to be unfit for the environment we'd like to maintain here. But that's really all I can say." The phone was rustling like she was about to close out on me, and I could not let that happen.

"Lois, I completely understand. I'm not going to ask you any more questions. Let's just say that I might draw the conclusions that he was found to be engaged in prohibited behavior, maybe drug use, or, um, *sexual* behavior. Would that be accurate?" I could practically hear Lois blush.

Long silence. "Well, the latter would be correct." *Boom.* "Lois, I just want to make sure we understand each other. Was Mr. Caruso maybe harassing a fellow employee in a sexually inappropriate way?"

"Well, it was inappropriate in that way, but it wasn't directed at anybody, umm, in particular. If I'm making myself clear."

This was getting very interesting. "Lois," I said, "I'm going to use a euphemism that might make this more comfortable—might I assume that Mr. Caruso was caught pulling the pud on company property?" I really hoped Lois had a teenage son, and I wouldn't have to get any more graphic—or technical. She conceded, but added, "My name is Lourdes, by the way."

Not good. Definitely a big fuckup. But I pushed forward. I wanted to be clear. "You mean, like Madonna's baby?" She laughed and said yes and before I blew it any more I squeezed out, "You should feel very good about this, ma'am," and got off the phone.

When I went to deliver the good news to George he was on the phone, so I left him a note. Sometimes the Agency tries to get pictures of subjects just for identity-verification, and in the glossy attached in my case file Mr. Caruso even looked like a pervert. I attached his greasy mug to a note that said, "George, he pulled a Pee-wee in a bathroom stall at work. Go figure."

My razor-sharp interrogation skills did not go unheeded. Eventually, George came to find me. I was sitting at my desk, where I'd been anxiously facing him for the past four days, and he threw me a bone. "Gray—I spoke to the client about that case. Thanks for not fucking it up." I felt my face go rosy. Our client ended up confronting Mr. Caruso about it, and he copped to the sullied truth. The clients went through with the deal anyway.

The Naked Truth

Having been warned about the Halloween party since practically the day I was hired at the Agency, I was expecting to be impressed. Nothing prepared me for it.

I waited until the eleventh hour—the day before Halloween—to pick out my costume, which I found by accident while walking to the subway after work. A brown suede and macramé halter top beckoned from the window of a thrift store called Grandma's Attic. I immediately conjured Cher and ran inside. The halter top was fifty-eight dollars, eighteen dollars over my entire Halloween budget, but I figured I didn't have time to be frugal at this point, since otherwise I had no costume to wear. I bought a long black wig and some brown leather bell-bottoms to match. I had some giant white plastic clip-on hoops from my dress-up days, and I wore some old platforms to seal the deal.

That day, Wendy, Renora, and I had to buy plastic cauldrons for candy and apple-bobbing. The largest costume-rental company in New York was next door to our building. Around Halloween, the lines of people seeking costumes snaked out the door around the block, but Tommy, our fixit guy, let us in by the back entrance. The place looked like the scene of a gruesome slaughter in the dressing room of an L.A. child star. It was swarming with pushy girls grading their boyfriends, as well as a chorus of grim reapers and cackling dwarfs. "Eww," Wendy whined. After we had arranged our witchy pots artfully, and I went to Cassie's to get dressed for the party, because, as usual, she didn't want to show up alone.

By the time I finished applying my fake lashes and putting bronzer all over my body, I barely recognized myself. I just needed the Sonny to my Cher, which really wasn't going to happen between now and later, so I'd asked Cassie to come. She was a 1970s prom queen, but her Salvation Army–bought silver pumps broke on the way down the stairs to meet me, and she had an identity crisis.

"Va-va-voom! You look like a hot piece of 1975 ass." She had on a gorgeous lavender polyester disco dress with a swishy pleated skirt and puffy three-quarter-length sleeves. The dress had silver zig-zags across the waist. Then I noticed she looked like she was about to puke. "What's the matter?'

"I can't wear this! I only have one heel," she wailed.

"Why don't you try on some other shoes?" I suggested.

"They don't match!"

Eventually, after much coaxing, she wore some black shoes she'd bought for a black-widow costume the year before.

Noah and Renora were on the decorating committee. All the furniture had been moved into the conference room. The entire loft was festooned with cobwebs, although, it occurred to me, many of these might not be decorations.

Everybody seemed to choose characters they already resembled, somewhat. Wendy was exercise guru Jane Fonda, after her teen-princess era and before she was a billionaire's wife. Her spandex bodysuit with its deep V-neck and stripes were set off by a pair of silver hand-knit legwarmers. Other girls gathered around to admire her impeccable rendition, completed by sweatbands around her wrists and head.

"I'm so into these legwarmers," she said to me, panting as she pumped her arms in the air as part of her aerobic-dancing routine. "I'm gonna wear them all the time. They're so *comfortable*!"

"Honey, you already wear legwarmers all the time," I pointed out.

Wielding a cane and a pipe, Linus approached us. He had shaved the top of his head and dyed the rest of his hair gray.

"Who am I?" he asked.

"I don't know . . . an old man."

"Amy, Amy Amy," he muttered, shuffling away from me. "That's obvious. But which *one*?"

"What are you, Rain Man?" It turned out he was Carl Jung.

Renora was a sexy romance novel cover girl. She'd bought C cup saline boob enhancers (they're called Curves), and stuffed herself into a tight and flouncy green velvet ball gown. She had a curly brown appliqué attached to her short hair. "Where's your Romeo?" I asked.

"Shhh." She pulled me aside. "I'm a little disturbed by his costume," she whispered. "I feel like he's *really* eighty years old."

"It is a little too good," I agreed. We watched as Linus stumbled by with Gus, dressed as a Hell's Angel; Evan, who was looking freaky as Gene Simmons in full ceremonial dress; and Nestor, who was Gonzo from the Muppets.

"Have you seen Sol or George?"

"No, but I heard. It's awful." At that moment I fleetingly spotted Sol cutting a rug on the dance floor. I didn't know it was Sol, though. He was wearing a woman's tennis outfit, and had a racquet in his hand. The costume was smudged with black paint. Every visible inch of skin on his body was covered with black paint, except for his eyes, white and blinking, like two gleaming sand dollars sinking into black velvet.

Evan came over and stood with us. "Pretty fucked, huh?"

"What *is* he?"

Evan pointed to Sol's back, where he had pinned a tiny black doll to himself, also outfitted in tennis whites. "He's the Williams sisters," he coughed.

"You're joking."

"I'm not." Sol was bouncing, apparently ignorant of his racist gaffe.

"That's not funny." Sol bounced over the dance floor, kicking his legs up with Jane Fonda and then pantomiming an atrocious serve over his head.

"Didn't blackface go out with the four humors and hydrogen-filled Zeppelins? There's something so completely wrong about that guy."

"How about everything?" he agreed. "Have you seen George?"

"No," I said, and Renora chimed in, joining us.

"I'll go get him." Evan went to get him, coming back a minute later with George naked but for a pair of CK boxer briefs and several little yellow Post-its stuck all over his body.

"Okay, fucksticks, what am I?" We all stared on, disbelievingly.

"The naked guy?"

"A pervert?"

"The guy at the party who drinks too much and makes a fool of himself?"

"All true, but that's not my gig tonight. C'mon, fishlips, you're smarter than that." He waited for another guess. "I'm the Naked Truth." On closer inspection, the notes stuck to him had things penned on them: I read them aloud, almost as a question.

"Girls don't swallow? I think I've found a factual error in your costume." I kept reading. "Yes, you do look . . . fatter? . . . Black men have bigger dicks? Your wife must love that one," I cracked. "How would you know?"

"What's up with Sol's costume?" Evan asked. "Isn't that, I don't know . . . politically incorrect? Offensive? Illegal?"

"Brown sugar, baby," he countered, smacking his lips in satisfaction.

"I can't believe I work here," Renora reflected later.

"I know."

I thought doing this kind of work would make me very powerful. Even if I saw a gruesome investigation in perfect clarity, it didn't matter. Our clients' interests dictated the response, and I was no more or less powerful. Or I'd take a really dull case and will it to be sensational, all in service of my hunger to be clever and almighty. In my own life, I was a terrible detective—I struck a hypothesis and found things to support it. Even in the face of a faulty theorem, I would pursue it like a demented, lovelorn fool. Perhaps the learning curve of the Agency had flattened for me. I loved my job, but wasn't sure I was any good at it, and I wasn't sure if it was good for me, either.

✪ TWENTY-TWO

> Actual life was chaos, but there was something terribly logical in the
> imagination . . . It was the imagination that made each crime bear its
> misshapen brood. In the common world of fact the wicked were not
> punished, nor the good rewarded.
>
> —OSCAR WILDE, *THE PICTURE*
> *OF DORIAN GRAY*

A Real Live Wire

Other trusted professionals include: hairdresser. Drug dealer.
Taxi driver. Therapist. In high school I took taxis from the subway
to my parents' house, which was a six-minute drive, five and a half
if I told him to take the shortcut through Garland Road and we
didn't hit a red light at Mill Street. Earl started driving me in sopho-
more year, and from then on if he was at the dispatcher when I got
off the train, he'd take me home. Multiply five minutes by five
times a week, and then by thirty-six school weeks, and you'll have
an idea why I got to know Earl pretty well.

"Yoo look like a really smaat one. And a sweethaaat," he said,
winking at me in the rearview mirror one ride home. He looked

like a young Don Knotts. His fingernails were bitten to slivers. His fingers were ropy and knotted, and his accent was classic Boston.

"Umm. Obviously you don't know me."

"It's ya ayes," he continued. "I've thawt a lat abowt this." His theory was based on a psychology class he had taken in night school at Salem State. "Thare's this dockta who sez you can read a person's face by thare facial moovements." This psychologist had classified every possible expression into an alphabet of emotion. Earl was already "a good judge of caarrocta," he added.

I watched his eyes in the rearview mirror. "See," he said, turning back to look at me for a second and then back to the road again, "if I contract my zygomatic maja and my orbicularis something or other, I'm haapy, and so orn and so fawth." One day on the way home from school, taking a shortcut, he pulled the car over to the side of the road and lifted a stack of papers off the front seat.

"I'm knawt that good a spella." He declared. "I got this papuh due in a week. Can you read it ova for me?"

I was too tired to refuse, so I read the whole thing in ten minutes, and learned to read cues from the backseat's reflection in the rearview mirror.

❧

The next time I went into Lucky Car Service in late November, Mussah told me that Moez had been in a car accident.

"Oh my God! Is he okay?"

"Yeah, he fine, but he total the car. He can't afford to use the car anymore. The insurance is too high and he got to pay for the damage now, too, so he move to Philly."

"Pennsylvania?"

"Yeah." And with that, Moez was gone.

Down with Dubya

The election of 2000 came just in time to salvage me from the doldrums of my disillusionment. It taught me to appreciate the little things, like how "families are where wings take dreams," or potential president-elect Al Gore brandishing a boner on the cover of *Esquire*. Politics had never been so fun, and I felt myself strangely privy to the whole affair, since on both sides it was moles, people like me, that the candidates were using to smear each other. I was shocked when Bush's DWI was heavy-handedly released. We could have found that in a few hours. Two weeks before the election, I made a color-coded map of the country, and, averaging the latest polling numbers from five I figured out who would take each state. By my most judicious calculations, Gore would win handily.

I spent election night with my ex-boyfriend Ben, who suffered my delusions of political grandeur. For some reason, I needed the anchor of his attention at moments like this, perhaps to counter the sting that could come from a defeat. We split a bottle of Clos du Bois at nine, when Gore won Florida. I licked the red sediment in a bloom-shaped deposit off the lip of my wineglass and marveled at how easy it was all going to be. Everything had gone according to my calculations: I had a logarithm for determining which polling services were more accurate and included them in appropriate rank, and I accounted for the precalculated margin of error for each figure, plus an additional conservative percentage for variance. With this kind of mathematics, I could forecast the future, foretell the climate, even constitute snow. At eleven the winds of fate shifted like a fickle downpour, and the networks took Florida back and put it in the "undetermined" column. By midnight, a barometric reversal had awarded Florida to George W., and Ben and I drank Brooklyn Pale Ale and flat Guinness out of the can and consoled ourselves that things could turn around. They did, at 2 A.M., and at 7 A.M., when I don't remember lying down in a devotional pose on my sheepskin in front of the television, they were still as uncertain as ever.

I'm what urban archivist Luc Sante has coined a "dirt broker." Or I might also be a missionary of facts, a crusader of certainty, or perhaps all of them. But part of my anguish after the election was the realization that, as Hendrik Hertzberg wrote in *The New Yorker,* "It will never be possible to get to the truth of this vote." I had abandoned my espousal of the indiscriminateness of being after I sold all my Derrida and de Man books after college. As an investigator, for all my digging, I've struggled with the reality that it's not possible to "get all the facts" or "generate the truth." The degree to which I'd forsaken my intellectual past was dramatic, and now it was all in jeopardy.

Circle Jerk

The office was abuzz with the topsy-turviness of the times. The tension was palpable. Now it wasn't just inside of me, it was in the office, it was everywhere. The markets were plummeting, the elections were a postmodern mess. We had all abandoned our Napsterizing to listen to live CNN feeds on the status of the elections. What else could go wrong? And then I noticed things in the office were strange. People were gathered at Evan's desk, and a hum of activity was transpiring in the conference room. I buzzed Evan.

"What's going on?"

"I think Assman's getting fired." I was stunned.

I made a bogus drop-off to Evan's desk so I could do a walk-by and peek into the conference room. Assman was sitting in there with George, Sol, and our accountant, Adrienne. I couldn't tell jack.

Ten minutes later, Assman picked up his messenger bag and stormed out of the office, face flushed, and Sol came out and walked toward—me! He swerved at Nestor's desk, and Nestor followed him into the room. "Jesus!" I heard Noah whisper.

I ran to the door after Assman. "Wait!" I caught him in the stairwell on the second floor. "What happened?" I asked him, as he turned his back on me and said, "They fired me. And my name is Matt."

━◘━

After the bloodletting at work that day, I met Cassie for drinks. First stop was one of our two Niagara-alternative haunts. Tom & Jerry, another Lower East Side bar—though totally unremarkable, it seemed to be a destination for a lot of my friends—happened to be just inside the perimeter of Cassie's approved barfly zone. Perky publishing assistants buzzed behind slouchy girls starting their own fashion labels and uppity personal assistants.

Cassie and I forged a path to the back of the bar, suffering sloppy gimlets and sharp elbows. "Ouch!" she hissed, shoving back at a girl in an asymmetrical cotton top with FERRAGAMO written on it and a single pigeon-feather earring fluttering out one ear. "Watch it, bitch!" the girl shot back at Cass, when we realized simultaneously it was Kim Deal, the guitarist from our favorite band in high school, the Breeders.

"Sorry," Cass said, shocked as we walked away, and she whispered, "I can't believe I cried at their show in high school."

I said, shell-shocked, "We should just go to Niagara." She assented.

We decided to get one drink first. The bartender was a cute Irish bloke with cool blue eyes. "What 'kin I get ya, ladies?"

"I'll have an Amstel Light." Cassie was doing some variation on the Atkins diet. A low-carb but not totally cold-turkey thing. She could eat buckwheat, for example, although it wasn't clear why she'd want to.

"I'll have the same, please." Still, I was intrigued. Plus I was feeling fat. Then I saw Renora coming out the bathroom at the back of the bar. She was holding her usual double shot of Jameson's and puffing on a cigarette.

"Renora!" She didn't see me waving at her, but instead walked over to a table behind a corner of the bar I couldn't see. Renora had told me she was hanging out with one of the many in her revolving door of male suitors tonight. But she didn't say she was coming to Manhattan.

I told Cass I'd be right back and went around the side of the bar and saw Renora leaning against the wall next to the bar, kissing someone—except it wasn't just someone. It was—could it be?— Linus. She was fooling around with . . . Linus? I was confused and disbelieving. Was she cheating on her English bartender boyfriend with Linus? And what about what he was saying the other day, about being "unburdened" and not buying into the female "art of ball bashing"?

I was going to turn around and pretend I wasn't seeing what I was seeing, but Renora looked up from their interlude, tongue wagging, and looked like she was about to faint.

She whispered something to Linus, who turned to look at me, and then they walked over together, Renora looking wobbly.

"Hi, Amy," Linus said sheepishly.

"I guess we're busted," Renora said.

"Sorry, I didn't mean to—"

"No, it's okay," Renora interrupted. "This was going to happen at some point. Just don't tell anyone at work. Please." She and Linus sat like strangers next to each other before she jumped up and handed me a glass of green fluid that looked like automobile coolant. "What is this?"

"It's absinthe?" I had heard absinthe was making a comeback, but I hadn't yet seen it make an appearance before.

"Will it make me insane?"

"No, it's different now. It doesn't have all those things in it that caused hysteria."

"I guess I already have that, anyway." I eyed the greasy-looking green fluid. "You know what, that's okay. I'll stick to beer."

I reemphasized my willingness to keep their secret, and went back to the bar. They made a mad dash for the exit. "What was *that*?" Cassie asked.

"Don't ask."

"Listen, while you were over there, some guy came over and said his friend was wondering if you had a boyfriend."

"Really? Was he cute?"

"Well, his friend was, but I don't know who his friend is. Plus they were standing over at that side of the bar, and they're not there anymore."

"Fuck."

We eventually made our usual deal with the devil and headed over to Niagara. It was a slow night. Stuart was standing in front of us at the bar, holding a shaker.

"Love the shirt," Cassie said to him cheerily, eyeing his blue-and-red embroidered bowling top.

"Really?"

"Yeah, it's cool."

"I think you told me that last time you were here," he recalled, leaning in to pour our drinks into ceramic half-coconuts.

"See," she said, "I *really* like that shirt."

"Hey," I threw in, frustrated, "I like your shirt, too." His scornful look seemed to say, "I like your friend Cassie's tatas, but don't flatter yourself, I'm not interested in yours." As usual with Stuart, he ignored me and kept his eyes on the prize. Thank God these drinks were free.

"So what is it about this shirt you like so much?" he said, leaning in and propping his chin on both palms right in front of Cassie's barstool, a bolt of light flashing off his shiny head as he moved.

"I've gotta pee," I said to the nobody that was listening, and I slipped upstairs to clear my head. As I walked down to the bar, I spotted Skye. She had already seen me, and she was with a boy.

"Hey, hon!" she cried, throwing her arms around my neck. "What are you doing here?"

"I'm with Cassie. The real question is, what are you doing here?" I wagged a suggestive forefinger at her.

"I was meeting my friend Peter." Peter was a supposedly really cute spiky-blondish-haired boy I'd never met before. "Hey," he said, extending his hand.

Skye said she had to run to the bathroom, and I was suddenly left alone with Peter, who seemed uncomfortable with our sudden proximity.

"So, how do you know Skye?" he asked.

When I was through answering that question, he pretended to check through his wallet and I pretended to be looking for someone. Finally I offered him a Tareyton, which he gladly took. When Skye finally came back, he seemed greatly relieved.

"Okay," she inhaled. "Well, it was nice to see you." Taking my cue, I returned downstairs to my lukewarm tropical nectar. Stuart had disappeared from behind the bar, and Cassie had abandoned her sidebar post. She did, however, leave a clue. On top of her jacket was a message in blue eyeliner on a yellow tiki cocktail napkin. It had tiny straw huts and dancing natives getting it on around the edges.

"Be right back," it read, in loopy blue kohl. The windows

separating the storage room were foggy, tiny veins of condensation running down the panes and over the doorframe onto the linoleum, where combat boots on dancing punk rockers smudged them away.

Getting Lucky

I got a message from Skye the next day.

When I called back, she didn't answer, so I started leaving a message: "Hey babe, it's me, I'm sorry I interrupted your date last night. Call me—"

She picked up the phone. "Amy? I'm so glad I got you! I need to ask you about something."

"Sure."

"My friend Peter really liked you last night."

"That's nice." I paused. "Weren't you on a date?"

"No!" she laughed. "We work together. We were having a meeting. He's the curator of the Art Cooper gallery. They have a few pieces of mine right now. Anyway, he asked me if you were dating someone and I said—I hope this is okay—I didn't think you were." It didn't seem possible to me that Peter, or any guy, for that matter, could not be in love with Skye. Although I believed that she thought they weren't on a date, I figured he must have secretly hoped it would turn into one. I simply wasn't buying that some cute guy could hang out with Skye and not be under her spell. She slayed men. Everyone wanted her.

"So, can I give him your number?" she pleaded.

"Are you sure he wants it?" I asked.

"Amy!"

I relented, but told her to give him my e-mail instead. I figured that if he'd gone to all the effort of asking about me, maybe he really was interested.

At my desk later, I heard the satisfying ping of incoming e-mail. I checked my inbox. There was a message from Peter. The subject line said, "AMY, AMy, Amy, amy." "Amy, I very much enjoyed meeting you the other night, and getting a chance to smoke your tobacco. I would leap through puddles (and risk a soaker) to see you again. If you're interested, maybe you'll send me your phone number. Hoping to get lucky, Peter."

My heart was in my mouth. I was touched. "Would you brave the Harlem Meer and risk the perilous jaws of the vicious mini-Alligator? If so, I'll meet you on the other side." Send.

That night, I sat in my living room and stared at the lights. Three spindly threads of spider silk fell around the center of the bulb right above me. The translucent fibers trembled faintly from the movement of air in the room. My breathing slowed. I saw a tiny dark spot emerge from the white-hot center of the bulb. When I looked directly at it, the speck practically disappeared against the light, but if I fixed my sight just to the right of it, I could see it more clearly, a tiny almond-shaped rhizome falling from the sky. It grew larger, and materialized as a quivering fine line around a smaller, darker nucleus. It was a tiny sac, pulsing slowly with the air, when the edge of the line was pierced and seemed to melt into a squirming larger dark blot. I rolled off the couch and watched as dozens of baby spiders pitched their worlds on tiny spindles thinner than eyelashes. Evidence of these little lives that, I supposed, could be done in with a hearty sneeze.

Yankee My Doodle

When Ben and I broke up, he had just come back from three weeks on location in upstate New York, shooting his second-year movie short for NYU's graduate film school. We had spoken occasionally, but I'd resolved myself to end it right before he left. I had found him, for, like, the fifth time, getting high in our apartment, drunk and stinking and laughing at me. I was years past my drug-experimentation phase, and tired of being the stern taskmaster girlfriend–slash-mommy to him. By the time he'd returned, I'd gone through my process of loss: sadness, anger, listlessness, weight loss, and then renewal. I felt hardened and excited about changing my life. We were a week away from our five-year anniversary. He came over to my tiny apartment, where, I'd assured him, I'd moved just months before "not because we're breaking up," but to have "more independence."

"You lied to me," he said, staring out the window.

"I'm sorry," I said. But at the time I didn't feel really sorry. I was over it—I thought. The conversation was short and not too painful. A week later, I was at work, still in publishing, when I got a call.

"Is this Amy Gray?"

"Yes, can I help you?" I answered dozens of calls daily from agents, authors, producers, editors and their assistants, and it could have been any number of legitimate persons on the line.

"This is John Marston, from Together Dating Service."

"What?" Together Dating Service was a fee-for-service dating company that had been running low-production-value ads in metropolitan areas, showing couples in grainy color video running over a greenish sand beach. If Together didn't work for you, you were entitled to a full refund of your $19.95 membership fee. "Why not get Together," they asked, "and have the life you know you deserve?"

"I'm not interested," I said, my finger hovering over the flash button.

"But you signed up for our service—is your address Dean Street in Brooklyn? Are you twenty-four and a hundred-fifty pounds?"

"I am not a fucking hundred-fifty pounds! What the fuck?

This must be a joke. I did not sign up for your service—and I'm—I'm not interested."

"Well, are you single?"

"Yeah." Why did I answer that?

"Maybe you didn't sign up for the service, but since you're single anyway, maybe you should try it. There are lots of great people in Together—"

"Well, no I'm not—"

"Maybe you and I could go out sometime. I work here, but I'm single too, and you have a nice voice."

"NO!" I was livid. "If you phone me again, I'm calling the police, asshole." I hit the line, and it occurred to me at that moment that it was Ben who had signed me up.

Two days later, I got home from work and there was a black bubble-wrapped package sitting in front of my door. I opened it to uncover a white box and, inside of that, several layers of tightly wrapped and taped tissue paper. Inside that was another box with gold embossing around the edges and a cellophane window to reveal its contents, a cylindrical baby-blue object that looked like a plastic cigar. I took it out of the box and saw the lettering across the bottom, "Batteries not included." It was a dildo! "That fucker," I thought, and picked up the phone to tell him what an immature, vengeful baby he was. But I dialed six digits and stopped and dropped the phone on my lap. I would not give him what he wanted—again. I would not.

❧

Lying on the couch, I felt a tickle on my neck and swatted mindlessly. On my hand was a tiny mash of spider. I thought about the snapdragons in my garden in summer and the baby spiders and the fragility of ecological equilibrium they forged in an unforgiving metropolis. Peter and I were like that, too. I resolved to tread carefully.

Where Wings Take Dream

Peter and I had e-mailed many more times that day, and he called me the next night. Thinking about Ben recently had made me feel a mix of pity and defensiveness. I never wanted to let myself come close to being the insentient punch line in my own life ever again. I still felt the need for armor, a chain mail suit of intelligence. Who was Peter, anyway? I felt uneasy. I, Spygirl, would find him out.

"So, you want to do something?" he asked.

"Yeah," I said, sounding unenthusiastic simply by trying to play it cool.

"I don't want to do something datey," he specified.

"What does that mean?"

"Well . . ." I immediately felt bad I'd asked this. What could he say? Eating out is the number-one date activity, but it's also biologically essential.

"Going out for dinner, or a movie," he said. "I don't know, really."

I waited. "So, do you have any unorthodox propositions?"

"Taking a walk? I could come over to your house and we could walk over the Brooklyn Bridge."

"I'd love to do that. That's a brilliant idea!" I had actually never done this before. He seemed bolstered by my enthusiasm.

"Well, thanks. I've been working on that concept for months."

"Nice one."

We agreed to meet at my apartment.

On Sunday at noon, I met Peter at the gate of my apartment

building. It was warm for November, in the sixties. Even so, he was wearing a T-shirt, entirely sweat through. We headed over to Adams Street and then onto the bridge. It was an exquisite day. We talked about our jobs; he told me about his gallery, how he'd come to have the idea for it and secure the funding. Not to be outdone by the land and sea, the skies over New York were their own bustling ecology. The blue was littered with helicopters, tiny toylike airplanes and huge dirigibles heaving across the sky; flocks of gulls, pigeons, and kites.

"Doesn't it seem as if nothing in New York City is undiscovered? Every inch is spoken for," Peter reflected, longingly.

I always think about lonely stretches of highway. Pieces of land that are forgotten and unloved with no prospects of ever being remembered. "What about that?" I pointed to a tiny square of green grass and a small rotting pier about a hundred yards away. He laughed.

"Should we go?"

"Sure."

"It'll be our own private square foot of Manhattan."

But when we walked off the bridge, we realized our square foot was nestled behind someone else's eight feet of chain-link and razor wire that held a truck lot.

"Maybe our square foot is actually under a red Mercedes big rig."

"Wait, I have an idea," he said. He ducked down the fence and reappeared skulking along its inside minutes later.

"How'd you do that?"

"It's magic," he said, waving his fingers like he was casting a spell.

"Okay, David Copperfield, enjoy yourself."

"No, there's a hole in the fence down here." He led me to a hole that was dug in the ground under the fence, and I ducked in.

By the time we were sitting in our own eight-by-five piece of grass, it felt luxurious.

"This is, like, the smallest little park in all of the world," he said. And then a big fat raindrop fell on my shoulder. Minutes later, we were sliding through the mud at the base of the fence. We ran like crazy, heading away from the river, the rain hitting us like fistfuls of gravel. By the time we ran into the Liquor Store Bar, my sneakers were sloshing loudly with all the water in them.

"Two Guinnesses, please," Peter asked the bartender, water puddling from his chin onto the oak bar below. That was the first of five pints each, whereupon we hailed a taxi, completely plastered, and went back to my apartment in Brooklyn. I played some Yo La Tengo for him, which he'd never heard before.

"Well, would it be too 'datey' if we have dinner?" I asked him.

He laughed. "I think we're ready." We went to a Vietnamese place in my neighborhood, and then to a bar afterward, where we sat knee-to-knee, warming up by a wood-burning stove at the back of the bar. At one point he took my hand, and before I knew it our cheeks were touching. From our first point of contact, a warm flush spread over me, spreading and sticking like hot red happiness.

He kissed me good night at my door. I ran into my room and flopped myself onto the bed. *Oh. My. God.*

❂ TWENTY-THREE

I'm the type of person who's willing to confront moderately awesome phenomena. . . . Chipping away at gigantic unproved postulates. Investigating the properties of common whole numbers and ending up in the wilds of analysis. Intoxicating theorems. Nagging little symmetries. The secrets hidden deep inside the great big primes. The way one formula or number or expression keeps turning up in the most unexpected places. The infinite. The infinitesimal. Glimpsing something, then losing it. The way it slides off the eyeball. The unfinished nature of the thing.

—DON DELILLO, *RATNER'S STAR*

Kicking Ass and Taking Names

"Aysome Graysom," Evan called to me from across the room. "What are you doing for New Year's?"

I groaned. "I dunno. Hopefully spending it with the quote-unquote perfect guy, love of my life, yang to my yin."

"I don't know what you're talking about. I'm available," Evan teased.

The ghosts of New Year's 1999 still haunted me, and I felt lackluster about planning another one. It had been a year since I started my job at the Agency and celebrated my last millennium New Year. The year had started with a lot of empty paranoia, but it ended in real chaos. You could hear it whispered by former CEOs who went home from work with pieces of paper that said zero, and Florida voters who dreamt of hanging chads and magazine-reading girls who didn't care anymore about assembling wardrobes that "go from workaday fun to nighttime glamour." People couldn't even agree on whether the millennium had begun. Since then, the market crashed, the democratic process had failed, and even baseball had a hiccup, pitting brothers against brothers in the Subway Series. We had even failed at achieving our own disaster; the Y2K Bug had been a bust.

Evan was trying to plan something at the Blue and Gold for everyone at the Agency, plus friends. "Preferably blond, single, slutty friends," he clarified.

"Evan, love, you're my only one."

"Nice one, Gray." The party, he explained, would be "chill." We would have the bar to our cheap, one-dollar-draft-slinging selves. "It'll be us, the St. Marks junkies, and the Tompkins Square winos," he declared. I filed it under "last-ditch options" and let the next five days fly by.

Romance Under a Kitchen Sink

Now I can see that my path to becoming a PI was circuitous yet inevitable. Like many young girls, I fantasized about spy work, fostering a sense of hearing particularly attuned to whispers and undertones. I culled the entire series of Nancy Drew mysteries, and held Harriet the Spy in almost biblical reverence, equipping myself with the available tools of documentation: a plastic phone, a note pad, binoculars, a Lucite hammer, and a screwdriver. (The purpose of the latter two: dismantling sinks, which seemed at the time like a probable enough occupation for a spy.) I spent my time mostly in the cupboard under our leaky kitchen sink and standing next to phone poles, where my cover as a Bell-Atlantic repairman, heightened by my snappy orange reflector belt (acquired for my new crossing-guard job) allowed eavesdropping and apparent obscurity.

Thrilled by the notion that I could use my wiles to glean weighty clues and grave intelligence, I became opposed to being told what to do, a trait that, for better or worse, still seems to linger and shield me like a security blanket. When my mother ordered me to set the table, for example, her directives evaporated into the wind: I was locked into my dreamy frequency. My new, loftier goals could take me into the kinds of forbidden places only boys went.

My neighbors, the Dickersons, had a backyard that bordered on ours. A newly forged covert sensibility kicked in when I initiated my first plan of real surveillance. Hiding behind the fence separating our houses, I lowered a plastic bucket into their yard. Inside was the first of a series of notes reading, "Hello. Who are you?" and then "Do you like frogs?" and then "I'm having a party right now. Come over." I will never forget the daily ritual of hoisting the bucket back up the next day, swelling with anticipation for the rejoinder within, a secret connection conceived in anonymity . . . that never came.

At dusk, I walked around the neighborhood, a neat oval of attractive shingled three-bedrooms with tidy lawns, and peered out into the yellowish-lit windows. I considered how I might penetrate that glowing world on the other side, how the secrets and rituals of these other families might be infiltrated. What did they eat for dinner? Did their mom wake them up in the morning like mine, chirping, "Rise and shine, darling!" How many minutes did they have to brush their teeth for? I came home and went to my room to use my dad's binoculars, looking for clues to life at the Dickersons'. Although I only observed the most insubstantial movements—a pair of kid's legs here, a streak of a mom's orangey mop there—they didn't seem to notice me. I hoped they would.

A month into my scheme, I was sniffed out. My mother came to my room one day asking, "Have you been throwing paper into the Dickersons' backyard?" "No," I said. "Well, even though you haven't been, don't anymore," she said. In truth, I had grown tired of my daily sacrament and was already planning further subversions and hatching more elaborate subterfuges. I was eight years old.

❧

Now the Harriet in me craved a huge calamity to reconstruct neatly from the ruins. She wanted the disorder followed by an orderly cleanup. A lightning storm in a bottle. A tempest in a teapot. But the mania of the millennium year was anything but. It was a nebulous kind of mess that was hard to put your finger on.

Harriet wanted the safety of becoming a trained observer of her own life, but while she was busy watching, no one was there to live it. Alas, it didn't work for her. I thought of Three-Ring Circus Guy creating fragments of his own life to live like movie stills. I decided to e-mail Peter. The suspense was killing me.

"What's your idea of a perfect New Year's Eve?" I wrote him.

"Curling up with a copy of some timeless prose like *Up the Butt* and diddling myself," he wrote back. This had to be the guy for me. He made me laugh more than Ben—no small feat.

I picked up the phone and called him. "Hey, what are you doing?"

"Hey!" He fell silent.

"Uh, that's okay, you don't have to tell me. For example, if you're on the toilet or sitting around diddling yourself."

"No. Sorry. I'm just working."

"Do you want to do something tonight?" I asked.

"I have to finish taking down a show here. I'll be done at tenthirty, eleven. Is that too late for you?"

I responded slowly, trying to be coy. "Nooo."

He waited to answer too. I imagined it was just enough time for a smile. "I'll be hungry then," he said.

"Me too."

"So bring your beautiful self to Casimir, and when I get there I want to find you sipping Merlot. And if you're wearing a skirt it wouldn't hurt."

I laughed. "I'll try to work my magic," I said. "On you, crotchless leather bell-bottoms might not hurt, either."

"Actually, I can say from experience, they would," he countered. I giggled.

Up, Up, and Away

I went home to change after work before I went to meet Peter. Resting on my couch, I squished a spider rounding my left upper arm. Hopefully, I thought, we're all more than hapless creatures quivering at the slightest ripple in the still air of an otherwise quiescent New York apartment.

Four hours later I sat at a small table in the side room at Casimir near the back corner. The space looks like a sultry salon in Prague. It's full of French, Turks, Israelis, Germans, and other foreigners leaning conspiratorially over tea-lit tables that bob as they move. The windows are steamy, posing a warm, damp defense against the bitterness outside.

I savored a cigarette and let myself revel in the romance of it all: meeting Peter, liking Peter, having a beautiful week and a half together. I looked around the bar and thought of all the other abandoned people. What a relief it was not to be one of them, even just for a week and a half. I observed a curly-haired man gesticulating uneasily to his British girlfriend. She argued back a few times and then marched out the door, giving him a good four-letter parting shot. I saw a petite woman frantically trying to rub a wine stain out of her skirt. When her boyfriend arrived, she batted her eyes and ignored it until he asked her, "What's on your skirt?" and she looked like she'd cry. I saw two New Yorkers arrive together. Sit down. Suck face for four or five minutes and then looking conjoined, leave. I saw—Moez?

Yes, it was. Coming toward me was Moez, my car driver.

"Oh my God!"

"Hello," he said, standing in front of me, smiling with his usual sheepishness.

"Hi, how are you?" I said, and without thinking I stood up and kissed his cheek, the cheek which I'd contemplated so thoroughly from so many backseats. He seemed to blush.

"I had accident."

"I know—are you okay? I was worried."

"Yes, yes," he said. "It was good. I realize that I need to stop doing what I'm doing, you know. I hate to drive that car, you know, so I been applying to school and I go back to Tunisia in a week."

I felt my heart drop a little. It was so much easier to imagine Moez tragically outdone by New York than leaving willingly. Leaving me.

"I get married," he said.

"What?" My shock was evident.

"Yes, my sister's friend. I met her a few years ago, you know. It's time to settle down, my sister says, and I miss my home." I wished him luck, and felt strangely relieved about the marriage thing. It was less romantic than the bildungsroman I'd scripted seconds before about a handsome, gentle young man returning to a bucolic life in the Promised Land after a punishing turn foraging for survival as a New York cabdriver.

At eleven-thirty Peter joined me.

"You're wearing a skirt," he said, fingering the edge of my sexy tight purple herringbone pencil skirt.

"Your crown jewels aren't on display," I protested.

"Umm, they will be later," he said. Soon enough I was completely entranced, forgetting all the other characters, foreign and otherwise, in that bar. Then I was only taking note of my own slow, hopeful breathing and monitoring the respiration and movements of one other person.

Peter and I woke up at ten and cuddled until eleven.

"I'm scared to let go of you," he said.

"I know," I said.

"Let's not," he said.

At noon he said he had to go to the gallery to put up a new show. I held on tighter.

"You can stay here," he said, kissing my arms.

"Really?"

"As long as you don't take the opportunity to read my diary and look through my underwear drawer."

"Why? What's in your underwear drawer?" I asked.

"Maybe I should send you home," he said, unpeeling himself from my embrace.

"Nooo, I'll be good," I begged.

At two he kissed me for the billionth time and brought me a cup of coffee in bed.

"So, when will I see you again?" He leaned over the bed as I sipped.

"I dunno."

"How about tonight?" he asked, smiling.

"That's two nights in a row."

"I know. It's a big move for us."

We agreed I'd call him around six.

Been Caught Stealing

Being in Peter's house without him was exhilarating. It required a confidence that was exciting to have conferred on me. I wore his boxers around the house, watched *Oprah*, ate some bran flakes, and admired his book collection. He had beautiful taste, effete and distinct. I wanted to live there and study his mind like gospel and commit it to memory and make it mine. I was touched by our sameness and thrilled by our differences.

By five I was bored and stir crazy. I got dressed and stood at the door, ready to leave, trying to think of what final discoveries I could make in my ephemeral moment in his house.

I couldn't think of any, but I decided to check my e-mail before I left. His computer was asleep. I hit the return key and listened to the quiet whiz as it reignited. H-o-t-m-a-i-l-d-o-t-c-o-m. There was a note from Peter with the subject "Lovely." "I've decided that this is what you are, so this is your new nickname, if you'll have it."

I wrote back, "With honor!" and sent it. Then I read that day's Salon.com postings—just a lot about the crumbling technology sector. And I was seized by a sudden panic that there might be something I needed to know about Peter that I might need to protect myself from and this might be my only chance to learn it. His warning not to go through his drawers hung in my mind, but I felt overwhelmed by fear.

I'll just check through some of his files, I thought to myself, clicking on his hard drive, and opening several documents only to quickly close them and think how stupid this whole thing was. I even found a letter, but it was eleven years old and who gives a damn. Then I spotted a file that said "Theoneyouleft," and I was riveted. I had to open it.

I gasped. The document was the sign I'd seen in the subway two months earlier. It was the love letter to a stranger that had made me cry then, and now, signed by theoneyouleftbehind.com. I studied the sign and couldn't make sense of it. If he could fall in love with a stranger like that, he was just like Edward, in love with reality-TV stars, or Alexis Whitcomb, in love with a pathetic shell of a person. I was disgusted that he could do it, but even more, I was furious with myself for erring. I put my coat on and prepared to storm out before I had one more impulse.

I did a search. One document was found. It was a diary entry. There was no date. He was talking about drinking late with his friend Haskell, going to Katz's Deli for an early breakfast at 5 A.M., and then wanting to call Skye. He couldn't get her out of his mind. I couldn't keep reading. Just as I suspected, he was in love with Skye, just like every other guy. Two drops of hot salty water rolled down each cheek. I finally slammed the door and wished he had been there to hear it.

I Never Want to Work in This Town Again

Outside I wasn't sure what to do with myself. The weather was bitter and punishing. Fighting intermittent rain and gales, I hiked over to Union Square and longed for something to catch my eye. In front of Barnes & Noble I braced myself against a blustery winter chill. In the window was a sleek, large-format volume called *In the Eye of the Storm*. I had seen that book before. When I was working in publishing. When I was a word detective.

I stepped inside to inspect the book. Opening to the acknowledgments page, I read, "Special thanks to Nathan Lazarus, my agent, Bill McGuire, my publisher . . ." The list went on and on. I was used to opening books immediately to their acknowledgments page. You could always determine who edited the book, who represented it. People don't know these things, but there are rules you learn when you work in the business of pushing books.

When I came in for my first publishing interview, I still had two weeks left of being a college senior. Boris, the other editor I would work for, asked all the questions.

"How do you feel about smoking?" he asked me, his impish grin revealing a gap between his front teeth.

Was this a trick question? A test of my current-events know-how? I was uncertain, but presented with the ridiculous self-possession only displayed by neophytes.

"Well, I think that the settlement with the Liggett group is a great first step. I hope that the other tobacco companies follow suit, since in the long run this saves everyone from years of litigating—"

"No, no, no, no," Boris boomed, slapping the table as he exchanged smiles with Gloria. "I mean, smoking as in *cigarettes*. As in being proximate to cigarette-smoking and the like."

"Oh!" I flushed. "I do it all the time. A pack a day." Gloria giggled as Boris told me I'd just barely missed losing the job.

"Want one?" he offered me, holding a Marlboro Red across the table.

"Oh, no. Not right now, thanks."

A year into my work, Boris had given me a manuscript to read, one that, as it happened, I actually liked. I sent him a baroque reader's report that ended with the imperative, "Reading *In the Eye of the Storm* is not optional. It is elemental." Until this point, I'd read dozens of proposals and been lukewarm about all of them.

This was my big ticket, what I imagined would be the fairy-tale beginning from whence my illustrious publishing career would grow.

I arranged the note and manuscript on Boris's desk to somehow stand out from the rest of the clutter. The piles on his desk were like archaeological strata: farther down, the rubber-banded and boxed stacks of paper had more yellowed edges, more cigarette burns, more stains from messy lunches. Finally I decided to put it on his chair. He didn't come in for two days after that. When he came in on the third day, he gave me a warning.

"Do NOT put any materials on my chair. Ever."

"Okay." Months passed. There was no word on my report. Finally, one day I was in his office, taking dictation for a rejection letter. "Capital 'R,' 'Regarding the matter of your submission, *comma,* I'm afraid this young writer has neither the pathos nor the gravitas that your enthusiasm led me to anticipate. *Period.* Alas, I'm afraid this is not right for me. My suspicions are that it will likely not be right for most mindful readers. In summation, dis ain't right for me." My inexpert prose was flowery, but Boris's was decidedly rococo. I respected his blend of highfalutin grandiose talk and street jive. As I scribbled this last line of his letter, I started to crack up.

He was laughing, too, until, apropos of nothing, he said, "That book, *In the Eye of the Storm*—it's crap, it'll never sell." I argued my point, saying he should give it a second read, but Boris was unmoving on the issue. So I dropped it—until we got a call from our publisher.

"I need to speak with Boris," he hissed.

After fifteen minutes of hushed conversation behind frosted-glass doors and some raised tones emanating from his office, Boris came out and asked me if I had that manuscript that I was "creaming over."

"Where's your copy?" I asked him, amused by the turn of events.

"I threw it away," he said between clenched teeth. It turned out there was a huge buzz about the book, and several publishers had made bids on it, none of which had been accepted. When the publisher called the agent and asked why he didn't have it, the agent said Boris had it.

I took a taxi home and got my report and the book, which I brought to the publisher. My publisher made an offer on the book a week later. Boris called me into his office.

"I don't want you to think that our buying this book has anything to do with my opinion about this book. It's still shit," he said warily.

I made a mental note to myself: Quit your shit job. Consider registering for that website called sendapieceofshittosomeone youhate.com.

Standing outside the bookstore, I noticed another book stacked next to *In the Eye of the Storm*. Dozens of copies of *Dot Comedy* towered like a grim reminder of romantic failure.

What a World It Would Be

After four cold hours walking around Manhattan with a head of steam, I decided to see Peter that night and confront him. I called him on my cell phone and we agreed to meet at his house at nine.

"Lovely?" he asked.

I stiffened. "Yes?"

"I have a surprise for you tonight."

"Oh. Really?"

"Wear something dressy." When I hung up I suddenly felt

guilty and doubted my intentions, but then I remembered the feeling of being duped and I braced myself and resolved to forge ahead.

After going home to Brooklyn, showering, and changing, I came back into the city and Peter met me at the Delancey Street subway stop near his gallery. He had some roses sticking out of his jacket pocket. "What are those?" I said, breathing heavily from the three flights to ground level.

"It's a pocket full of posey. For you."

I half laughed, but my petulance seemed to boil right over the surface. Still, Peter didn't seem to notice. He blew air in my ear and hailed a taxi.

"Are you excited to see where we're going?" he asked.

"Sure," I said, staring out the window. Soon we pulled up to a façade in Tribeca that looked dark and severe, the windows great arcing panes of darkened glass.

"Do you know where we are?" he asked.

"Nope."

"It's Bouley Bakery. It's one of my favorite restaurants in the city." We were seated in a romantic banquette near the back. I barely remember the food, but I tried to order the most expensive things, thinking, "He'll be sorry." I noticed a pained flicker cross Peter's face when I loudly asked for a glass of their "most expensive" aperitif.

Afterward we stood outside the concrete building, back where we started. The tidal wall gave way. Whatever muscle had kept me from screaming and running out on him, from hanging up on him or telling him to kiss my ass, snapped. Did he think I was stupid, I wanted to know, did he think that I wouldn't know he really wanted Skye, and how long did he think he was going to have to date me to get her and I would never touch anybody who was so lowly and desperate they posted want ads on the fucking subway to get laid. I remember that Peter looked scared and then said, "I can't believe you looked on my computer."

I had an excuse for that, but he had already made up his mind.

"You think you're fucking Nancy Drew? You don't know anything!" he shouted. "You are a scared, pathetic, cruel person. You clearly expect from everyone what you get from the fucking psychos you investigate, and it's made you crazy!"

For an amount of time I couldn't begin to calculate, I stood there sobbing. He must have left at some point. I called Cassie. I was so cold that my blue fingers could barely manipulate the digits.

When I finally got through she asked, "Hey what's up?" in her usual chirpy voice.

"Kiiin I come oveeerr?" I wailed.

Cass answered the door looking serious and I burrowed into her shoulder, crying. She hugged me. "I'm sorry, Amy," she said. She was wearing the red sweater.

Peggy Lipton Ain't Got Nothing on Me

Back in the office, George and Sol seemed giddy with the promise of a sanctioned night of drinking away from screaming kids, curfews, and work. George called me over. "Listen, Gray, I need you to do me a favor."

"Sure."

"I've got this computer guy coming in and I want you to talk him up."

"About what?"

"Nothing. Just flip you hair or something to, you know, get his attention. Every time they come, they spend about two minutes on the server and it breaks again."

"Okay."

"I want him to stick around and fix this thing till it's really done." It briefly occurred to me that this was probably an inappropriate request, but I liked my assignment nonetheless.

When the computer guy came into the room, nobody looked up but me. I smiled, crossing the room to ask, in my gee-whiz voice, "Hello. May I help you?" His face smacked of total system failure. Did not compute. "My name is Amy, by the way." I figured it couldn't hurt to amp it up. His features were skewed across his face, almost like objects sliding off an overturned table. He screwed his mouth in a chewing-type motion before he answered, his beady black eyes moving slowly and listlessly over the office, "Yep, yep, yep." I brought him over to the server, which was housed in the broom closet, and leaned seductively against one of the circuit boxes inside.

"It must be fun, fixing computers and stuff." I was stretching, but Computer Guy wasn't biting; he didn't even look at me. He unloaded his fanny pack of itsy-bitsy screwdrivers and sat on the floor, muttering "Yep, yep, yep" occasionally. Finally, I turned back to my desk, where George came and chastised, "I thought you were going to turn it on."

"I'm sorry. He's cataleptic. It's weird. I don't even know if he's a Homo sapiens." This was particularly humiliating for me, who needed to feel like I had some wiles left in my crazy self. But not even the IT guy was fooled by me.

"Just homo, maybe," George responded, laughing himself all the way back to his desk, as the computer guy tooled away, never knowing that all this laughter was about him.

Are We Having Fun Yet?

I called Cassie before the big night and invited her. Skye said she'd try to be there, but she had a dozen other parties she was juggling, including a thing David Blaine had invited her to at Studio 54. Jeremy was invited, too, and he e-mailed back asking if there'd be hot chicks. "We make no statements regarding the number of invited females or their scores on the bootylicious meter," I wrote back.

When we left work that night, Renora, Evan, George, and Linus had said they were coming, and maybe, it had been rumored, the famous Berks might show. It would be quite a night, but somehow much less than I'd hoped for only a week ago.

For the New Year's festivities, the Blue and Gold staff had taped a cardboard star covered in tinfoil to the St. Pauli Girl bar tap. On the way over, Cassie had been agonizing about how she looked. "I wish I just knew what the lighting was like in there," she complained. "I mean, is it bright, fluorescent?" "Is there a mirror in the bathroom?" "How dark is it?" "Like, really dark?" "Like, a yellow dark or a red dark?" How was I supposed to know she'd want to do bar reconnaissance? When we got there, she seemed underwhelmed. "You call this dark?" she guffawed. I closed my eyes and prayed for her to get laid tonight.

Evan was already there. "Laaaadies," he sang, slinging an arm and a spattering of beer over each of us. "You're looking loooveleee tonight." He was already hammered, and was fond of vowels when he was drunk.

Wendy was at the bar, having it out with Sol and Morgan. I left Cassie in Evan's sloppy hands and wandered over to referee. "A. Gray, maybe you can help us here."

"Doubtful," I clipped.

"Come on, come over here." Sol had his arm around me, too. The Agency had never been so full of love. "You can help us." Sol's eyes rolled back, and for a second I thought he was going to throw up on me, but instead he said, "Is it true that Renora is in love with Assman?" I smiled.

"I cannot tell a lie," I said, grinning.

Morgan groaned. "I'm participating in conjuring the voyeuristic equivalent of a car wreck," he whined. Then he smiled. "But I still want to stop and stare, damn it." Wendy and I exchanged shocked glances. I had never heard Morgan swear before.

"There is *no way*," Wendy said, shaking her head. "I just know Renora's taste. She likes nerds. It's, like, impossible." She folded her arms, which had cute little sweatbands on them. I was more than happy to disseminate misinformation on this subject, but I had no idea how the rumor got started, since I hadn't told anyone about our conversation. Unless Renora told someone and they'd got it wrong, didn't know how my Assman fetish had gotten shunted onto Renora.

By a quarter to midnight, I had accumulated a bizarre array of friends and friends of friends. I had e-mailed the invitation to everyone in my address book, thinking nobody would show. Jeremy was there, doing shots and sharing stinky spliffs with Noah. Skye seemed to have forgone for a second chance with David Blaine. She was sitting at the bar flanked by Vinny and some other lusty fans.

Sol was handing out twenties to all of us for shots, since the bar didn't have credit tabs. "Can I have some dough?" I asked him. He was ho-ho-hoing as he pulled a wad of sticky twenties from his pocket and gave one to me, to Evan, to Wendy. Another sweaty fist pushed its way into the fray.

It was Dan. He pulled his ubiquitous headphones off his head.

"Dude," he said with a salute.

"Hey," I said sadly.

"I hope you don't mind me coming, but your e-mail said there'd be all your foxy female coworkers—"

"Wait—I said that?"

"Yeah." He pulled a crumpled e-mail printout and handed it to me. "No, I'm joking. Just to bring light to the whole Renora thing. I wasn't hitting on her—"

"Don't worry about it," I interrupted. "It was stupid, really."

But he wouldn't let it go. "I just—I felt like you completely cut me out, for no reason. I was guilty before being proven innocent. And then I didn't even get a chance for a defense."

"I'm sorry," I said. "I guess I'm trigger-happy. Or gun-shy. Or once bitten, twice shy. Some shit like that."

He laughed. "I didn't want things to end . . ." He hesitated.

"I know." Out of the corner of my vision I saw Cassie coming toward me. "It's hard to start over in these situations, but I have a friend who I think you could really fall in love with, and she's a lot saner than me. Plus she makes more money—when she's working."

"She doesn't work?"

"She got laid off."

Dan grinned. "So did I. My dot-com went under."

I quickly introduced Cassie to Dan. I was brusque. "Dan, meet Cassie. Cassie, Dan. You guys should date each other, and you both just got fired, so you'll have plenty of time."

While Cassie and Dan got to know each other I overheard George and Sol having a rhetorical tussle about Froot Loops.

"See, 'Froot''s not a word," Sol was explaining. "It doesn't mean anything."

"It is a word, you're saying it. It's their legal loophole." George giggled. "No pun intended."

"But it's not if you see it spelled. When deaf people buy Froot

Loops they can't read the word 'Froot,' they just hear it. It's a direct attempt to misguide consumers. The *Oxford English Dictionary* should file a class action suit for trademark infringement and defaming their product."

"Fruit doesn't belong to anybody."

"I don't know, looking at Noah I would beg to differ. Ha-ha-ha!" Sol had a breakfast-size box of cereal on him, and the next thing I knew my bosses were closing their eyes and tossing back some Loops as part of a taste test to see if Froot, like fruit, came in different flavors, or was just different colors.

A few beers later I found myself immersed in conversation with Evan about the breakup.

"Don't laugh," I warned, "but I think he could have been the one." The Guinness had lubricated me well. I was foaming at the mouth.

"Yah, you blew it, big time!"

"Evan! You're not supposed to say that!"

"But it's true," he said. "I'm telling it like it is. You can't let this make you think everyone is an enemy. This job isn't the real world, A. Gray."

"What am I supposed to think when every folder that crosses my desk is a lunatic? Ahhhh!" I yelled in frustration and dropped my beer accidentally on Evan's steel-toed shoe.

"Jesus effing Christ. You need a reality check, A. Gray. It's not the job, it's you." He hobbled away, cursing.

"Whatever," I called after him. "I don't need to take advice from a guy—"

Before something irreversible escaped me I pointed over to the coin-operated bronco-riding machine along the side of the bar.

"Look!" I said pointing. Leaning against the harness, their heads tilted together like two contemplative cowboys, were Renora and Linus. Kissing.

"Whoa." Suddenly Gus and George and Sol and everyone were crowded together cooing and yelping to embarrass them. Renora looked up from their embrace and started laughing.

"This is not pay-per-view," she said.

"I'm not paying," George countered.

"But you're cheating on your one and only Assman."

"I'm not doing anything of the sort," Renora explained, before giving me a shrug and announcing, "*Amy* was hot for Assman, not me," at which point the bar devolved into whoops and cries and chants of "Amy and Assman sitting in a tree." I was laughing so hard I almost forgot my broken heart.

I felt a hand on my shoulder.

I turned around.

It was Peter. His hair sparkled with moisture. "Hi," I said, startled.

"Ho-ho," Sol was chortling. "Who the hell are you?" he said, pointing at Peter. "I don't know you."

"Sorry, he's with me," I said, dragging him over to the side of the bar. "What are you doing here?"

"I don't know."

We stood looking at each other silently.

"Anyway, it looks like you've moved on pretty quickly with this Assman character."

My right lip curled. "Are you serious?"

Peter was tired-looking. A patina of sweat gave him a greenish mother-of-pearl veneer.

"I just hope you vetted that guy, 'cause it sounds like he must have a lot to hide, with a name like that." He was shaking now.

"Peter, I'm so sorry."

"You don't know where that Ass has been," he said, getting nasty.

"Stop it, please." I didn't know Peter could get angry like this.

Maybe I'd figured if he liked me there must have been something wrong with him. But now he was ripshit, and there was something animating and vital about it. He was telling it like it was, and I respected him for it.

"Please, listen to me," I said. "I think I've gotten confused over the last twelve months about what I expect from people. Taking this job, I wanted to make myself completely safe from disappointment. The truth is, you're never totally safe, and by not trusting you I put myself in the way of much greater harm, the harm of not recognizing something great if it kicks me in the ass."

Peter was stone-faced.

"You're right to be angry with me, and if you never talk to me again I'll always be sorry and I'll always miss you and I'll never begrudge you for it. I messed up."

Peter was looking distracted. Suddenly he walked away from me, and I stood there stunned. He came back a minute later, with a double shot glass in each hand.

"What are these?" I asked. He pointed to Sol, standing away from us. Sol pointed at me and winked. Peter said that Sol had told him to tell me we needed liquor and he'd advised us to make love, not war.

"What is it?" I asked sniffing it.

"Just drink it, Miss Marple," he said, and with that the smoky alloy went down my hatch and my frozen-over vascular system felt melted around the edges.

"Come outside," Peter said, leading me outside the bar and under a streetlamp. His hair was electric and yellow. He looked like he was on fire with the tawny glow from above.

"You totally betrayed me," he said. I nodded my hanging head in agreement. "And you also did a shitty job of investigating." I looked up. "The subway sign was a project I did at SVA. There was no woman on the F line. There was nothing. The project was to find people like you, people who imagined clues where there were none, who saw themselves as players in other people's fantasy lives. This wasn't about me, it was about you."

We were silent for a minute. "What about Skye?" I asked.

"What about her?!" he bellowed. "There was a time when I thought I had more feelings for her. It lasted about a day. That was four and half years ago. Don't you think if I had wanted to act on it I would have?!"

I absorbed his fury solemnly.

"You think you're so fucking clever, we'll you PI-ed yourself into quite a fucking situation here." For what felt like the longest time we stood unspeaking, and I waited for the ax to fall.

"But, for whatever reason, probably because I, like you, am a fucking romantic, and you're smart and beautiful and funny and fun and I think I see something in you I want, I can't turn away."

I looked up at him.

"I want to forget this and I want you to never do this again."

He pulled me close and rubbed his eyes on my shoulder, and we stood outside the bar for the longest time, kissing and whispering "Never" a lot. At one point Sol ran out with a cymbal and banged it in my ear, and Evan shuffled out holding Skye's hand. Otherwise, as I stood there with Peter I put my trust not in facts, and not in dreams, but in the pure, true feeling that siphoned from my gut and drove all the way to my fingertips and beyond me onto the light. Soon the ringing cheers of the revelers within spilled outside, at first muffled and then thunderous: eight . . . seven . . . six . . . five . . .

And then it started to snow.

⌁ ACKNOWLEDGMENTS

The author wishes to thank the following people: Jessica Power, Charlotte Herscher, Amber Smith, Rob Haskell, Deborah Rubin, Lauren Redniss, Abigail Gray, Nick Harder, Robert Grover, Sylvie Rabineau, Keri Selig, Ed Redlick, Becky Hartman-Edwards, Jill and David Adler, Barbara Hart, Bernice Gray, and everyone at the Agency.

Particular thanks to my supremely clever editor, Bruce Tracy, and my fabulous and unwavering agent, Betsy Lerner, as well as Katie Zug and Erin Hosier. Most of all, thanks to my parents.

✪ ABOUT THE AUTHOR

AMY GRAY spent three years working as a private investigator in New York City. She previously worked in book publishing. She has been profiled in *W* magazine, *The New York Times*, and *Glamour*, among other places. She graduated from Brown University, and lives in New York.